AQA

GCSE

Media Studies

Make the Grade!

Mandy Esseen

Martin Phillips

Lesley Wisson: Chief Examiner

www.heinemann.co.uk

✓ Free online support
✓ Useful weblinks
✓ 24 hour online ordering

01865 888118

Heinemann

Part of Pearson

Contents

Pop music

Advertising and marketing

Radio

External Assessment

Controlled Assessment

Glossary

CD-ROM contents

You will find a CD-ROM in the back of this student book. On it is an electronic version of this book and a range of resources to help you with your GCSE Media Studies course. Wherever a resource appears, you will find detail on this in the student book in the 'CD-ROM Extra!' feature.

Free External Assessment Topic on-line support

To access our unique Exam Café go to www. contentextra.com/ gcseaqamediastudies and enter the username: gcseaqamediastudies and password: Heinemann.

Introduction

Media Studies is one of the most exciting subjects available to students today, partly because it has so much variety but mostly because it is current and relevant to you. It reflects the world you live in and by studying this subject you are helping to make sense of the world you inhabit.

What will you be studying?

The following section outlines what your AQA GCSE Media Studies course includes.

Key Concepts

There are four key media concepts which form the basis of the subject content of your course. They are:

- **Media language: forms and conventions**: this is the language of the media. It doesn't mean just the words people use, but also the way in which media texts are put together. It is how a media producer manages to put across the same message to millions of people. It involves colours and lighting and mise-en-scène.

- **Institutions**: this is who makes what and for whom. It is a study of, for example, who owns which newspaper and who decides what goes in it. Or who makes a particular film and how it reaches the cinema near you. Or who makes the advertisements that keep repeating in your head. Or who makes the rules and regulations governing the media. And it is about who makes the money out of the media business, because that is what the media is, business – big business!

- **Audience**: this is the study of you, the audience, the consumer, the people who listen to the local radio stations or buy the latest magazines. You will learn how the media producers manipulate their audiences into following a particular fashion or trend or how you are targeted to buy the latest CDs or DVDs, or watch the latest blockbuster film.

- **Representation**: by examining how you see the world and how the world sees you, you will understand how representations work. You will study the world of stereotypes and hidden messages that help audiences to consume the media.

It is not always easy to separate out the study of each of these concepts. But if you remember how to address each concept, you are well on the way to being successful in this subject.

Media forms and platforms

In your AQA Media Studies course, you will be studying media 'forms'. This means you will be studying different areas of the media. You will have to cover a minimum of three media forms in the course of your study. These include:

Moving image

Moving image can be broken down into several media platforms such as magazines, television or radio. You can study television but focus on television programmes, or television advertising, or television news. You can study film, including how a film is made, how it is distributed and how it is exhibited, but you can also study the genre of film.

Sound

Almost every area of the media can be broken down, so sound, another media form, can be separated into radio programming, news, advertising or comparing local and national stations.

Print

Print, another media form, can be broken down into newspapers, magazines, comics, advertising, etc.

New technologies

You will also study new technologies such as podcast and blogs, to name but a few. The case studies in this book provide a regular and explicit focus on cross-media aspects in the context of the relevant chapter.

The case studies in this book provide a regular and explicit focus on cross-media aspects in the context of the relevant chapter.

How will you be assessed?

Your AQA GCSE Media Studies course is divided into two main sections: Controlled Assessment and the External Assessment. In brief, your course looks like this:

Controlled Assessment: understanding the media

In the Controlled Assessment section, you will have to complete three assignments following a simple format: APE! That is:

- analysis
- production
- evaluation.

This way you cover all the Assessment Objectives and, hopefully, get high marks.

The areas of media study are chosen (by your teacher) from assignment banks provided by the Awarding Body, AQA. These help to direct your study so that you don't waste too much time completing work that is not relevant to the assessment. These banks of topics cover all the media forms and will provide something to interest everyone.

The three assignments are not carried out in isolation but as a result of several weeks of study of the topic areas. In this way you are as knowledgeable as you can be and you will fully understand the topic you are working on.

Course component and outline	% of your GCSE	Marks (and Assessment Objectives)
Controlled Assessment **Three assignments:** • Assignment 1: Introduction to the media • Assignment 2: Cross-media study • Assignment 3: Practical Production and Evaluation	60%	• Assignment 1: 15 marks (AO2 and AO3) • Assignment 2: 30 marks (AO2 and AO3) • Assignment 3: 45 marks (AO3 and AO4)
External Assessment **Two tasks**	40%	• Two tasks: 30 marks for each (AO1, AO3, AO4)

TIP

See pages 181–191 for detailed guidance and ideas for the External Assessment.

Assignment 1: Introduction to the media

This assignment focuses on the analysis and production of a media text within a specific genre and media platform.

This assignment will focus on **media language** and **audience**, so you might look at analysing two advertisements from the television *or* a magazine and decide how successful they have been and then produce your own advertisement targeted at a specific audience. Alternatively you might choose to deconstruct the covers of two DVDs and explain how they attract and appeal to the target audience and then design your own DVD cover, again targeted at a specific audience.

Assignment 2: Cross-media study

This looks at two different ways of reaching an audience. You will have to study how different media texts depend upon each other or how a media message can be communicated across different media platforms.

The main concepts that you will focus on in this assignment are **representation** and **institution** (although of course media language and audience may also crop up).

You will be expected to analyse two different responses to two different texts based on the same idea and then undertake two planning tasks based on a common idea across two platforms. For example, you might choose to look at how a particular news story has been covered on television news and in a newspaper *or* how a print magazine and a webzine contrast and compare. The production tasks will be planning tasks so, in this instance, you will only be expected to show the television news storyboard for the opening headlines and a design of the front page of a newspaper showing the placing of the main headlines.

Assignment 3: Practical Production and Evaluation

This is where you will be expected to decide on your major production piece. You can work in a small group but you will be assessed on what *you* do, so make sure all your pre-production planning is clear and keep good notes of the decisions and reasons why you chose to do things in a certain way. The evaluation must be entirely your own work and no copied parts should be included.

You are going to be assessed, not just on how creative and imaginative you can be within the chosen topic area, but also on how effectively you can produce the media text using the appropriate codes and conventions and using the right media terminology. Original material is always the best option, so you should go out and take your own images wherever possible and always write original copy.

For this assignment you will be asked to create a media text, taking it from conception to realisation, in other words, to produce your media text from your very first thoughts about it. You will need to consider all of the media concepts in this assignment.

As an example, you might want to study film trailers for a particular genre and then storyboard and film your own 120-second trailer. Then, of course, you need to evaluate it. You might decide to study the talk-based radio stations in your area and then script and record a 5-minute extract (only fading in and out the songs) and then evaluate it.

External Assessment: investigating the media

This part of the assessment is designed to test your critical and planning skills. You will be asked to create a planning task and offer some evaluation for it. You will be expected to address all of the main media concepts but only AO1, AO3 and AO4 of the Assessment Objectives. This is the part of the course that is like an exam, because you will have to do the test under exam conditions (although after preparation).

> **TIP**
> See pages 18–19 for detailed guidance and practice for the External Assessment.

The External Assessment topic

You will know the topic of the External Assessment well in advance of taking the test, so preparation can begin early. Then, nearer the assessment date, you will have several weeks of study devoted solely to preparation of the assessment.

You will have a media text or stimulus material given to you about a month before the actual test, in order for you to undertake your own research and preparation for the test. You will then have to sit a 90-minute assessment, answering two unseen tasks based on the pre-released topic.

Assessment Objectives

Assessment Objectives are the criteria that the Awarding Body, AQA, uses to assess your capabilities. There are four Assessment Objectives in GCSE Media Studies. It is useful to remember what these are so that you are sure to cover them when you write your assignments or design your media products.

The Assessment Objectives are:

- **AO1: Knowledge and Understanding** – this is what you know and understand about the media texts you are studying and the organisations that make them. You will be expected to use the right terminology, for example, or be able to deconstruct a media product thoroughly.

- **AO2: Analysis and Response** – this is being able to really evaluate something, rather than just describe it, and make your own responses to the media you are studying.

- **AO3: Research and Planning** – this covers all the planning you do to understand how and why something was created for the audience to consume.

- **AO4: Production and Evaluation** – here you will be expected to make media texts and be able to evaluate their success against your own research.

Your teacher will be able to explain how these Assessment Objectives work in more detail, but don't forget about them, and remember that they are the criteria you will be tested against.

And finally ...

You won't regret taking AQA GCSE Media Studies. It is a hugely enjoyable subject and makes the best of the knowledge and expertise you already have as consumers of the media. Don't be afraid to ask questions, but be prepared to research the answers yourself. Keep your eyes and ears open and listen out for any media debates you might come across in the news.

The media are all around us but, armed with your GCSE in Media Studies, they will make more sense and you will know how to cope with them, using your critical and analytical skills.

Film

Your learning

In this chapter you will learn about:

- film theory: genre, narrative, representation
- film technology in relation to film-making, marketing and viewing
- film promotion, looking especially at posters, trailers and websites
- the cross-media nature of film including marketing and distribution, advertising, magazines, the Internet and television
- studying films: making films and textual analysis – a case-study approach.

Genre

In film, exploring the ways certain **conventions** or **characteristics** are used to create style and appeal is important.

ACTIVITY 1

1 Working on your own, write down your two favourite and two least favourite films.

2 Now combine your chosen films into two class lists.
- Do the same types of film – such as adventure, fantasy, science fiction, romantic comedy and Westerns – appear on both lists?
- Were the same types of film popular with both boys and girls?

Did you find it easy to say what types of film were your favourites? If so, it is probably because you already know a lot about **genre** (a French word meaning 'type'). You can probably tell, from a few seconds of a TV trailer or even from a poster, what genre a new film is likely to be, and you will have certain expectations as a result.

What film genre do the following words suggest:
- explosions
- car chases
- time pressure?

You probably thought 'Action' before you even read the second word! Media producers rely on your ability to recognise genre when they promote new films, to arouse **audience** interest, expectation and anticipation.

Key terms

Genre conventions or **characteristics**
The typical features in a film which show the audience what genre it is.

Genre A type of media text (programme, film, CD cover, etc.) with certain predictable characteristics.

Audience People who are reading, looking at, listening to or using a media text.

Films are often a mix of several genres – known as cross-genres or **hybrid** genres – to attract the widest possible target audience. For example, *Cloverfield* (2008) seems to be a simple action movie aimed at fans of the action genre. However, it also uses the genre characteristics of:

- science fiction – the largely unseen threat is an alien monster
- documentary – the footage is shot on a documentary-style hand-held camera
- teen horror movie – the characters are all young people who face unexpected and tense threats.

ACTIVITY 2

1 *Work in pairs. Make a table like the one below to show the characteristics of four popular genres: romantic comedy, Disney animation, science fiction and horror.*

Genre	Typical setting	Typical characters	Typical plots	Typical props	Typical themes
Romantic comedy		Young man, young woman	They meet, hate each other, coincidences throw them together...		

2 *Now share your answers with another pair. Add any good ideas that you missed.*

CD-ROM Extra!

Trailers
Open the CD in the back of this book and click on the icon below to open a link to see some examples of film trailers.

HTML

ACTIVITY 3

1 *Watch three or four different film clips or film trailers.*

- *How soon can you identify which genre each one fits into?*
- *Does it demonstrate cross-genre (hybrid) characteristics?*
- *What type of audience will each one attract? For example, young or old, male or female?*

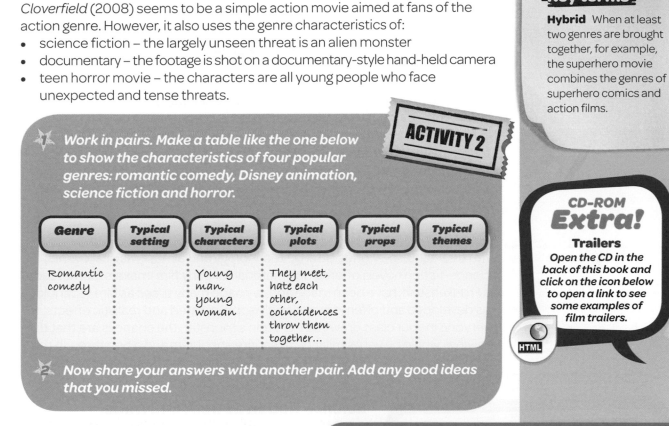

Science fiction is a genre that has at its heart some form of technology which is not yet possible, but which could be one day. It is a popular genre, although it has not always drawn the huge audiences it does today. For that reason, it is an interesting genre to study, to see how it has developed and from what roots.

The roots of science fiction

Literary heritage

Science-fiction novels were popular long before film was even invented. Early sci-fi novels include *Twenty Thousand Leagues Under the Sea* by Jules Verne (1870) and *The Time Machine* (1895) by H.G. Wells. Even earlier, Mary Shelley's *Frankenstein* was published in 1818 when she was only 21. It is an early example of a hybrid, it being part horror and part science fiction. It told the story of a scientist who discovered how to create life and make a creature in his own likeness, with terrible consequences.

Early science-fiction films

With their fantastic worlds, strange technology and almost magical events, science-fiction novels offered rich material for early film-makers. Some, such as *Frankenstein*, have been made and re-made many times as film technology has developed and offered increasingly sophisticated and realistic effects. If everyone in your class drew Frankenstein's monster, the chances are that the drawings would be very similar (with square shoulders and a bolt through the neck!) and based on the first film representation of the monster, played by Boris Karloff in 1933!

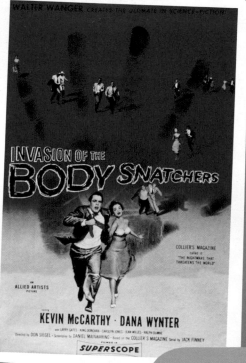

Science fiction as a social symbol

Because science-fiction narratives often include exploration, danger and new technology, they have been used to explore issues causing concern in society. For example:

- *Invasion of the Bodysnatchers* (1956) seemed to be about an alien invasion, but was also about the McCarthy trials in the 1950s, when many American citizens were questioned about their possible Communist sympathies.

- American science-fiction films in the 1950s and 1960s, such as *Dr Strangelove or: How I Learned to Stop Worrying and Love the Bomb* (1964), explored the fear that nuclear technology would result in the destruction of the world.

- The X-Men comics, and later the film trilogy, seem to be about humans and mutants, but are also texts that have been used to explore attitudes to prejudice, such as racial hatred.

If you can, look at some X-Men comics together with some scenes from X-Men the movie. How do these science-fiction texts communicate messages about human prejudice?

ACTIVITY 4

The blockbuster science-fiction film

Until the early 1990s, science-fiction film was regarded as a minority genre which only longstanding fans watched. Then James Cameron produced the special effects-driven *Terminator 2* in 1991, Steven Spielberg produced *Jurassic Park* in 1993 and Roland Emmerich wrote and directed *Stargate* in 1994. All these films were marketed to audiences as cross-genres of action with science fiction. With a big budget and special effects, Emmerich followed *Stargate* in 1996 with *Independence Day*, and science fiction was established as a hugely exciting and action-packed genre for teenagers.

Science-fiction films continue to be big hits today

ACTIVITY 5

⭐ *Using the Internet as a starting point, find out as much as you can about the big blockbuster science-fiction films from the past few years. Which directors and stars have become associated with science-fiction films?*

⭐ *Which science-fiction films do you think most teenagers prefer? Can you explain why?*

⭐ *Try to decide what top five ingredients make a science-fiction film really popular.*

Grade Studio

Examiner's tip

Understanding how representation works is essential. For example, think about body language: you *know* when someone is angry or happy; think about *how* you know.

Lara Croft in *Tomb Raider* – hero not heroine?

Representations in science fiction

Representation is an important word in media studies. Representations of people are usually designed to make them as believable as possible, but if you look closely at representations of key social groups, such as women, men, teenagers, ethnic groups, old people, you will see that they are often quite **stereotypical**. Many representations of teenagers show them as being disrespectful, moody and selfish – this is obviously a very narrow view of teenagers!

ACTIVITY 6

1. Look at a range of film clips in two or three science-fiction films. Try to identify different ways in which people are represented.

2. Now refine your observations by making a list to show how similar social groups (women, men, teenagers, ethnic groups, old people) are generally represented.

3. Try to suggest examples of representations that are not stereotypical but seem to be genuinely convincing and 'realistic'.

When discussing character it is helpful to consider the views of Vladimir Propp, a theorist who wrote about characters in narratives. He suggested that every story had characters in certain roles: hero, heroine or princess, villain, donor or mentor and helper (see below to find out more about these roles). Science fiction can represent groups of people in unusual ways by allowing them to fulfil unexpected roles in societies that are wholly invented, such as the character of the alien.

Representations of women

Science fiction has offered women the opportunity to break away from the stereotypical role of the heroine as a helpless 'princess' who needs to be rescued by the hero. Ripley in Ridley Scott's *Alien* (1979) and Sarah Connor in *Terminator* (1984) were given lead roles who had real power and strength and were often central to the meaning and development of the narrative. It could be argued that such women play the hero role rather than the heroine.

ACTIVITY 7

In small groups, find out about some or all of these characters. Present your findings as a display of images with accompanying factfiles.

- *Lara Croft in* Tomb Raider *(2001)*
- *Sarah Connor in* Terminator 2 *(1991)*
- *Ripley in* Alien Resurrection *(1997)*
- *Lyndsay in* The Abyss *(1989)*
- *Princess Amidala in* Star Wars I, II and III *(1999, 2002 and 2005)*
- *Trinity in* The Matrix *trilogy (1999–2003)*

Representations of aliens

One of the most interesting conventions of science fiction is the presence of some amazingly memorable aliens! Try jotting down as many as you can in one minute.

Sometimes taking 'human' form, sometimes robot, sometimes imaginative life-forms from other planets, aliens allow film-makers to explore different patterns of behaviour, language and customs. The essential thing about aliens is that they are different from us. It is not hard to see that aliens are often used as a symbol for themes of belonging and for being different. They can also be a way for film-makers to explore social problems, such as prejudice, in a subtle way.

ACTIVITY 8

1. *Create your own alien. You can make it friendly or hostile, but you must label your design by pointing out key features that make it different from a human. Before you start, consider what you've already learned about the representations of aliens!*

2. *Extend your design by writing a paragraph describing how the alien responds to humans, and what would happen if it came to Earth.*

3. *Other commonly found representations in science-fiction films are: scientists, **stock characters** and captains or other leadership figures. Choose one of these representations and analyse its role in one or two films of your choice. Share your findings with the class as a presentation or display.*

Key terms

Stock character A supporting character who is often quite stereotypical and whose job it is to support the lead characters, to be saved by them or to die!

Analysing science-fiction films

Analysing a film is similar to reading a book, and calls upon similar analytical skills. First, however, you must know the key features of film language, and then be able to work out what it means. Use this checklist to help you to look for the most important features in a science-fiction film:

- *Characters* (including aliens) will have clear roles and purposes in the narrative.
- *Costumes* are important – especially in future worlds.
- *Settings* (the locations where the action takes place) are part of the created world and often involve **special effects**.
- *Colours* are important and are often symbolic. For example, neon green often symbolises 'the alien'.
- *Soundtrack* is a vital clue to suggesting mood, theme and key moments.
- *Conventions* such as space, jargon, gadgets, weapons, etc. all build up the understanding of the narrative.
- *Special effects* may play a huge part – look out for animation, CGI (computer-generated imagery – see page 120, clever use of camera angles, action sequences.

Key terms

Special effects Exciting and dynamic visual or sound effects used to create impact in films.

Grade Studio

Examiner's tip

If your work in Activity 10 is going to be part of a Controlled Assessment assignment, you will need to include your pre-production research. Include all the work on deconstructing the films you studied in order to understand the codes and conventions.

ACTIVITY 9

Practise your analytical skills in science fiction. Watch clips from a range of science-fiction films. Make notes on the conventions, themes and characters as you go, using a table like the one below. An example has been given to get you started.

Name of film	Conventions	Themes	Characters
Sunshine	Space travel Cut off from Earth	How far humans will go for new experiences	Captain Space crew

You could present your notes as an essay, report or presentation. Try to explain what common themes you recognised, what you noticed about characters and anything you noticed about different approaches to the science-fiction genre.

ACTIVITY 10

Prepare a developed film pitch, based around the following idea:

New technology has made space travel even easier. Led by a female Captain and a male First Officer, NASA launches a revolutionary spaceship that can travel through the universe using the technique of 'space-folding' making it possible to travel vast distances. The journey is very exciting, and takes the crew to a new world where the inhabitants have strange but seemingly peaceful customs. The humans then realise that all is not as it first appeared and must work out a plan to escape and get back to Earth – but not without tragedy, love and an unexpected twist of fate before the end of the film.

1. *Give your film a title and explain its meaning.*

2. *Cast the main parts and explain your choices.*

3. *Outline the narrative more fully, explaining all the interesting details.*

4. *Design the film poster.*

5. *If you are going to develop this work into a Controlled Assessment piece, plan the promotion campaign for the film. This could include: storyboard or trailer, merchandise designs, soundtrack CD cover and DVD cover.*

If you are stuck for a title, you may wish to use 'Beyond the stars' or 'Far from home'

Narrative

Understanding **narrative** is an important part of any Media Studies course – this applies to many media texts, and not just film.

How narratives are organised

When discussing narrative, it is helpful to consider Russian theorist Tzvetan Todorov. He devised a way of analysing narratives according to the way they move forward through different stages. Todorov suggested that many narratives, regardless of their genre, could be broken into specific stages for analysis. Read the stages below then the extract that follows.

> **Todorov's Narrative Stages**
>
> **Equilibrium** – the setting is established, key character(s) are introduced and the storyline is set up.
>
> **Disruption** – oppositional character(s) appear and the story takes a particular direction.
>
> **Recognition of disruption** – the lives of characters and events are interwoven. Tension builds throughout this section, which is often the longest.
>
> **Attempt to repair disruption** – the highest point of tension after which there is a change in dynamic.
>
> **Reinstatement of equilibrium** – matters are sorted out, problems are solved and questions answered.

Emily was tired of watching wimpy princes trying to get rid of the local dragon, so she decided to have a go herself. She soon came upon the dragon, who was singeing the top of a freckle-faced boy's head.

Being a resourceful princess, Emily set a trap for the dragon and then tricked him into following her.

'You're just a silly girl, and even though it's hardly worth it, I'm going to toast you to a crisp and have you for pudding!' boomed the dragon. Just then, the branches he was standing on gave way, and he fell down a very deep well, his fire put out once and for all.

Emily returned to the boy.

'What's your name?' she asked.

'Prince Matthew,' said the boy.

'That'll do nicely,' said Emily. 'Where do you live?'

'In Happy-Ever-After,' he replied.

'That'll do nicely too,' said Emily.

And with that, she and Matthew rode off together to Happy-Ever-After.

You may well ask why this children's fairy story is in a book on GCSE Media Studies. The answer is that the **narrative structure** suggested by Todorov fits this story perfectly.

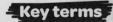

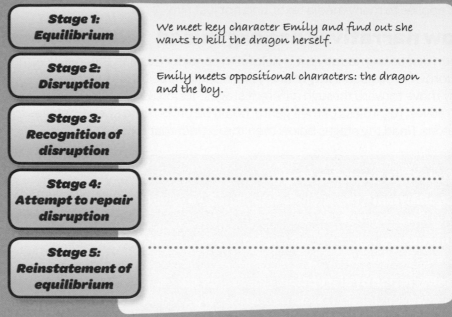

1 Create your own chart to show how the theory can be applied to Emily's story. The first two sections have already been done to help you.

Stage 1: Equilibrium	We meet key character Emily and find out she wants to kill the dragon herself.
Stage 2: Disruption	Emily meets oppositional characters: the dragon and the boy.
Stage 3: Recognition of disruption	
Stage 4: Attempt to repair disruption	
Stage 5: Reinstatement of equilibrium	

2 Work in a small group to identify each of the stages in two films you know well.

3 Watch a short narrative – a cartoon would be a good text to use. Analyse its narrative structure by breaking it down into its five stages.

4 Think of your own simple narrative featuring a small boy or girl. Write a 50-word story that follows this narrative structure and read it to a partner.

Playing with narratives

Not all narratives fit into the straightforward structure suggested by Todorov, especially if they are trying to do something different or unpredictable. For example, in the film *Back To The Future* (1985) directed by Steven Spielberg, a boy travels back in time to meet the scientist who invented time travel. The stages of the narrative in this film are not in chronological order. Can you think of any other examples of unpredictable narratives?

The correct term for something that does not fit a recognised theory is a **subversion**. You may recognise these subversion techniques:

- *Flashback* – where a section of the film is referred back to, for example, *The Incredible Hulk* (2008) directed by Louis Leterrier.

- *Flashforward* – where a section of the film from the future is shown before it would normally have happened, for example, *Inside Man* (2006) directed by Spike Lee.

Key terms

Subversion When a technique is used which does not fit a theory or the usual way of doing something (for example, when a twist takes the narrative in a new direction).

- *Twist* – where part of the film (often the end) is unpredictable or even shocking, for example, *The Happening* (2008) directed by M. Night Shyamalan.
- *Parallel narratives* – where the lives of characters move alongside each other for some of the film without them meeting, for example, *Crash* (2004) directed by Paul Haggis.

Audience involvement

Audiences enjoy texts most when they are really involved in them. When they are genuinely hooked into the text's narrative and development, it is as if they are actually part of it. You can see why this is so important – someone who is really involved in a text is much less likely to switch it off or put it back on the shelf.

Here are some techniques that help an audience to become involved or positioned in a film or television text.

- Point-of-view shots – the camera adopts the position of a character within the text. This can be an over-the-shoulder shot, looking at whatever the character is looking at, or a shot from the point of view of the character. This is particularly powerful when the character is experiencing a strong emotion – the viewer is more likely to feel their emotion when taking their point of view.
- Reaction shots – the camera moves to an extreme close-up of a character's face to show their reaction to something that has happened.
- Insert shots – this technique gives the audience extra or privileged information that one or more characters may not yet know, for example, in a two-set scene with two characters in different locations. The audience knows what is happening to each of them when the characters themselves do not.
- Shot reverse-shot – the camera alternates between two characters to show their building relationship (whether positive or negative), often as a conversation is taking place between them. This is a common technique in dramas where the inter-relationship between characters is important. The camera acts as a third person in shot reverse-shot, giving the audience the impression that they are turning their heads from one character to the other.

Reading facial expression is crucial to understanding a character's reaction

These three images demonstrate the shot reverse-shot technique

Divide into groups. Look again at Emily's story on page 9. Each group should prepare to re-tell the story, using one or more subversions. Change the original version so that the narrative no longer follows the same path. The following suggestions may help you:

- *Flashback* – start the story from the moment when Emily is facing the dragon.
- *Flashforward* – begin the story with a dream sequence in which Emily faces a fire-breathing beast.
- *Twist* – Emily does not have to be human!
- *Parallel narratives* – tell Emily's story side by side with Prince Matthew's (or the dragon's) story. This could make the audience feel differently towards them.

A minicam

ACTIVITY 13

⭐ Watch a series of three to five film clips from the genres of science fiction, romantic comedy and horror. Identify as many techniques of audience positioning as possible.

② Using a still camera, create a series of shots which demonstrate each of the audience positioning techniques. Display them in your classroom with an imaginary narrative situation written underneath each one. You can see an example in the photographs on page 11.

Additional camera terms and definitions

A lot of time is spent on setting up every scene in a film. It is important to position the cameras in just the right way to capture on film exactly what the director wants the audience to see. In addition to the techniques mentioned already, here are some other camera shots that you will be able to identify in the films you study.

A steadicam

Camera term	What it suggests
Establishing shot	The camera is set far back to show or to emphasise setting or location rather than the subject.
Slo-mo	A moment which is replayed very slowly.
Pan shot	The camera moves horizontally, taking in all the details along the way.
Tracking shot	The camera moves alongside characters using either a hand-held technique or smooth dolly tracks.
Zoom	The camera focuses in on, or out from, a subject by using a telephoto lens.
Minicam	A tiny camera is placed in an unusual place for effect.
Steadicam	A weighted camera is strapped to an operator to allow hand-held but controlled movement.

Intertextuality

Have you ever experienced the thrill of watching a film and recognising a reference to another film? This type of link between two texts is known as an **intertextual reference**.

Do you recognise the phrase 'I'll be back'? Where have you heard it? It is, of course, used in all *Terminator* films, but has also been used intertextually in other films such as *Last Action Hero* (1993) when Arnold Schwarzenegger says 'I'll be back... Ha! Bet you didn't expect me to say that!'

The UK Film Council reported in 2007 that 'I'll be back' is the most often used line from a film in everyday conversation!

Intertextual references can be visual as well. You can find a good example of this in *Toy Story 2* (1999). The toys are riding around Al's toy barn in a Barbie tour guide car and Rex the dinosaur is running behind them, his reflection clearly seen in the wing mirror. This is an intertextual reference to the scene in *Jurassic Park* (1993) when the T-rex can be seen in the wing mirror chasing the tour guide vehicle – in this case, with the intention of eating the passengers!

The story of *Bridget Jones's Diary* (2001) is full of intertextual references to Jane Austen's *Pride and Prejudice*, although the settings and the characters of the heroines could hardly be more different. The basic storyline is similar: girl meets and hates boy but after many mishaps realises his true worth and marries him.

Key terms

Intertextual reference When one media text mimics or refers to another media text in a way that many consumers will recognise.

TIP

Using a chart, table or annotation to present textual analysis for research and planning tasks will help you to keep under the word limit for controlled assessment tasks.

ACTIVITY 14

⭐ *Watch the first ten minutes of one of these films:* **Star Wars IV: A New Hope** *(1997),* **The Truman Show** *(1998) or* **Saving Private Ryan** *(1998). Look for evidence of genre characteristics, narrative structure, audience positioning and carefully set-up camerawork.*

⭐ *Present your findings as a table, chart, report or essay. For example, you could set out your findings in a table like the one below.*

Film	Genre characteristics	Narrative structure	Audience positioning	Camerawork
The Truman Show	Orchestral music, realistic setting and convincing dress codes suggest a drama			The camera is used in very unusual ways – first as a way of positioning the film audience, but also (through secret mini-cameras) to show what the TV audience are seeing

Film technology

Film-making technology

Today most directors use small, light (and very portable) cameras for filming, which also allows for digital editing software to be used. Such editing is known as non-linear editing, which means that footage can be shot, cut up and ordered out of sequence on a computer. Because it is fairly easy to use, it has led to a massive rise in low-budget, independent films being made. You may be an independent film-maker yourself, or you may have simple film-making technology in your school or college. (See the Controlled Assessment chapter pages 192–216, which include ideas and tips for film-making.)

Film-viewing technology

Screen size, sound quality and the comfort of film viewing have changed remarkably over time. Look at and discuss the three different film-viewing places pictured below. How do these different places affect your appreciation of the film?

A traditional
Odeon cinema

The IMAX cinema
in London

A state-of-the-art
home cinema system

Film flashback

When you look at any key area of Media Studies, it is always a good idea to understand its background. For film, it is important to have a grasp of how the film industry's technology has changed over time in response to changing patterns of audience response and expectations.

Charlie Chaplin in the silent film *The Gold Rush* (1925)

1894

First moving pictures were screened to audiences. They were very short and featured actual events happening, so they were called 'actualities'. Examples included *The Sneeze* and *The Kiss*.

EARLY 1900s

Films became longer and began to tell stories. Some even used early special effects. A good example is *A Trip to the Moon* (1902) by Georges Méliès. Films were silent, with on-screen text.

Hollywood began to dominate film production by setting up powerful (and rich) film studios. This was known as the Studio System.

1927

The first 'talking' film – *The Jazz Singer* – was released, changing film production for ever.

1930s

The first films to use Technicolor were produced. Two good examples were Oscar contenders *Gone with the Wind* and *The Wizard of Oz* in 1939.

1950s

The popularity of epic films resulted in screens being bigger – an early form of today's widescreen technology.

1977

Star Wars IV: A New Hope was the first film to use Dolby surround sound.

1982

Disney's *Tron* was the first film to use CGI (computer-generated imagery).

1999

Star Wars I: The Phantom Menace was the first film to be filmed mostly using digital cameras – which meant that digital editing was used too.

2001

We will see more developments that will make films seem increasingly realistic. IMAX 3D screens will use Sony's new stereoscopic Real-D technology to make film viewing a virtual reality experience!

2008

Christopher Nolan's *The Dark Knight* was the first film to use IMAX technology in the shooting of the film.

21ST CENTURY

Peter Jackson used breakthrough CGI technology, called motion-capture animation, to create the realistic character Gollum for *The Lord of the Rings* trilogy. He did this by putting sensors on actor Andy Serkis and recording his movements onto a computer-generated character.

CGI was used to create this sabre-toothed tiger in the 2008 film *10,000 BC*

Film promotion and marketing in the 21st century

Film posters

Posters and trailers have been used to promote films for many years, but the nature of film marketing and promotion has changed a great deal since the 1990s. However, posters are still a vital part of the marketing process, so it is always worthwhile studying their key **conventions**.

Poster conventions

- an eye-catching image or images — often related to characters (and the stars in the film) or the setting of the film
- the title of the film, carefully constructed in terms of font style, colour, size and placement: a lot of thought goes into the title – it is meant to be memorable, and also to suggest the genre of the film
- a tagline for the film – which is like the catchy slogans of advertisements – offering another clue to the genre and main themes or content of the film
- the names of well-known or key people connected to the film. These are usually the lead actors but may also be the director or producer.
- **endorsements** from other media productions (for example, *Empire* magazine) giving their comments such as 'an unmissable film'
- details of any award nominations or awards that the film has already won. These will be placed clearly on the poster.
- The production 'blurb' — information, in tiny print, that lists the production and distribution companies as well as other information.

Key terms

Conventions The typical characteristics of a particular type of text.

Endorsement Giving approval to something.

CD-ROM Extra!

Film posters
Open the CD in the back of this book and click on the icon below to see enlarged versions of the film posters on page 17.

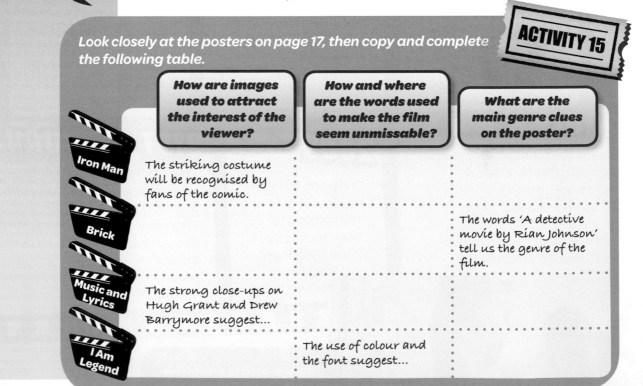

ACTIVITY 15

Look closely at the posters on page 17, then copy and complete the following table.

	How are images used to attract the interest of the viewer?	How and where are the words used to make the film seem unmissable?	What are the main genre clues on the poster?
Iron Man	The striking costume will be recognised by fans of the comic.		
Brick			The words 'A detective movie by Rian Johnson' tell us the genre of the film.
Music and Lyrics	The strong close-ups on Hugh Grant and Drew Barrymore suggest...		
I Am Legend		The use of colour and the font suggest...	

ACTIVITY 16

Using your table from Activity 15, compare how at least two of the posters on page 17 use different techniques to appeal to their audiences.

As you present your answer, it might help you to think about where you might see film posters. For example, an obvious place is in the cinema itself, where they are usually to be found on walls, or blown up to become 3D cardboard displays. However, they also appear on billboards or bus shelters.

Film trailers

Trailers are an important part of film marketing. They are similar to advertisements in that they promote a product – in this case the film. Trailers often have big budgets because film studios understand that the trailer is one of the most important ways of creating immediate interest in a film before it is released. Like posters, there are often several versions of trailers made – the earlier ones are known as 'teaser' trailers, because they are meant to tease audiences with only a few exciting details. Closer to the release date, trailers give more information, including the all-important release date.

Look closely at the following list of trailer conventions:

Trailer conventions

- Trailers include key moments from the film which are not placed in the sequence of the film, and do not give away any crucial plot details (some trailers are criticised for giving away too many details).

- The title of the film is not usually put on screen until the end of the trailer, often followed by a release date.

- The names of the main stars are put on screen early on in the trailer. This is important as it lets audiences know who they can expect to see in the film. Audiences will often decide they want to see a film just because of the stars in it.

- Sometimes the names of the director and/or producer are included, with phrases such as 'from the director/makers of....' This helps the audience to make connections between the film being trailed and previously successful and recognised films.

- Many mainstream films will use a powerful voice-over that draws our attention to the key points of the film.

- On-screen text gives important information about the film, including the stars, director/producers, tag line, title and release date. Notice the style of this text and how it is often accompanied by a musical beat.

- Music is essential in trailers as it can suggest the genre, style and plot of the film. Look at how music is used cleverly to bring all the elements of the trailer together.

1. *Watch at least four film trailers. Choose one of them and make a timeline of the key moments in it.*

2. *Watch all four trailers again. Give each one a star award (five stars is the highest rating) according to how much you feel you want to see the film after watching the trailer. Explain your reasons for giving the awards.*

3. *Choose one trailer again. Use the Internet to find the promotional poster that corresponds to the film trailer you've chosen.*

   - *Make a table like the one below to show the main similarities and differences between the poster and the trailer. Some ideas for the I Am Legend film trailer have already been given to get you started.*
   - *Can you suggest reasons for the similarities and differences?*

CD-ROM
Extra!
Trailers
Open the CD in the back of this book and click on the icon below to open a link to see some examples of film trailers.

HTML

Grade Studio

Examiner's tip

How you deconstruct media texts is an important part of your assessment. Get it right and you get higher marks!

Key terms

Typography The choice of font style and size, graphic design and layout.

I Am Legend	Poster	Trailer
How stars/ characters are represented	A single image of the lead star is shown as the central image – the film is using the star's 'pull' to attract audiences.	The lead star is shown in a series of shots with other actors – the trailer shows us how the star interacts with others and what his/ her character type is.
Use of **typography**	The poster uses a classic black serif font that suggests the serious and realistic nature of the film – it also supports the idea of the word 'Legend' being grand and memorable.	
Genre clues		
Narrative clues		
Characters and relationships		

Film website – the Internet

This section has already pointed out the importance of Internet technology in film marketing. Most films today have their own websites with 'extra features' to interest audiences, such as games, facts and trivia about the film, background details on the stars and hyperlinks to the director's commentary, etc.

The Indiana Jones website generates huge interest as the films have been so popular

Film-related websites are also important in giving information to film fans. For example, imdb.com is one of the most visited websites. If you visit the site you will see that you can find out details of any film:

- that has been made
- is being made at the moment
- is planned for production in the near future.

You can research actors, directors, producers or any other film-related personnel. It is an extremely educational (and quite addictive) site.

ACTIVITY 18

This activity encourages you to visit and use imdb.com. When the home page comes up, simply look in the search box menu and select the word 'Titles' for a film or 'Names' for a star or director, then type in the title or name in the box next to it to start your search.

You could create 'factfiles' as a class and make a display of the details you discover.

Film-related magazines also have their own websites that are popular with audiences. *Empire* magazine, for example, offers readers and non-readers of the print-based magazine the chance to subscribe to empireonline.co.uk. This site is a weekly updated review of newest releases, awards and 'in-production' projects. It is rapidly becoming more popular than the magazine itself!

ACTIVITY 19

1. *Choose an unreleased film and find out as much as you can about it from your chosen website. Ask yourself the following questions.*
   - *Does the site try to influence your opinions about the film in some way?*
   - *Are there interactive links within the site to, for example, trailers or interviews?*
   - *Does the site give any exclusive information or gossip about films/stars/directors, etc?*

2. *What are the strengths and weaknesses of the site?*

3. *Practise your research skills. Think of a director or actor. Look them up on imdb.com and write down any new information you have gained about them. You could present your findings in a short presentation to your class, including clips of films with which they have been associated.*

4. *Compare your research with information given in a film-related magazine. What are the main similarities and differences between the two media areas relating to film?*

CD-ROM
Extra!
Empireonline
Open the CD in the back of this book and click on the icon below to open a link to empireonline.

HTML

Distribution

Distribution varies from film to film. Films with big budgets may, in Britain, start with release in big London cinemas and then go on general release. Films which are less highly financed will appear at selected cinemas. Some films never make it to the cinema and go 'straight to DVD', either because their quality is thought to be poor, or because there is no money to promote them.

Spending huge amounts of money on making and promoting a film which is expected to be a blockbuster is no guarantee of box-office success. There have been many expensive flops, for example, *Waterworld* (1995), starring Kevin Costner. The film, which was said to have cost over $150 million to make, was disliked by the critics and was not an immediate success with the public (although it is believed to have made money eventually through DVD sales etc.).

Leonardo DiCaprio signing autographs for fans (2007)

There have been surprise successes too. The box office success of *William Shakespeare's Romeo and Juliet* (1996), directed by Baz Luhrmann, was so unexpected that not enough prints of the film were available! One of its stars, Leonardo DiCaprio, became a box-office draw and appeared soon after in the successful film *Titanic* (1997) which won 11 Oscars.

British film *The Full Monty* (1997) was a surprise hit for another reason. It was a low-budget film, so little money was spent on publicity and there was limited distribution. It proved to be a huge hit, mainly because people who saw it found it funny and moving, and told their friends to go and see it. Before long, the film was packing out the cinemas all over Britain and it enjoyed success in the USA too.

Film classification

Before any film can be shown in the cinema or sold as a video or DVD, it must be assessed by a regulatory body to decide which age group it is suitable for. The BBFC classifies films, while OFCOM rates videos and DVDs. You can see the BBFC classification scheme below.

 Universal: suitable for everyone.

 Video release particularly suitable for pre-school children.

 Parental Guidance: anyone can see the film, although some material may be unsuitable for children.

 Children under 12 can see the film only if accompanied by an adult.

 Not suitable for people under 15.

 Not suitable for people under 18.

 Video can only be sold through a licensed sex shop.

ACTIVITY 20

Many critics and parents have suggested that the film The Dark Knight should have been given a 15 certificate instead of a 12A because of its suggestions of violence rather than actual violence. One scene of particular concern was when The Joker holds a knife in a man's mouth, although the audience never sees any actual violence.

Why do you think suggested violence could have a harmful effect on some audiences?

CD-ROM
Extra!
The Dark Knight podcast
Open the CD in the back of this book and click on the icon below to listen to a podcast on The Dark Knight.

Film podcasts

Podcasts are audio or audio-visual files which are distributed through downloading or streaming to mobile MP3 players or personal computers. Links to the podcast are usually found on the podcast's website, and are often free to download.

Podcasts are proving to be increasingly relevant in the media area of film. As well as channel re-broadcasting podcasts such as BBC iPlayer, which offer users chances to see films on TV they have missed, film distribution companies sometimes use podcasts as a way of promoting new films, making interviews with stars available and offering film fans a way of responding to new films.

In addition, and making the most of the popularity of film review magazines such as *Empire* and TV review shows, there is a growing interest in film review podcasts. BBC iPlayer, for example, broadcasts a review podcast in its Arts, Media and Culture section, although the most popular example is the Mark Kermode and Simon Mayo Film Reviews podcast. Broadcast originally on Radio 5 Live, the podcast which is free to download is continuing to attract growing numbers of a wide range of users.

ACTIVITY 21

Click on the Mark Kermode and Simon Mayo Radio 5 Film Review podcast link on the CD-ROM and listen to the discussion.

1. *Discuss in a small group the main films reviewed in the podcast. What factors do you think Mark Kermode looks for in a good film? What factors make him critical of a film?*

2. *Working with a partner, choose two films – one of which you both love, and one of which you do not rate highly. Record yourselves discussing the films, as if it were going to be a new podcast, giving reasons for your opinions, and backing them up with references to other films too.*

3. *Share your recordings as a class, and make suggestions to each potential podcaster on ways to improve the quality/humour/clarity of the podcast.*

CD-ROM
Extra!
Film podcasts
Open the CD in the back of this book and click on the icon below to open a link to BBC Radio 5's Mark Kermode and Simon Mayo's Film Review podcast website.

This case study considers the cross-media aspects of the film industry.

Merchandise

Films sometimes use promotional toys, gadgets, clothing, franchise deals with food companies, etc. to help market themselves. Sometimes we can own a film, wear a film, take our pens to school in the film pencil case and even *eat* the film! For example, McDonald's often have a deal with Disney where they will pay Disney for the right to give away small film-related toys with their Happy Meals, thus making the meals more appealing and selling more of them. As a result, both McDonald's and Disney profit from the arrangement.

It has been claimed that the global sales of Harry Potter merchandise have made J.K. Rowling almost as much money as the sales of the books themselves. Harry Potter has become a worldwide name thanks, in part, to such a successful international marketing campaign.

Advertisements

Visiting the cinema is an experience that is pleasurable on many levels. Not only do we have the opportunity to watch eagerly awaited films on huge screens with surround sound while sitting in a comfortable seat (with a specially shaped armrest to hold a large fizzy drink!), we can also see the latest big budget advertisements – often as a version made especially for cinema viewing – as well as 'forthcoming releases' (trailers).

When media industries set up relationships with each other (for example, the advertising and film industries), and where each industry offers something to the other, it is called media synergy. Advertisers pay film distributors to advertise their products before their films are screened and, as a result, there is more money for films to be made.

Magazines

Film-related magazines also have an industry relationship with film distributors (another example of media synergy). Distributors are responsible for the marketing of a film and also for setting the release date. They buy space in film magazines to help promote their film and, in return, the magazine sells more copies based on the amount of 'inside information' on up and coming films. Sometimes this can lead to magazines running two different front covers in order to promote sales even more. For example, at the end of 2006, *Narnia: The Lion, the Witch and the Wardrobe* was due to be released on 8 December, while *King Kong* was due to be released on 15 December. *Empire* magazine ran one version of the December issue with a lion on the front, and another version with a gorilla.

The TAGLINE uses the BUZZ WORDS 'amazing' and 'special edition' to make the audience feel that they are getting something unique and valuable. The phrase 'sci-fi' stands out in blue to make a link between the whole edition and the genre of science fiction.

The TITLE BLOCK is red SANS SERIF font on a blue background which suggests both technology and masculinity. The tagline above also links the title block to the genre of science fiction.

A typical Empire magazine cover

AMAZING SCI-FI SPECIAL EDITION!

DECEMBER 2008
£3.90
$9.99 USD

EMPIRE

empireonline.com

The WEBSITE makes it possible for the audience to connect to the publishing company and to see more details about the magazine online.

The words 'Meet the new Spock and Kirk' are like an instruction. Film fans may recognise the names of the characters as the Captain and First Officer of the famous Starship *Enterprise*.

MEET THE NEW SPOCK AND KIRK!

PLUS!
QUANTUM OF SOLACE REVIEWED
PAUL NEWMAN REMEMBERED

The CENTRAL IMAGE uses a challenging DIRECT MODE OF ADDRESS of two actors looking straight at the reader in character.

STAR TREK

CHRISTMAS BLU-RAY GUIDE!
DARK KNIGHT SHAWSHANK GODFATHER & MORE!

The title of the film acts as ANCHORAGE text for the central image which may call on their FORE-KNOWLEDGE of the huge TV show and film franchise.

ON BOARD J.J. ABRAMS' ALL-ACTION EPIC!
ON SET WITH THE DAY THE EARTH STOOD STILL
THE FIRST WORD ON TERMINATOR SALVATION
TEN THINGS YOU NEED TO KNOW ABOUT AVATAR

A series of PUFFS are used to inform readers about articles connected to key film areas: behind the scenes insights, reviews and polls.

A special Blu-Ray guide emphasises the magazine as leading the way with film technology and quality films.

★CASE STUDY★
ACTIVITY

Look at the film pages in a range of magazines.
These could include Empire, Total Film, Total DVD, Heat, *the* Guardian Weekend *magazine, etc. Discuss how films are marketed in these magazines. You might like to consider the following areas:*

- *How many pages are there in the magazine?*
- *Who is the likely target audience of the magazine?*
- *How many pages are devoted to film?*
- *How many films are given space in the magazine?*
- *Choose one or two films that are found in most, if not all, the magazines. Compare the different responses of the reviewers to each film.*
- *Choose your favourite review from one of the magazines. Analyse its style and the techniques it uses to appeal to its readers.*

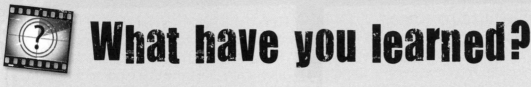

What have you learned?

In this chapter you have learned about:

Texts

- Analysing narratives
- Analysing and comparing posters and trailers
- Exploring websites
- Looking at the construction of film magazine covers

Media language

Genre

- How film genres use clear characteristics to allow audiences to classify and engage with them
- How sub-genres and cross-genres develop
- Case study genre – science fiction. How genres develop over time
- How to include an understanding of genre in coursework

Narrative

- How linear narratives are organised
- How non-linear narratives use subversions
- The importance of character types and their function in narratives
- The importance of audience positioning in narratives

Representation

- How representations lead to stereotyping
- How different social groups can be categorised through representation
- The representation of women in science fiction
- The representation of social issues and events in science fiction

Audiences

- Thinking about target audiences
- Considering audience appeal
- Exploring audience responses and needs
- Discussing the effects of film classification on audiences

Institutions

- Film technology in relation to film-making, marketing and viewing
- The key dates of the film industry
- Film promotion, looking especially at posters, trailers and websites

Cross-media

- The cross-media nature of film including:
  - marketing and distribution
  - advertising
  - magazines
  - the Internet
  - television

Television

Your learning

In this chapter you will learn about:

- television history – public service and commercial broadcasting
- TV production
- the regulation of TV channels and programmes
- channel identity
- analysing opening sequences
- television genres and their appeal to audiences
- the cross-media nature of television

ACTIVITY 1

1 *Keep a TV diary for a few days (but not more than one week). Note down:*
    - *when you watch and for how long*
    - *which programmes you actively try to see*
    - *where you watch*
    - *whether you watch alone or with others.*

2 *What would you miss most if you had to spend three months without television:*
    - *particular programmes or types of programme*
    - *the coverage of particular events*
    - *particular channels?*

3 *Do you think having access to the Internet makes having a television unnecessary? What are the main attractions of each?*

UXBRIDGE COLLEGE
LEARNING CENTRE

Television – a brief history and introduction

From Activity 1, what did you learn about your own viewing habits? Most programmes attract quite specific audiences, and many of the programmes you watch will be aimed at you, the **target audience**. Other programmes you watch are influenced by other factors. For example, you may not have as much choice about what you watch if you are watching television with your family. Who is in charge of the remote control in your home?

If you watch a media text such as a TV programme with focus and attention, it is called *primary* consumption. If you are doing something else (such as homework) while the television is on, it is called *secondary* consumption.

Secondary viewing

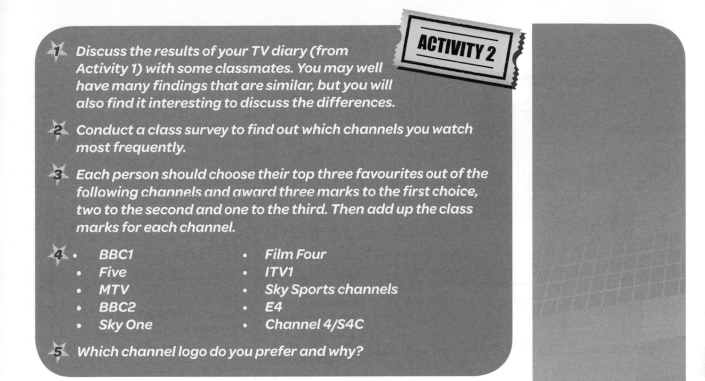

1. *Discuss the results of your TV diary (from Activity 1) with some classmates. You may well have many findings that are similar, but you will also find it interesting to discuss the differences.*

2. *Conduct a class survey to find out which channels you watch most frequently.*

3. *Each person should choose their top three favourites out of the following channels and award three marks to the first choice, two to the second and one to the third. Then add up the class marks for each channel.*

4.
   - *BBC1*
   - *Five*
   - *MTV*
   - *BBC2*
   - *Sky One*
   - *Film Four*
   - *ITV1*
   - *Sky Sports channels*
   - *E4*
   - *Channel 4/S4C*

5. *Which channel logo do you prefer and why?*

Did you find it hard to imagine life without television? You may well have several television sets in your home, including one in your bedroom! Your TV diary will already have shown you how often you turn to the television for your media entertainment.

Less than 60 years ago, it would have been unusual for a family to have even one 20 cm wide black-and-white television set – and it could only transmit one channel! To get a clear idea of the major developments in television history, look at the timeline on the next page.

Television is less than 100 years old

UK television timeline

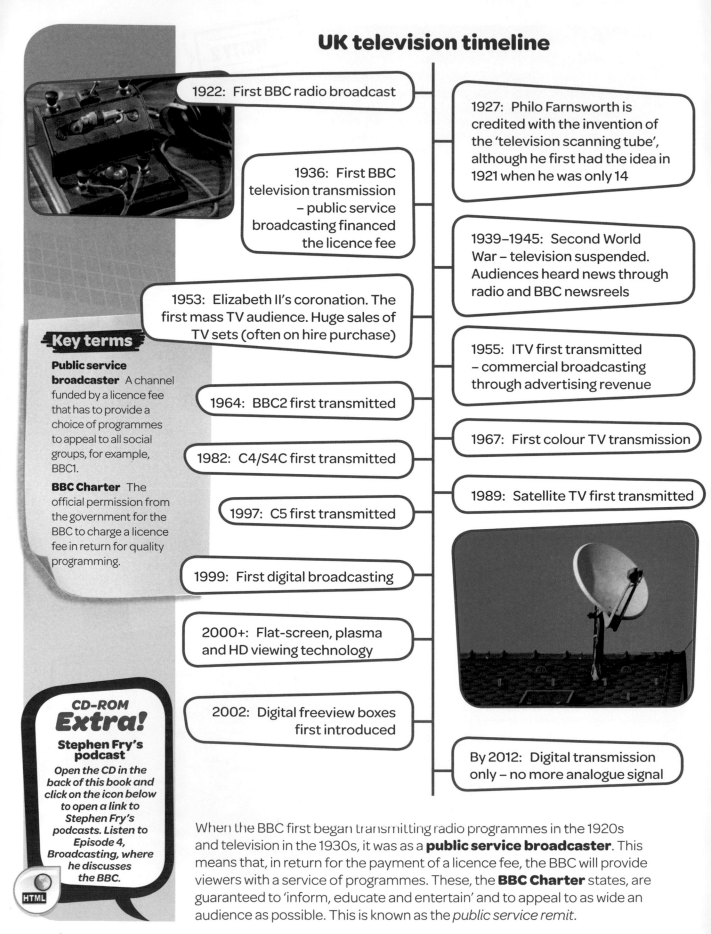

1922: First BBC radio broadcast

1927: Philo Farnsworth is credited with the invention of the 'television scanning tube', although he first had the idea in 1921 when he was only 14

1936: First BBC television transmission – public service broadcasting financed the licence fee

1939–1945: Second World War – television suspended. Audiences heard news through radio and BBC newsreels

1953: Elizabeth II's coronation. The first mass TV audience. Huge sales of TV sets (often on hire purchase)

1955: ITV first transmitted – commercial broadcasting through advertising revenue

1964: BBC2 first transmitted

1967: First colour TV transmission

1982: C4/S4C first transmitted

1989: Satellite TV first transmitted

1997: C5 first transmitted

1999: First digital broadcasting

2000+: Flat-screen, plasma and HD viewing technology

2002: Digital freeview boxes first introduced

By 2012: Digital transmission only – no more analogue signal

Key terms

Public service broadcaster A channel funded by a licence fee that has to provide a choice of programmes to appeal to all social groups, for example, BBC1.

BBC Charter The official permission from the government for the BBC to charge a licence fee in return for quality programming.

CD–ROM
Extra!
Stephen Fry's podcast
Open the CD in the back of this book and click on the icon below to open a link to Stephen Fry's podcasts. Listen to Episode 4, Broadcasting, where he discusses the BBC.

HTML

When the BBC first began transmitting radio programmes in the 1920s and television in the 1930s, it was as a **public service broadcaster**. This means that, in return for the payment of a licence fee, the BBC will provide viewers with a service of programmes. These, the **BBC Charter** states, are guaranteed to 'inform, educate and entertain' and to appeal to as wide an audience as possible. This is known as the *public service remit*.

When ITV first began transmitting television programmes in the 1950s, it was as an independent **commercial broadcaster**. Independent television channels are paid money in return for time slots that advertisers use to promote their products. Such time slots vary in price depending on whether they are during **peak time** (6.00 p.m. to 10.30 p.m.) or not.

1. Look at the television schedule for any day of the week in a TV listings magazine. Count up how many programmes on BBC1 and BBC2 are informative, educational and/or entertaining (you may wish to look at the information on the Uses and Gratifications Theory on page 76 before tackling this activity).

2. Now look at the programmes that are on the commercial channels listed in Activity 2 during peak time. Can you identify any types of programme which are especially popular?

3. Discuss as a class or in small groups whether the BBC should be allowed to continue charging a licence fee. Use information from this activity and the class survey. Start by looking back at your schedules and try to find out what programmes the BBC offers that are different from commercial channels. You may also want to interview your teachers and ask them about their views on the BBC.

What do you think would happen to viewing choices if every channel was funded by advertising revenue? Advertisers are most interested in buying time slots around or during peak time programmes, when most people are watching. This puts pressure on commercial broadcasting channels to produce more and more of the types of programme that are most popular. What could be the effects of this?

Television production

Television programmes are either made directly by television companies or commissioned from smaller freelance companies. Every role in the making of a TV programme is important – ranging from those in **pre-production** through to **production** and **post-production**. Look at the list of some of the key roles shown on the next page – which ones do you think are the most important? You will find a more thorough list on the CD-ROM.

Key terms

Commercial broadcaster A channel funded by money from advertising, for example, ITV.

Peak time The hours between 6.00 p.m. and 10.30 p.m. when most people are watching television and viewing figures are at their highest.

Key terms

Pre-production Activities at the beginning of the production process, e.g. ideas, bids for finance, storyboards, scriptwriting, planning and designing, set construction, casting and rehearsals.

Production Shooting in purpose-built sets or in outside locations.

Post-production Activities at the end of the production process, e.g. editing, sound dubbing, credits, marketing and promotion, focus groups, trailers, articles and features.

Key roles in television production

Executive producer arranges finance and oversees the whole project, including editorial decisions.

Producer/Director is responsible for the setting up and shooting of every scene.

Researcher for example, ensures all details of location, sets, props and costume are appropriate and accurate for the style and time period of the programme.

Scriptwriter writes the script for the programme; this could be from an original idea or an adaptation.

Camera operator responsible for setting up every shot in a scene. This may involve working with other operators for techniques such as shot reverse-shot.

Editor takes the 'raw footage' shot each day and edits it into a sequence of scenes that tell the story. This can also involve adding music, fades and dissolves.

Production assistant looks after all administration, including scripts and running orders.

Actors/performers create believable characters. The success of a programme can depend on audiences appreciating the actors' performances – they are often the most memorable feature of a programme. This also applies to presenters. The most successful programmes usually mean stardom (and pay rises!) for the lead actors or presenters.

All of the above roles are important at different times and in different ways. Ultimately, it is the performance in front of the camera which attracts and keeps audiences, but for those performances to be outstanding, the team behind the camera need to have first done their specialist jobs. A television production is a complex task and planning is absolutely vital. However, some things are unpredictable, no matter how good the plan.

What can go wrong

- Multiple takes are often needed to 'get it right' in front of the camera – look at 'blooper' programmes, which are about moments when actors and presenters do not get it right.

- Live audiences: unpredictability on the part of guests and audiences and having to manage large numbers.

- The weather: some programmes have to be cancelled or postponed if weather conditions are not just right.

- *Eastenders* is filmed three months ahead but it is designed to look as though it is happening today. This is difficult when seasons change in that time!

- Illness or scandal: a key character or presenter may be too ill to appear or may be involved in some public scandal.

- Skill and teamwork are needed to get over production problems as they arise. For example, in *Doctor Who*, the eruption of Vesuvius in Pompeii in AD79 was filmed in 2008 in South Wales!

The powerful WWII scenes at Dunkirk in the film *Atonement* (2007) were actually filmed at Redcar on the North-East coast of England

Television regulation

Whenever you study a media industry, it is always important to consider how the industry is regulated in order to protect audiences from potentially offensive or harmful material.

The regulatory body, Ofcom, has the responsibility of ensuring that TV and radio audiences are protected in areas such as taste, decency, fairness and privacy. If Ofcom decides that a programme does not uphold these standards, they can insist either that a programme is cancelled or that a warning is given at the beginning of the show.

The most vulnerable group in terms of being potentially affected by programme content is young children. Terrestrial television stations use the **watershed** to give parents the chance to ensure their children do not see adult material, such as explicit language or violence. Do you think broadcasters ever stretch the watershed agreement?

One problem that Ofcom faces is how to regulate television programmes that are increasingly viewed over the Internet. There is no clear regulation of programmes that are **downloaded**, and this means there is a chance of audiences, especially children, seeing programmes that would normally be censored by Ofcom.

8.00 Holby City
Change of Heart. The desecration of his wife's grave leaves Linden deeply upset. Jac, meanwhile, probes Joseph for news from South Africa, before a turn for the worse sees her rushed into theatre.

Michael Spence	Hari Dhillon	Maddy Young	Nadine Lewington
Jac Naylor	Rosie Marcel	Donna Jackson	Jaye Jacobs
Mark Williams	Robert Powell	Daisha Anderson	Rebecca Grant
Connie Beauchamp		Jayne Grayson	Stella Gonet
	Amanda Mealing	Jamie Norton	Dominic Colchester
Elliot Hope	Paul Bradley	Barry Carter	Francis Magee
Joseph Byrne	Luke Roberts	India Carter	Christina Baily
Linden Cullen	Duncan Pow	Liam Harris	Craig Stein

Writer David Lawrence; Producer Jane Wallbank
Director Daikin Marsh (S) (AD)   6536
Amanda Mealing answers One Final Question: page 162

9.00 Criminal Justice
DRAMA OF THE WEEK

RT CHOICE 2/5. Newly arrived in prison, Ben has already but unwittingly made a deadly enemy. Meanwhile his defence team strikes a deal with the prosecution – but it's one that will require him to tell a lie. Continues tomorrow at 9pm.
For cast see Wednesday/Thursday (S) (AD)   6772

8.00 Today at Wimbledon
The ladies' quarter-final action plus a preview of tomorrow's corresponding men's matches.
Repeated tomorrow at 10.30am (S)   4178
Watch again over the next seven days, after 12 midnight, at www.bbc.co.uk/iplayer

9.00 Duncan Bannatyne Takes On Tobacco
DOCUMENTARY OF THE WEEK

RT CHOICE Multi-millionaire *Dragons' Den* veteran Duncan Bannatyne, himself a former smoker, travels to Africa to find out why increasing numbers of young people are taking up the habit. There he meets children as young as ten who not only smoke, but try to make their living from selling cigarettes. Having gathered evidence of one British-based firm's extraordinary marketing practices, the uncompromising Scot prepares to confront the company on his return to Britain. Showing in the *This World* documentary strand.
Director Alison Pinkney; Producer Debbie Christie (S) (AD)   7642

Channel identity

All television channels try to create a recognisable channel identity for themselves, so that audiences will feel a sense of familiarity and loyalty to the station. They create this identity by using:

- short snippets of music
- special graphics using the channel logo (called screen idents)
- seasonal idents
- certain types of programme, including flagship programmes for which the channel is known.

The identity of BBC1

The BBC is the oldest and most established broadcaster in the UK. As a public service broadcaster, BBC channels try to convey a high-quality image to their audiences, in order for them to feel the licence fee is worthwhile. They convey this image by creating a strong channel identity.

A recent series of on-screen **idents** for the BBC has been based on the symbol of a circle. Peter Fincham, Controller for BBC 1 in 2008 said, 'In an increasingly competitive marketplace, a channel needs to stand out from the crowd and I believe our new identity is just what's needed for BBC 1. The circle, which is at the heart of this campaign, has been familiar to BBC 1 viewers over the years, but what we've got here is modern, forward looking and surprising.'

The on screen idents are set in everyday and realistic locations, but show people or animals doing extraordinary things. The idents cover everything from daredevil motorbikes to synchronised hippos. It's warm and it's dynamic.

Other features of the BBC

- The BBC is well known for particular programmes, such as news and current affairs, documentaries, drama, sport and children's programmes.
- The BBC promotes itself in creative ways. In 1997 the BBC used Lou Reed's song 'Perfect Day' to show how the BBC promotes different types of music. The promo ended with the text on screen: 'Whatever your musical taste, it is catered for by BBC Radio and Television.'
- Flagship programmes include *The Evening News*, *Blue Peter*, *Doctor Who*, *Eastenders* and any big budget period/classic dramas.
- There are special promotions for forthcoming programmes, for example, Wimbledon, Christmas specials and even especially dramatic episodes of familiar programmes such as *Eastenders* or *Doctor Who*.

BBC1 is famous for its series *Strictly Come Dancing*

Key terms

Ident Like a logo, an instantly recognisable feature of the film, character or company, for example, the Hulk's green fists.

CD-ROM
Extra!
BBC Perfect Day Promotion
Open the CD in the back of this book and click on the icon below to open a link to the BBC's Perfect Day promotion.

HTML

Explore the BBC website. It is one of the most visited websites in the world and is updated every minute. You may like to think about the following:

- *What are the most eye-catching features on the page?*
- *What is the lead story? If you check again later, has the story changed in some way?*
- *There are several interactive features on the site. Play with some of them and give your verdict!*
- *Experiment with how iPlayer works. Why do you think this is a good feature for the BBC to promote?*
- *Follow a link to a radio-related link, for example, 'The Best of Chris Moyles' podcast. How does it relate to the radio station itself?*
- *Scroll to the bottom of the site, and open the 'About The BBC' link. Read through this information – you will find it supports this chapter on television very well.*
- *Present or discuss your findings and opinions about the site.*

CD-ROM
Extra!
BBC website
Open the CD in the back of this book and click on the icon below to open a link to the BBC website.

HTML

A Channel 4 on-screen ident

Channel 4

Channel 4 started in 1982 and had a reputation from the start for making challenging programmes that targeted a wide range of audiences. It is a commercial broadcaster, but has a strong public service image. The original, animated logo using early computer technology came to be seen as the embodiment of a channel that was constantly re-inventing itself and challenging the expectations of its viewers.

More recent on-screen idents have seen the Channel 4 logo being created out of unusual objects, such as skyscrapers, hedges and electricity pylons. You could try creating a new ident for Channel 4 or another channel.

Other features of Channel 4
Channel 4:

- is the only terrestrial channel deliberately to target teenagers with programmes such as *T4* and *The Tube*
- has launched sister channels that have their own identity:
  - More 4 is for serious programming
  - E4 is for lighter and youth programming
  - Film 4 is a dedicated film channel
  - 4Music is an independent radio channel
  - 4oD is an 'on demand' service that allows viewers to see any programmes from the last 30 days

- is more independent than the BBC and is able to take more risks in subject matter with, for example, controversial documentaries
- airs popular big-budget American dramas such as *The OC, ER, Entourage, One Tree Hill* and *Brothers and Sisters*
- launched a new music channel – 4Music – on Friday 15 August 2008
- makes and funds films
- has flagship programmes – *Hollyoaks, Skins, Richard and Judy, Friends, Big Brother, Channel 4 News.*

ACTIVITY 6

Explore the Channel 4 website. It is a site that really reflects the identity of the channel itself. You may like to think about the following:

- *How is the page organised?*

- *How are audiences encouraged to interact with the site (and even with Channel 4 itself)?*

- *Scroll to the bottom of the site and open the 'Advertising on 4' link. Read through this information – what do you learn about Channel 4 as a commercial broadcaster?*

- *Scroll to the bottom of the site, and open the 'About C4' link. You will find the information supports this chapter on television very well.*

- *Stay inside the 'About C4' link. Under the 'Useful Links' tab, open the '4 Producers' link, and then click on 'Commissioning'. Here you will find some fascinating material which tells you how and why Channel 4 makes certain programmes.*

- *Present or discuss what you have learned about Channel 4.*

Analysing opening sequences

Consider the key concepts of **genre**, **narrative** and **representation** in relation to television programmes. In many ways we could say that:

- genre shapes the codes/key features in a television programme
- narrative shapes the structure and organisation of the programme
- representation shapes the messages for the audiences of the programme.

Analysing television **opening (or title) sequences** is a useful way of thinking about the ways in which programmes as a whole are constructed with meanings for their target audiences. They are used to create instant identity and appeal.

CORONATION STREET

ACTIVITY 7

Look at the still frame shot from the opening sequence of Coronation Street. What clues does it give you about the programme? Copy and complete the table below (you'll see that some examples have been added to get you started). If you are able to watch the opening, you'll be able to pick out many more points!

What you can see	Clues about the programme
The camera shows us the key features of the area: the terraced housing and cobbled streets.	Establishes that the programme is set in a traditional area with a sense of community.
The title of the programme.	Coronation Street is written in a white, traditional font to emphasise the traditional nature of the programme.

Just from the still frames of an opening sequence, it is possible to start making observations about genre, narrative and representation.

Television genres and audiences

ACTIVITY 8

1. Watch a variety of opening sequences. Explore what is suggested to audiences through visual images and soundtrack. Consider:
   - the clues that suggest the genre of the programme
   - how location and time are established
   - how groups of people are represented, if at all
   - how the soundtrack gives clues about the content of the programme
   - how any lettering used relates to the style of the programme.

2. Storyboard *the opening sequence of a news or current affairs programme set in your local area (see pages 106–107 in Chapter 5 if you need help with storyboarding). Think about all the features you looked out for in the sequences you watched. You might like to think about:*
   - *the kinds of issue and event that local viewers would be interested in*
   - *the presenter of the programme*
   - *the style of reporting*
   - *music and graphics that reflect the style of the programme*
   - *the role of local residents.*

ACTIVITY 9

1. *Look at a daily TV schedule in a newspaper. Focus on BBC1, BBC2, ITV1, C4 and Five. List all the genres that you can find, such as situation comedy and news. Make a note of how many of each you can find. Discuss the genres that are most popular with teenagers.*

2. *In small groups, think of a new TV programme aimed at and featuring teenagers. Write down what genre the programme belongs to and when it will be shown. Add any other important details, such as what will happen and who will feature in it. If you wish, you could develop the news/current affairs programme idea from the previous activity.*

3. *Present your ideas to the rest of the class and listen to the ideas of other groups.*

4. *Think about all the ideas put forward. What were the most noticeable similarities and differences? Were there any particularly popular genres of programme? Why might that be?*

Key terms

Storyboard The key moments of a story shown using images and notes – see the example on page 107.

Examiner's tip

Storyboarding is a key media skill. Use this for reference if you use storyboarding in any Controlled Assessment assignment.

Examiner's tip

You could possibly use your findings in Activity 9 in a Controlled Assessment assignment. It is a good example of Assessment Objective 3 (AO3) research. These research methods are also good practice for the research you will need to undertake in preparation for the External Assessment.

Scheduling

You will probably notice that some television genres are more popular than others, and that these are often scheduled during peak time. Scheduling is an important strategy that broadcasters use to encourage as many people as possible to watch their channel. Techniques used to do this include:

- *Hammocking* – a new or less popular programme is scheduled between two high ratings (very popular) programmes. The idea is that viewers will keep watching the new programme after the first one has finished since they will be waiting for the third programme anyway.

- *Pre-echoing* – high ratings programmes are often advertised days before they are scheduled and early on during the actual day of transmission. This is to create a sense of excitement and expectation in audiences and also to attract new audiences.

- *Theming* – having special theme days, or theme weeks, such as 'Shark Week'.

- *Stacking* – grouping together programmes with similar appeal to 'sweep' the viewer along from one programme to the next.

- *Bridging* – when a channel tries to prevent the audience from changing channels on the hour or half hour. This can be achieved by:

  - having a programme already under way and something compelling happening at the 'changing point'

  - running a programme late so that people 'hang around' and miss the start of other programmes

  - advertising the next programme during the credits of the previous one.

E4

8.00 Friends
Series seven. Rachel bumps into an old college friend. (S) (AD)
8.30 Chandler turns to Joey and Ross for some much-needed help. (S)
9.00 Scrubs
New. 9/11; series seven. *My Dumb Luck* The board attempts to force Dr Kelso into retirement and JD and Turk try to show up Dr Cox when he is unable to diagnose a patient. (S)
www.radiotimes.com/scrubs
9.30 My Name Is Earl
9/22; series three. *Randy in Charge* Earl creates a sketch to deter kids from a life of crime. (S) (AD)

The Uses and Gratifications Theory

TV programmes are produced by teams of people who conduct extensive **market research** in order to find out what different audiences want to see on television. They are aware that audiences use the media to satisfy certain needs or requirements. Blumler and Katz discuss audience demand in their Theory of Uses and Gratifications (see page 76). To summarise, they suggest that audiences need to:
- be INFORMED and EDUCATED about the world
- IDENTIFY with characters and situations
- be ENTERTAINED
- use the media as a talking point for SOCIAL INTERACTION
- ESCAPE from their daily lives.

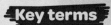
Key terms

Market research
Finding out what audiences like or dislike about aspects of the media through interviews, surveys and focus groups.

1. Look again at a TV schedule. Can you identify any obvious scheduling techniques? For example, can you spot channels using the hammocking technique?

2. Now apply The Uses and Gratifications Theory to the television programmes and genres you have just identified. This will help you see which audience needs are being met by each genre. Put your answers for each television programme you have chosen into a table like the one below, adding ticks where appropriate.

	Inform	Identify	Entertain	Social interaction	Escape
Uses					
Gratifications					

Television drama

Television drama is a hugely popular television genre, attracting wide-ranging audiences simply because there are so many different dramas to choose from in terms of both style and content. Since it is such a large genre, it is useful to divide it up further into **sub-genres** such as crime drama, medical drama and docu-drama, in order to look at it more closely.

Key terms

Sub-genre Genres can be divided into sub-genres, for example, teen comedies are a sub-genre of comedy (see Chapter 1: Film for further details).

TV Drama

Crime drama

Medical drama

Docu-drama

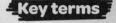

Desperate Housewives is a very popular television drama

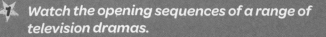

1. Watch the opening sequences of a range of television dramas.

2. Complete a copy of the diagram below, showing the typical sub-genre conventions or characteristics. One has been done for you already. You may need to add more arms or boxes.

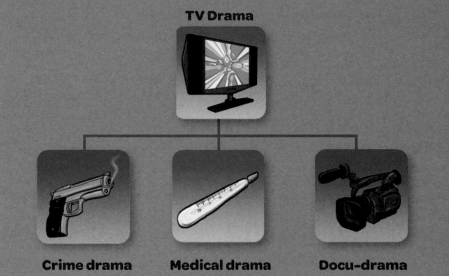

TV Drama

Crime drama Medical drama Docu-drama

3. What other impressions do you get from the opening sequences? Try to add in more notes on your diagram about any of the following areas: music, striking images, on-screen text.

4. Discuss with a partner what storylines are suggested by the openings. What clues tell you the kinds of story that will be important in the programmes? Look out for where the camera spends extra time, giving importance to certain moments and particular characters and their stories.

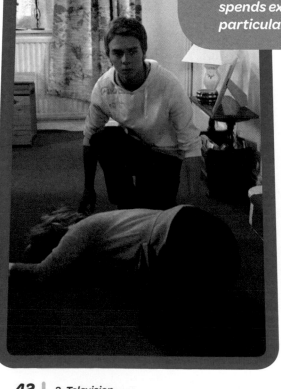

Coronation Street villain

Camerawork

Some types of camera shot are used a lot in television drama. The aim is to make it seem as though the audience is either 'there' in the scene through point-of-view shots or 'looking on' through the use of lots of close-ups and shots through windows and doors. (You may like to look at the section on audience involvement on page 11 in Chapter 1: Film.)

Characters

Having central characters that the audience can get to know well is essential to television drama. These may play certain roles in the story, for example, heroes, villains and helpers (see page 103). However, often, realistic characters are harder to categorise into character types, since in real life people tend not to be heroes and villains!

Play a game with a partner. (Alternatively, you could make this a whole-class activity with rounds and a final winner.)

1 **Each person must choose two characters from different well-known television drama series.**

2 **Think of three facts about each character and give them one by one to your partner as clues, starting with the most difficult. Your partner must guess who your chosen characters are. Award 5 points for guessing with just one clue, 3 for two guesses and 1 for three guesses.**

Analysing character can focus our attention on one or more of the following important areas:

- the character's role in the drama
- their relationship with other characters
- the ways that the actor brings the character to life:
  - use of voice or accent
  - movement and gesture
  - emotional power to engage with the audience.
- the impact of the character on audiences over a long period of time.

The audience can usually spot two main types of character in a drama – those who are less important and are there for 'padding', and those around whom the main narrative(s) centre. For example, in a medical drama the patients are only shown for part of one programme, whereas the hospital staff are seen week after week. The less important characters are less developed and often more **stereotyped** than the main characters or **central protagonists**.

Setting

The location of a TV drama is important in establishing a sense of a real place where the story can exist. Many regional features may well appear, such as landmarks and the local accent, dress and customs of those who live there.

Characters in soap operas become very familiar to their audiences

Ramsey Street – the famous setting for the Australian soap _Neighbours_

> ### Key terms
>
> **Stereotyping** Grouping people together according to simple shared characteristics, without allowing for any individual uniqueness.
>
> **Central protagonists** Key characters around whom the text and narrative are centred.

These features are included to encourage a strong sense of engagement with the world of the drama, the characters and their lives. Fans of TV drama sometimes write to their favourite characters, forgetting that they are played by actors and do not really exist!

One of the most important features of the majority of television dramas is that they create realistic worlds that audiences can believe in.

Soap opera

Soap opera is one of the most popular sub-genres of drama on television. It has its own set of conventions, all of which are designed to make viewers believe that the world of the programme really exists.

Radio soap opera *The Archers* is the world's longest running radio soap and was first aired in 1950

Soap operas began as serialised dramas, first on radio and later on television, paid for by washing-powder manufacturers. It became clear that the audience for daytime soap operas – housewives at home during the day – also enjoyed dramas based in hospital wards and in doctors' surgeries. Before long, soap operas appeared during peak-time viewing. Early examples included *The Archers* on Radio 4 and *Coronation Street* on ITV, which became popular in the 1960s and still have appeal today.

Recent UK soap operas include *Eastenders*, which began broadcasting on BBC1 in 1985, and *Hollyoaks* on Channel 4, which began life in 1995. *Desperate Housewives* and *Ugly Betty* on Channel 4 are popular American dramas that also have large followings.

Ugly Betty is popular with teenage audiences

ACTIVITY 13

Find out more about soap operas. Research the most important and popular soaps and how they have developed since they were first transmitted.
For each series, try to find out:
* *when the series started*
* *where it is set*
* *any ways in which the series has changed over the years.*

Soap operas usually have a **multi-stranded narrative** where there is more than one story in one episode. The most important narrative in any particular episode usually acts as a cliff-hanger to keep audiences interested until the next episode. These narratives are interwoven or mixed together; it is possible to draw a special chart called a **cross-plot** to make it easier to analyse how the narrative works and which characters are given the most screen time.

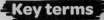

ACTIVITY 14

Use the chart below to help you create your own cross-plot of an episode of your favourite soap opera. The cross-plot outlined is from a fictitious episode of a soap opera set in Cardiff.

1. *Start by watching the episode and making a list of all the scenes featured and what happens in them. There could well be more than 15.*

2. *Draw a chart like the one below that includes the main characters and three to five of the most important storylines in the boxes on the left. Make a column for each scene.*

3. *Put an X in each scene where a character from a particular storyline is featured.*

4. *If a character also appears briefly in another scene/storyline, put a small asterisk (*) in that scene.*

The Bay 17/09/2009	scene 1	scene 2	scene 3	scene 4	scene 5	scene 6	scene 7	scene 8	scene 9	scene 10
STORY 1 – James Burgess The rugby tickets	X		X	*		X		X		X
STORY 2 – Carys and Chris The misunderstanding			X		X		X		X	
STORY 3 – Mrs Hendrikson Bomb scare at the assembly building		X	*	X					*	

Now that you have created your own cross-plot, you can analyse the ways in which the different storylines are interwoven, and how certain storylines dominate the episode.

- What do you notice about the pace and frequency of scenes towards the end of the episode?
- Which storyline does the episode end on?
- Why do some characters appear in more than one storyline?

Other important characteristics to look for when analysing soap opera are:

- a strong sense of realism in the setting and atmosphere
- a difference between the stable, regular characters (usually the inhabitants of the town/area/district) and the visiting characters who are just there for one or two episodes (usually visitors to the central location, as well as friends, relatives and 'love interests' of the inhabitants)
- sets that are carefully planned to be as believable as possible; décor, props and the behaviour of people in them are designed to convince the audience that they really do exist
- a central meeting place where characters can join together and interact
- episodes that usually follow the pattern of a normal day, i.e. morning until night.

Grade Studio

ACTIVITY 15

1. *You could now watch two different British soap operas, trying to identify as many of the above characteristics as you can.*

2. *If you have time, you could also watch one popular British soap opera and one American soap or drama. Then compare the storylines, characters and settings. Try to think of reasons to explain the main differences between them.*

ACTIVITY 16

1. *Find two pages from TV listings magazines that have features/articles on two different soap operas.*

2. *Stick them onto A3 paper and annotate them, pointing out all their typical features and the ways the dramas have been made to seem interesting and appealing, for example, by focusing on the dramatic developments in the storyline of a regular character to encourage viewers to want to see what happens to them.*

Lifestyle programmes

There has been a huge explosion in the number of lifestyle programmes in the last 20 years and more recently there have been lifestyle satellite channels such as Discovery, Lifestyle and UKTV Food that only screen lifestyle programmes.

A lifestyle programme might be described as one that focuses on home, garden, food and family concerns. They have proved popular with a range of audiences, especially since the early 1990s. The main target audience for these programmes tends to be homeowners, but programme makers keep trying to make them appeal to teenagers too.

Most terrestrial channels have their own food programmes, and while DIY shows are usually screened during the day, food programmes are often screened during peak time since they attract a high number of viewers.

Food programmes were originally targeted at 'housewives at home', and many still appeal mostly to female viewers who are traditionally seen as the 'food preparers'. But more recently there has been such a rise in male celebrity chefs, that male viewers have become more interested in cooking! And the number of boys taking Food Technology GCSE courses has increased recently by more than 30 per cent.

ACTIVITY 17

1 *You may well be familiar with at least some of the following food programmes. List those that are familiar to you, putting them in your own order of preference. Explain why some are more familiar to you than others.*
   - **Masterchef**
   - **Ramsay's Kitchen Nightmares**
   - **Nigella Express**
   - **The F Word**
   - **Saturday Kitchen**
   - **Delia**
   - **Jamie at Home**
   - **Hell's Kitchen**
   - **Ready, Steady, Cook**

2 *Lifestyle programmes are not often targeted at teenagers, but this is not because teenagers are not interested in their family, their surroundings or the food they eat! Outline your own lifestyle programme that you feel will appeal to a teenage audience. Think about the following aspects of the programme:*
   - *the presenter*
   - *the main focus areas*
   - *the music and guests*
   - *the channel and scheduling*
   - *the production values – are these programmes expensive to make?*

TELEVISION
CASE STUDY

TELEVISION WEBSITES

This case study discusses some of the cross-media aspects of television websites. The iInternet has had a very big impact on television and is a good example of cross-media. In the same way that magazines and newspapers have their own interactive websites, television channels and even television programmes have their own sites that are full of extra facts, information and interactive games.

Skins

This chapter has already looked in some detail at the BBC and C4 websites, but most individual programmes also have their own websites.

★CASE STUDY★ ACTIVITY A

Look at the information below on the Skins website. Then, choosing either the Skins website or another programme website, explore it. Present your findings, explaining how the website makes connections to the programme and yet also offers something different.

http://www.e4.com/blog/skins-news/posts/1-10/view.e4

Skins
Blog
The gang
Episode guide
Pictures
Video
Music
Skins needs you!
Series II picture recap
On your mobile

Blog archive

▸ January
▸ February
▸ March
▸ April
▸ May
▸ June
▸ July
▸ August
▸ September
▸ October
▸ November
▸ December

Posted by: Skins   on Wed Apr 16, 2008 at 11:37 am:

In January 2007 we were introduced to Tony Stonem and his crew. It seems like before then TV trailers were something as basic and run of the mill as a set of clips showing you what was coming up. How very old fashioned. Then Skins came along, and we took one look at that house party trailer and realised:

1   We needed to get out more.
2   We wanted to get to know these misfits (and ask them where they got their clothes from).
3   That song by that band Gossip was really rather good.

Skins has proved to be a big hit, both as a TV drama and a website

Big Brother

Love it or hate it, everyone has heard of the reality television show *Big Brother*. Screened on Channel 4, along with sister programmes on E4, the show has helped to make reality television one of the most popular television genres of the 21st century.

Big Brother's popularity

From May to September 2008, *Big Brother 9* was transmitted every day to an average of 5 million viewers, which was perceived as a disappointment compared to the ratings of previous years. Nevertheless, *Big Brother* has proved itself a guaranteed audience attraction for Channel 4 and Endemol (its production company) for a number of years, and is part of Channel 4's identity, combining an eye with the Channel 4 logo.

The reality TV show began in 2000 and was the first of its kind in terms of the genre of reality TV. Since then, the show has been transmitted each summer with its simple formula of a group of 'ordinary' people who have been thrown together in 'the Big Brother house' completing tasks and bidding for public approval, with those least popular being voted out each Friday evening, during an 'eviction show'.

The show is referred to by Endemol UK executive Tim Hincks as a 'banker' for the channel, 'just like Wimbledon or *EastEnders* is to the BBC'.

Cross-media in Big Brother

Part of *Big Brother*'s appeal is its effective use of cross-media to self-publicise. It transmits partner programmes alongside the main show on C4 – 'Big Brother's Little Brother', 'Big Brother's Big Mouth', 'Diary Room Uncut' and 'Big Brother's Big Ears' are all screened on E4 and are designed to target a younger audience as they are more 'edgy' and controversial – often being screened after the watershed.

Big Brother's website

Big Brother runs a successful website throughout the duration of the show's run. When the programme began in 2000, the *Big Brother* website accounted for 99.8 per cent of all traffic and was accessed by over 2 million visitors, one in five of all UK home surfers (according to research firm Net Value).

CD-ROM
Extra!
Big Brother website
Open the CD in the back of this book and click on the icon below to open a link to the Big Brother website.

HTML

Today the site is highly interactive and invites the comments and opinions of site users. It includes a mixture of audio sound bites, video clips and text news reports on the housemates, as well as links to other C4 programmes and interactive games.

★CASE STUDY★
ACTIVITY B

Visit the **Big Brother** *website*. What do you think is its most interesting feature?

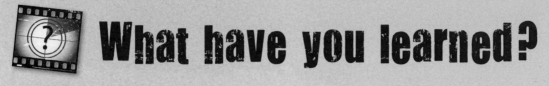

What have you learned?

In this chapter you have learned about:

Texts

- Analysing openings
- Analysing narratives
- Looking at the construction of drama, soap and lifestyle programmes

Media language

Genre

- How television genres use clear characteristics to allow audiences to classify and engage with them
- How sub-genres and cross-genres develop
- Case study genres – television drama, soap opera and lifestyle programmes
- Cross-media case study – How programmes develop and change over time

Narrative

- The construction of television narratives
- How to use cross-plotting to analyse narrative construction

Representation

- How different social groups are represented in programmes
- The representation of characters, settings and issues in different genres
- The changing nature of representations on television

Audiences

- Who is watching and when
- Considering audience appeal
- Analysing audience responses and needs

Institutions

- Television regulation
- Television technology in relation to production and key roles in making programmes
- Public service and commercial broadcasting
- Scheduling techniques

Cross-media

- The cross-media nature of television including:
  - channel identity
  - magazines and comics
  - the effects of advertising revenue
  - related websites

News

Your learning

In this chapter you will learn about:

- the different use of codes and conventions by media organisations who present the news
- how audiences are targeted and retained by news media organisations
- the changes in the news media brought about by new technology
- how the content of the news is influenced both by the institutions or organisations that produce it and by those that provide news stories
- how the representation of individuals and groups in the news is only one of many possible presentations.

News – an introduction

News is big business. A desire to find out what is happening in the world seems to be an important part of many people's daily lives. Some people get this from newspapers, others from the television, radio or the Internet. So why are we all so interested in one form of news or another? It's probably because human beings have an in-built love of stories: news stories sit alongside soap operas, novels and Hollywood movies as narratives, or stories.

Once they have found out about what is happening, people will often quickly form an opinion about the events of the time. Should the Prime Minister resign? Is knife crime among young people a sign that society is collapsing into chaos? Is *Big Brother* a good thing? The news keeps us thinking about these issues, which we then discuss with our friends at school, in the hairdressers, in the café, in the taxi or wherever. Now we can even share our views with the whole world by blogging, although this can have its downside, as American journalist Ed Murrow points out:

> *'Just because your voice can now reach halfway round the world, it doesn't mean you're wiser than when it only reached to the end of the bar!'*

Examiner's tip

When looking at news, you need to consider the cross-media aspects of it.

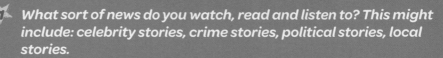
With a group of at least two others, explore your own news consumption by discussing the following questions:

1. *What sort of news do you watch, read and listen to? This might include: celebrity stories, crime stories, political stories, local stories.*

2. *How many of the following news media do you use and how often do you use them?*

- *National TV news. Do you usually watch one particular channel? If so, why?*
- *Local TV news.*
- *The Internet. Which sites?*
- *National newspapers. Which ones?*
- *Local newspapers. Which ones?*
- *National radio. Which stations?*
- *Local radio. Which stations?*
- *Do you find local or national news more interesting?*

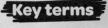

Key terms

Circulation The number of copies of a newspaper which are sold.

Readership The number of people who read the paper. This is usually higher than circulation, as several people can read the same paper.

This photograph appeared in the *Illustrated London News* in 1892. It shows the Duke of York (later King George V) and other officers on board *HMS Melampus*

Newspapers

Despite competition from TV, radio and the Internet, 300 years after the first newspaper was produced, a printed daily newspaper is not yet a thing of the past. It is true that there is a constant and steady decline in the **circulation** of newspapers. All but one of the main national dailies sold fewer copies in the year up to June 2008. Some are in steeper decline than others.

The only 'winner' is the *Sun*, which showed an increase of 0.81 per cent, while its main rival, the *Daily Mirror*, was down by 5.97 per cent on the previous year. However, in June 2008, ten and a half million national daily newspapers were still sold in the UK every day. This means that the **readership** of these papers could be 20 million or more – a third of the population of the country.

A recent survey asked adults aged 16–34 which words they associated with each of radio, television and newspapers.

- Newspapers were thought to be 'informative', 'serious' and 'influential' by more people than radio and television.
- 42 per cent agreed that 'newspapers are an important part of daily life'.

A timeline of the British press

Today's newspapers are colourful, full of pictures and have Internet versions. This constitutes a big change which has happened very quickly. For the first 200 years of their 300-year history, newspapers were mostly printed with a few black and white pictures.

1702
First daily paper *Daily Courant* founded (last published in 1735).

1785
The Times is first published: UK's oldest surviving daily newspaper.

1791
Observer founded: UK's oldest surviving Sunday newspaper.

1806
First use of illustration in *The Times*: Admiral Lord Nelson's funeral.

1855
Repeal of the Stamp Act opens the way for cheap, mass-circulation newspapers and modern newspaper design, using spacing and headlines.

1844
First story based on telegraphed news printed in *The Times*: birth of a son to Queen Victoria at Windsor.

1832
First recorded British newspaper cartoon, published in *Bell's New Weekly Messenger*.

1889
Early use of photographs: Cambridge and Oxford boat crews, in *Illustrated London News*.

1900
Daily Express launched: first national daily to put news on the front page.

1903
Daily Mirror launched: first daily illustrated exclusively with photographs.

1963
Sunday Times launches a magazine-style colour supplement.

1994
Electronic Telegraph launched: first British national on the Internet.

1991
Press Complaints Commission replaces the Press Council for more effective press self-regulation.

1987
First women editors of national newspapers in modern times: Wendy Henry (*News of the World*) and Eve Pollard (*Sunday Mirror*).

1999
Metro launched: a daily newspaper distributed free to travellers on the London Underground.

2003
The first broadsheets go tabloid: the *Independent* and *The Times*.

2008
All major newspapers now have Internet versions which are fast becoming more important than the printed versions.

As photography became an important part of the way people could perceive the world, newspapers adapted and the 'pictorial' content gradually increased. The industry remained male-dominated until recently. Competition from other media eventually forced changes on a reluctant press.

Key terms

Broadsheets Traditionally, newspapers printed in a large format (pages of 37 cm by 58 cm); they are considered to be more serious in content than tabloids than broadsheets.

Tabloids Traditionally, newspapers with pages half the size of broadsheets; they are usually more highly illustrated and can be less serious in their tone and content than broadsheets.

Demograph The type of audience watching or reading a media product.

Upmarket People who are comfortably off with a reasonable income.

Downmarket People who have smaller incomes and less money to spend on anything beyond the basic living requirements.

Red tops Tabloid newspapers with red mastheads.

Masthead The title of the newspaper which appears in large type at the top of the front page.

Targeting their audience

There are two main types of newspaper. They used to be divided into **broadsheets** and **tabloids**. Although this definition was based on the size of the paper they used, with broadsheets being much larger than tabloids, only a few papers still use the largest format. Most broadsheets are now a compact size. Nevertheless, the term has stuck.

There are also generalisations about the type of person who reads each sort of paper which are based on audience research. Broadsheets are associated with people in well-paid jobs who represent an **upmarket demograph**. Tabloids are associated with less well-off readers, or a **downmarket** demograph.

The five daily tabloids can be subdivided into two groups:

1 The *Sun*, *Mirror* and *Daily Star* are called the **red tops** because they have red **mastheads**. These papers report on politics and international news but generally include more gossip about celebrities from the pop or film world and sleaze or scandal of any sort. Stories are written simply and are quite short. Red tops tend to have more pictures than other papers, particularly the broadsheets. Their main aim is to be an easy read.

2 The *Daily Mail* and the *Daily Express* are often called the 'middle market' dailies. They target a readership somewhere between those of the red tops and the broadsheets. They print plenty of news and features for people wanting a paper that is not too gossipy or trivial, but they also have a variety of lightweight articles and pictures.

www.dailymail.co.uk

As well as entertaining, the tabloid papers line up behind one of the two major political parties. At one time only the *Daily Mirror* was a Labour-supporting tabloid. In 1992, the Labour Party was widely expected to win the General Election. But after John Major's surprise victory for the Tories, the *Sun*, which had supported the Conservatives, claimed that it had won the election for them. An important triumph for the Labour Party was to convince Rupert Murdoch, the owner of the *Sun* (as well as *The Times*, *The Sunday Times* and the *News of the World*) to change sides and back Labour. Five years later Labour romped home to a big victory – and the *Sun* could claim to have swung the election again.

Broadsheets

The five quality papers have higher news content, usually higher prices for each copy and lower circulation figures than the tabloids.

*   *The Times* is the oldest of all the dailies; it used to have the reputation for being rather stuffy and the 'voice of the ruling classes'. In 1979 it was bought by Rupert Murdoch's News International company and is now a genuinely modern paper, but still with more of an 'establishment' view than some others.

*   The *Daily Telegraph* is the broadsheet with the highest circulation. It is a strong supporter of the Conservative Party. Still broadsheet in size.

*   The *Guardian* is usually described as a liberal or left-wing paper.

*   The *Independent* is the newest of the national dailies, set up in 1986 and intended to be independent of any one political party's viewpoint.

*   The *Financial Times* is the only national daily to be printed on pink paper. It reports mainly on business and economic news, although it does have other news, including a sports section. Still broadsheet in size.

Ethnic newspapers

As Britain is home to an increasingly diverse number of cultures, there is a variety of newspapers to serve these audiences. The *New Nation* describes itself as 'Britain's number one black newspaper', while the *Asian Times* claims to be 'Britain's leading Asian newspaper'.

Look at the online versions of one tabloid and one broadsheet daily national newspaper.

Examine the content, layout and advertising on each site. To what extent do you think it is correct to say that the broadsheet is appealing to an upmarket audience while the tabloid targets a downmarket demograph?

Newspaper language

The 'language' of newspapers is not just the words that appear in them. As with other media languages, it includes the pictures that are used, different font styles and sizes in text and headings, and the way these things are put together in the layout of the page.

No aspect of the way newspapers are put together is an accident. At every stage of production people are making decisions which affect the way the paper looks, reads ... and sells!

The copy

Copy is written by journalists called reporters. Writing for newspapers is very different from the sort of writing done by, say, a novelist. News reporters need to get across the maximum amount of information in the shortest possible time. They also aim to get the 'bare bones' of the story established in the first sentence or two – if you are hooked into the story from the very start you will carry on reading.

Here is an example from the *Daily Mail* on Monday, 21 July 2008:

Happy hours and 'supersize' wine glasses could be banned in an admission that the 24-hour drinking experiment has failed

Journalists are taught to KISS – Keep It Short and Simple. They used also to be taught to get the 'Five Ws' – Who? What? Where? When? Why? – into the first sentences of their story. Now styles of writing for newspapers have moved on. Trying to pack in all five Ws made for indigestible sentences and this rule is not always followed to the letter.

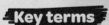

Find three different newspapers and look at the opening two sentences from the main front-page story in each. How many of the Five Ws has the reporter managed to get into the story?

The pictures

The first newspapers printed 300 years ago had few pictures – and those pictures were drawings because, of course, the camera had not been invented. Nowadays news photographs play an important part in the whole look of a newspaper, especially the front page.

Look at the image below to see how *The Times* set out its front page reporting on one of the biggest international news stories of recent times. The event was highly significant in the Western world. Almost anyone who was alive at the time remembers exactly what they were doing when they first heard the news of the terrorist attack on New York's twin towers.

Front page of *The Times*, 12 September, 2001

Look at the front page on page 57, paying special attention to the photograph.

1. What is it about the photograph that helps to create an impact on the reader?

2. Why do you think the **picture editor** chose this particular image? What does the photo tell us about the story?

Captions

People say that 'a picture is worth a thousand words'. Certainly the photograph of New York after the attack on the twin towers on page 57 says a great deal about the event. The **caption** that goes with a photograph is also important because it can **anchor** a meaning – it tries to push the reader towards one **angle** by providing an interpretation for them.

Key terms

Picture editor The person responsible for choosing the photographs that go into a newspaper.

Caption Descriptive words next to a picture.

Anchor To pin down a particular meaning of a drawing or photograph, often by adding a caption.

Angle The particular point of view a newspaper wants its readers to take on a story.

Street scene in Khayelitsha, South Africa

Look at the photograph above. There could be a number of interpretations of this image. However, choosing suitable captions could alter the way people read it.

- *South Africa's government has managed to re-house many of its people from tin shacks into solid, brick-built houses*: this caption gives a positive slant on the picture.

- *Unemployment still blights South Africa's townships*: this caption gives a different, more negative meaning.

A

1 Look at the photographs A and B. For each one, write two possible captions to appear in a newspaper of your choice. One should give a positive angle and the other a more negative angle.

2 In pairs or groups, take a series of photographs around your school site. Make a wall display or a website featuring these photographs, giving them captions which alter the way the viewer might interpret them.

B

Headlines

Good headlines are crucial, especially on the front page. It's the headline which will draw a purchaser's attention to the paper when it is on the shelf among its competitors. Broadsheet editors will try to draw readers to their stories by using concise (brief) headlines which sometimes also give the newspaper's angle on the story, but tabloid headlines are large and catchy.

The *Sun* has become famous for its controversial headlines. Although these can be amusing, they sometimes cross the line from humour into bad taste. In 1989 the paper printed the headline 'THE TRUTH' above an article about the Hillsborough football disaster in which 95 Liverpool fans were killed. The *Sun*'s 'truth' was that the disaster was caused by drunken Liverpool fans behaving badly. Sales of the paper in Liverpool collapsed, with many newsagents refusing to stock it.

Some of the techniques headline writers use include:
- abbreviating names, for example, BECKS for David Beckham
- parodying well-known phrases, for example, BRAWL OVER BAR THE SHOUTING
- Incorrect or invented spelling, for example, GOTCHA
- puns (play on words), for example, BOOTIFUL – winning goal in a Cup Final
- rhyming, for example, FAME GAME TURNS VERY LAME.

> *Look at some back copies of tabloid front pages and try to find examples of each of the headline techniques listed above.*
>
> **ACTIVITY 6**

Layout

When all the copy is written and all the photographs have been chosen, the final choices concern how the page is to be laid out. Layout is a key part of the battle to grab the reader's attention and hang on to it.

The front page from the *Daily Mail* on page 61 has been marked up with the terms used by **sub-editors** to describe modern newspaper layout. The sub-editors of the paper set out the pages on a computer screen which breaks the page into a series of columns called a page grid. In the past, pages were almost always set out in columns, with nothing breaking the grid pattern. Modern page design often allows both photographs and text to spill outside rigid columns to create dramatic visual impact.

Newspapers are constantly researching the ways in which people *read* pages. They have found, for example, that:
- headlines near photographs are read more than those placed further away
- using colour does not make a story more likely to be read
- people reading a paper look at most of the photographs, artwork and headlines – but much less of the copy.

Above all, a newspaper wants to achieve an individual visual style. This is about individual preferences.

CD-ROM
Extra!

Newspaper front pages

Open the CD in the back of this book and click on the icon below to open a link to some front pages of the Daily Mirror. These may help you with Activity 6.

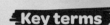

Key terms

Sub-editor The person responsible for the layout of a newspaper.

Masthead

Dateline

Front cover flash

Splash head full caps

Strapline

By-line

Page lead

Support story

Underscored

4 colour pic

Caption

Cross-reference

Daily Mail

MONDAY, JULY 21, 2008

www.dailymail.co.uk   DAILY NEWSPAPER OF THE YEAR 50p

NEW 18-DISC COLLECTION

FREE DVD
BLEAK HOUSE

Another sensational FREE costume drama for you to collect

PART ONE

PICK UP FROM TESCO OR WHSMITH OR WE CAN POST YOU THE WHOLE SET   DETAILS PAGE 30 P&P PAYABLE

Three years after relaxing drink laws, ministers signal U-turn

TIME'S UP FOR HAPPY HOUR

By **Michael Lea**
Political Correspondent

HAPPY hours and 'super-size' wine glasses could be banned in an admission that the 24-hour drinking experiment is failing.

Labour's hopes of creating a Continental-style cafe culture have not materialised since licensing laws were relaxed nearly three years ago.

Instead, booze-fuelled violence and alcohol-related deaths, injuries and illnesses have surged.

Now, having previously refused to heed warnings from police and doctors, ministers are preparing a climbdown by toughening up the laws on alcohol sales.

Key measures are likely to include:

■A ban on happy hours and cut-price promotions;

■Pubs and clubs ordered to serve smaller measures of wines and spirits as standard;

■Cigarette-style health warnings on cans and bottles, extending a voluntary scheme where containers show the units of alcohol;

■Loss-leading alcohol sales by supermarkets may also be targeted.

The moves will build on a review by the audit firm KPMG into the link between price promotions and alcohol abuse, which could be published this week. Ministers have been dismayed at the lack of voluntary action from the drinks industry. Some pubs have extended happy hours

Turn to Page 4

Kate McCann: The inquiry into her daughter's disappearance is to be closed

New agony for Kate as Maddie detective cashes in

SEE PAGE FIVE

The features of newspaper layout

Below and opposite are two front pages designed by the Sun to show how their paper might have reported famous moments from history, using modern page design techniques.

Choose two other events from the list of historical events below and design your own tabloid front page.

- The assassination of American President John F. Kennedy in 1963.
- The end of the Second World War in 1945.
- Neil Armstrong becomes the first man to walk on the moon in 1969.
- Elizabeth I becomes Queen of England in 1558.
- Nelson Mandela is released from jail in 1990 after 27 years.

Sir Walter Raleigh brings potatoes and tobacco to England from the Americas

THE Sun

Friday, November 25, 1859   Penny farthing   THOUGHT: SPEAK FOR YOURSELF

ARE YOU A CHIMP OFF THE OLD BLOCK?
SEE PAGES 4 AND 5

Monkey nutter

Barmy boffin Darwin reckons we are all descended from apes

MAD scientist Charles Darwin caused fury last night by claiming we're all descended from APES.

By JEAN POOLE

Darwin, 50, makes a string of outrageous allegations in his controversial book On The Origin Of Species, which sold out on its first day yesterday.

Darwin **SCOFFS** at the 'Adam and Eve' theory of mankind's creation. He says the real answer lies in the **FOSSILS** he once studied on a sailing trip.

The barmy boffin, from Shrewsbury, reckons all animals 'evolve' — becoming more and more refined and advanced over thousands of years. This is all thanks to "natural selection" which means only the fittest and best examples of a species survive to breed and pass on their successful characteristics.

Darwin avoids mentioning man in his book, concentrating on plants and animals. But experts say he **MUST** believe in mankind being merely advanced apes, or his theory doesn't hold water.

Furious scientists last night insisted Darwin did not have a shred of real evidence. And Church chiefs said he was belittling the Bible and the importance of man over animals.

Buffoon as a baboon . . . how he'd look

Charles Darwin writes *On the Origin of the Species* in which he outlines his theory of human evolution

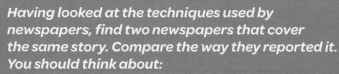

ACTIVITY 8

Having looked at the techniques used by newspapers, find two newspapers that cover the same story. Compare the way they reported it. You should think about:
- *the pictures they have used*
- *the type of language they have used*
- *what view they have taken about the story.*

CASE STUDY

REPRESENTATION IN NEWS

*In this case study we will consider the cross-media nature of representation in news. The key concept of **representation** is an important one for all Media Studies students to understand. In studying the news, representation is about understanding that news stories are a representation of events, and the people and ideas who are part of those events. Someone has always made a choice about the pictures that represent the story and the words used to link with the pictures. If the choices made had been different, the representation would have taken on a different meaning.*

Key terms

Representation How people, places, events or ideas are represented or portrayed to audiences in media texts. Sometimes this is simplistically through stereotypes so the audience can see immediately what is meant, and sometimes the meanings are less obvious.

Putting people, events or ideas into categories is a part of the way representation works. When we see repeated representations of famine-stricken children in Africa, those images can begin to affect the way we think about that continent. The generalisation that 'Africa equals Poverty' means we might be surprised to learn that, for example, there are many highly successful hi-tech businesses and entrepreneurs in Africa. It doesn't fit with our 'common sense' view of Africa – a view fuelled by endless repetitions of the same images in the media.

An example of the way the media can deal in negative representations has been the coverage of young people in 'hoodies'. Such people are not usually shown sympathetically; they are usually associated with stories of disturbances or petty crime, even though most young people who wear hoodies are normal, law-abiding citizens.

So it is important to explore news stories to judge the extent to which they contain a point of view. Television news broadcasters are required to ensure they show *fairness* and *balance* in their treatment of stories. A balance of opposing viewpoints should be included in contentious stories. Newspaper reporting is not always as balanced.

One group who are often targeted by media campaigns are so-called 'benefit scroungers'. Michael Philpott was an individual who found himself labelled in this way by the national newspapers.

CD-ROM
Extra!

Central Television
Open the CD in the back of this book and click on the icon below to see a Central Television clip. This will help you with the Case Study Activity.

SHAMELESS

£26,000 a year benefits but scrounger who has 14 children wants MORE of your cash and moans: Britain has let me down

BY JOHN CHAPMAN

A LAYABOUT with 14 children by five different women last night demanded a bigger council house for his family.

Unemployed Michael Philpott claimed that he has to sleep outside in a tent because of his 'overcrowded home'.

The 49-year-old, branded Britain's biggest scrounger, even accused the country of 'going down the pan' because his plight was being ignored.

Philpott, who pays £68 a week for his three-bedroom house, receives £26,500 a year in benefits. Now he wants a six-bedroom home for his children, wife and heavily pregnant lover.

But last night his antics met with outrage. Tory MP Ann Widdecombe said: 'This man beggars belief. It's the most preposterous thing I have ever heard of'.

★CASE STUDY★ ACTIVITY

1 *Look at the newspaper piece about Mr Philpott.*
- *What opinions are expressed about him?*
- *What words are used to stir up the emotions of the readers?*

2 *Before it was picked up by the press, this story was originally covered by Central Television's regional news programme. In response to viewers' emails, they ran a follow-up to the story on 22 March. Watch the clip from Central Television on the CD-ROM.*
- *What representation are we given of Mr Philpott in this news coverage?*
- *From what you are told in the article, make a list of the facts we know about Mr Philpott.*
- *Now list the way opinions about him have been used to make us think about him in a particular way.*
- *Would you say it is a 'positive' representation or a 'negative' one? You should support what you say by giving detailed examples from the actual news story. This should not just include the words from the script which has been written for the piece, but also where the crew have placed Mr Philpott, what other things appear in the shots, the tone of voice and types of question asked.*
- *To what extent do you think the piece on Mr Philpott succeeded in presenting all sides and leaving the audience to judge for itself?*

The selection process

Where do news stories come from?

Every story and item of news that you read in a paper or on a website, hear on the radio, or see on television, has a source. In an age with 24-hour rolling television news, it is easy to imagine that all news journalists rush around the globe, chasing action-packed stories about war, crime or other high-profile events. While this may be true for a few of the top reporters, most journalists, and particularly those working on local newspapers or local radio, will spend their whole time on their local patch.

Journalists get their stories from a variety of sources:

- *News agencies* – such as The Press Association and Reuters Association Press which supply news from all over the world.
- *Reporters* – the BBC has the biggest range of reporters based all over the globe. The smaller the organisation, the fewer reporters there are to cover events.
- *From each other* – foreign television, the national press and radio all provide stories. Stories from local television stations and newspapers sometimes appear on national television or radio news.
- *Freelance journalists* may approach a station with a story, or may be commissioned to research one.
- *Processed news* – this is gathered from items such as press releases, agendas for council meetings, and police, fire and rescue services voicebanks.

How are news items chosen?

With so many sources of news, there are far more stories than can be included in the papers for one day or a half-hour television news bulletin. The people who select the news have to consider the whole audience and provide news which has relevance to the mass audience in the case of something like the BBC's *Ten O'Clock News* or the local community for a local radio station.

CD-ROM
Extra!
News sources
Open the CD in the back of this book and click on the icon below to see a clip of a news editor explaining news sources and selection.

It is your job to choose the story which will go 'at the top of the show' for tonight's BBC Ten O'Clock News, and a further three stories which will be the major news items of the day. Read through the possibilities below and choose your top story and the three stories that will follow it.

Story	Images available to support the story
The cost of living has risen for the fourth month in a row.	**Stock footage** of supermarket shelves, petrol stations, high street stores.
Prince William has a new girlfriend.	Twenty seconds of shaky footage from a camera held above the heads of a crowd as a girl rushes out of her house and into a car.
Fourteen people die in a mud slide in Colombia.	Aerial footage of the scenes of devastation. An interview with a woman who has lost her home.
Liverpool FC pay a record transfer fee to Barcelona for a striker.	Archive footage of striker playing for Barcelona. Press conference where manager introduces new player.
An important Tudor palace is on fire.	Mobile phone footage from a member of the public taken from some distance away from fire.
Fifteen soldiers are killed in an attack on their barracks in Afghanistan.	Video phone link to reporter at the scene. Still images of the barracks after the blast.
The Mayor of London is caught speeding on the M25.	Press conference where Mayor apologises.
Channel 4 announces a new reality TV show where contestants are isolated in a series of igloos in Greenland.	Stock footage of the Arctic Circle. Interview with Channel 4 Head of Programmes.

Key terms

Stock footage Material held in a library which shows something relevant to the news story but was not filmed specifically to go with it.

Grade Studio

Examiner's tip

It is helpful to understand *how* news stories are ranked. Their importance relates to the types of people involved, the times of day the news is broadcast and the different places where the news is broadcast to.

Key terms

News values Things that help a story get into the news.

When you were deciding which of the stories to include in Activity 9, you probably asked yourself about the importance of the stories to the audience who watch the programme and balanced that with the visual material you had to support the story. Like news journalists anywhere, an important part of your decision will have been based on **news values**.

Most journalists will tell you that selecting the right stories for the day is a matter of experience and instinct. However, in a famous study in 1973, researchers Galtang and Ruge found that certain factors help a story to get into the news.

The text below outlines the factors that Galtang and Ruge identified that determine which stories get into the news.

Timescale – a murder is committed and discovered quickly, so it fits the timescale on which news organisations work. An increase in gun crime, which happens over a long period, will only get reported when there is a series of gun-related crimes.

The size of an event – a rail crash killing 25 people is big news; a train derailment with no injuries is not.

Surprise – was the event unexpected?

Predictability – if the news organisations expect something to happen, then it will. A big anti-capitalist demonstration planned for central London will get reported, even if it passes off peacefully, because the news organisations expect violence and send journalists to cover it.

Continuity – a running story, like a war, will continue to be covered.

How clear the event is – news need not be simple, but a very complicated story will probably be left out.

Reference to elite people or nations – news about the USA or the US president is more likely to get covered than similar news from Costa Rica.

Key terms

Gatekeeping Where reporters or editors block certain issues but allow others through into newspapers or news broadcasts.

This process of selecting and rejecting items for the news is called **gatekeeping**. The gatekeepers who make the decisions will be influenced by their own backgrounds and education.

Branding TV news

There are television channels which are entirely devoted to up-to-the-minute, round-the-clock news coverage. Like any part of the television industry, news is thus big business. It is important for each channel to develop its own distinctive **branding** so that viewers recognise it and – hopefully – identify with it enough to show *brand loyalty* by regularly tuning in to the station to watch its news programmes.

In the early days, the news was usually read by a white male in a suit and tie, sitting at a desk. There were few additional pictures and hardly any on-screen graphics. Things are dramatically different today. Cameras shift position around news presenters who are often a male/female partnership. They sometimes come out from behind their desk and walk about the studio, talking to their audience in a conversational way.

Modern-day news on Channel 5

Elaborate sets are designed to give a distinctive tone to the type of news coverage the station is providing. Printed information is often scrolled across the screen, giving facts about stories other than the one being focused on by the presenters.

An important part of the Media Studies Key Concept of media language is the idea of *mise-en-scène*. This French expression literally means 'put in the scene'. It helps us to explore how scenes from film and television convey their meaning by looking carefully at the *connotations* brought into our minds by the sets, props, lighting, type of actors/presenters and costume. For television news, the visual look of the set and the presenters' clothing will match the expectations of the target audience and the tone the programme hopes to set.

ACTIVITY 10

You have been asked to design the set for the launch of a news programme which will be shown at 6 o'clock on ITV 3. It is attempting to attract a younger audience in the 16–34 age range.

1. *Decide on the name you will give your news programme.*

2. *Draw up some ideas for what the set will look like, thinking very carefully about the furniture, the colours of the set and especially what will appear on the large plasma screens to be sited behind the presenters.*

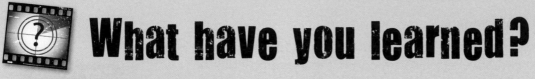
What have you learned?

In this chapter you have learned about:

Texts
- How newspaper stories are constructed
- Analysing stories from different news media

Media language

Genre
- How the news media have changed across time
- How the style and content of different news media allow audiences to classify and engage with them
- The branding of television news

Narrative
- The construction of narratives in the news media

Representation
- How individuals, ideas and groups are represented in the news media

Audiences
- Who reads and watches which news media
- How the news media address specific audience demographs

Institutions
- Sources of news in the news media
- The news values that influence which stories get into the news

Cross-media
- How new technology is affecting the way news media operate

4 Magazines

Your learning

In this chapter you will learn about:

- categorising magazines
- analysing magazine covers and contents pages
- who reads magazines, when, where and why
- values and lifestyles
- describing audiences
- stars and celebrities
- magazines and advertising
- online magazines.

Categorising magazines

ACTIVITY 1

1. *Why do you choose the magazines you read?*

2. *Do you always read the same magazines or do you choose a different one each time?*

3. *Where do you read them?*

4. *Do you read magazines while you are doing something else, such as talking with friends?*

Go into any supermarket, newsagent or garage. The choice of magazines is staggering. Looking at the way they are displayed will help you to understand what types of magazine there are.

Magazines displayed in a store

TIP

Start a topic notebook to jot down your thoughts and ideas in response to the questions in activity 2. This could be used as evidence of production research or for a textual investigation. See the material in the chapter on Controlled Assessment at the end of this book.

ACTIVITY 2

Conduct some research into the magazines on sale by going into your local newsagent or supermarket. Stand back and look at the rows of magazines on the shelves.

1. *What are your first impressions of the display?*

2. *How have the magazines been arranged?*

3. *Do any colours stand out strongly? Which ones?*

4. *What features on the covers tell you what time of year it is?*

5. *Do any faces appear on more than one magazine? Whose?*

6. *Which subjects or themes are covered by more than one magazine?*

Key terms

Categorising
Ordering or grouping similar texts, for example, magazines, according to the features they have in common.

Lifestyle magazines
Magazines dealing with many topics and issues to appeal to a wide audience.

Specialist magazines
Magazines focusing on a particular area of interest to appeal to a narrow or niche audience.

Cover price The price charged for the magazine that is displayed on the front cover.

Target audience
The specific group of people that a media text is aimed at.

One obvious way to start **categorising** magazines is to split them into general interest or lifestyle, and specialist groups. General interest/**lifestyle magazines**, such as *Glamour*, have a broad range of subject matter, covering many topics and issues. **Specialist magazines**, such as *Digital Camera*, are tailored to a particular area of interest. Think about the magazines you read – which category do they belong to?

ACTIVITY 3

1. *Work in a pair or small group and decide whether each of these magazine titles is in the general interest or the specialist category. The first two have been done for you.*

General interest magazines	Specialist magazines
OK	Empire

- OK
- Empire
- Good Food
- New Woman
- Rugby World
- PC Format
- Heat

- Radio Times
- Men's Health
- Match of the Day
- Angler's Mail
- Digital Camera
- Family Circle
- Bob the Builder

- Hair
- Stuff
- Inside Soap
- Mizz
- Glamour
- NGamer
- Woman's Own

Remember that there are also many other ways of categorising magazines, perhaps by **cover price**, **target audience**, *or in terms of the companies that publish them.*

2. *Look again at the list of magazine titles. Choose another way of categorising them. You may need to go back to your supermarket or newsagent, speak to magazine readers or look up titles on the Internet – each title usually has its own website.*

Analysing magazine covers

Magazine publishing is a hugely profitable media industry. It is also very competitive. You will have realised from your research activities so far that a key technique used by magazines to attract and address their audiences involves capturing their interest on the shelf.

Now you are going to look closely at a magazine cover and analyse its features. This is an excellent way to find out what messages a magazine is conveying to its audience. To be successful, a magazine must establish a close, personal and almost friendly relationship with its readers. This is called the **mode of address**. On the cover on page 74, the central image is photographed looking straight out at the reader; this is known as a *direct* mode of address and suggests she is establishing a personal relationship with the reader with whom she is on friendly terms.

Before you look at the annotated magazine cover, make sure you understand some of the other terms used in the annotations. It is always important to use the correct terms when you analyse a media text:

- **seasonal theme**: when the colours and contents of a magazine relate to the time of year; for example, red hearts and features on love and romance in February for St Valentine's Day
- **mise-en-scène**: the way in which every element of the text is arranged to create meanings
- **anchorage text**: writing that fixes the meaning of an image (also known as a caption)
- **buzz word**: a word that stands out on the text, for example, 'Free'
- **key signifier**: the first thing on a cover that attracts the eye – it could be an image or words
- **puffs**: information on the front cover that is about the inside contents of the magazine (also known as 'coverlines')
- **superimposition**: when images and words are laid over each other. Often the title is partially covered by the central image – it is assumed the audience will recognise the title anyway.

Grade Studio

Examiner's tip
Using the appropriate terminology accurately is a good way to earn more marks.

The model, Courtney Love, is celebrity who uses DIRECT MODE OF ADDRESS and looks straight at the reader to establish a relationship with them.

The TITLE BLOCK is white SERIF font which suggests longstanding, high quality sophistication. The name *Elle* is the French word for 'she' and suggests high class, as well as a focus on fashion which is associated with France.

The magazine WEBSITE makes it possible for readers to go beyond the hard copy of this edition and read the online version too.

The ANCHORAGE TEXT links the central image to the topics of the article on Courtney Love. It uses the RULE OF THREE for interest.

The main PUFF emphasises the need to follow and imitate the latest fashion trends closely.

The advice to readers on style and wearing fashion is an example of the U and G theory, where audiences will choose a text that they can identify with and that will help them belong socially.

Words like 'rules' and 'great style' make the reader feel that the advice on fashion and accessories in this magazine is going to be valuable in their own lives.

Featuring stars and celebrities are very popular with female readers. It is an example of media industries using each other to increase their profits.

The free hair stylist is an INCENTIVE to encourage readers to buy the magazine.

It is rare for a central image to be seen in full length. Here, Courtney Love's 'look' is like a representation of what Elle magazine suggest the reader should be wearing.

ELLE

ELLEUK.COM

50 RULES OF GREAT STYLE

TRULY MADLY COURTNEY
Up all night with
ROCK'S COOLEST BLONDE

20% OFF UNIQLO FOR EV...

YOUR PERSONAL STYLE ISSUE
HOW TO FIND A LOOK YOU'LL LOVE EVERY DAY
HAIR: THE CUT & COLOUR TO SUIT YOU
HIRE A HIGH-STREET STYLIST FOR FREE

Now have a go at analysing a magazine front cover yourself. *PC Gamer* is a specialist computer games magazine aimed at 16–35-year-old males. Try to identify how the cover has been designed to appeal to its audience.

- Remember to use the appropriate terms whenever you can.
- Look back at how the cover on page 74 was analysed if you need help.

PC Gamer's readers are mostly male computer games fans aged 16–35

Who reads magazines?

Considering the ways in which audiences read or watch different media texts is an important part of Media Studies. The best way to start is with YOU, since so many texts are aimed at people like you. You are part of the powerful 14–18-year-old audience, and media producers are keen to know what you like and what you want.

Can you think why your age group is so powerful? The main reason is that, even though you don't usually earn large sums of money, what you do earn is virtually all **disposable income** – there is only you to spend it on. After all, most young people do not have to pay for food or housing, so media producers want you to spend your money on their products. Producers also want readers with spending power to attract advertisers who **subsidise** the cost of production. The money that advertisers pay for space in print-based texts is used to reduce the selling price. Without subsidy, print-based media texts would cost over twice as much. We'll look more closely at the relationship between magazines and advertisers later in this chapter.

Why do people consume media texts?

Some media theorists have suggested that media audiences make *active* choices about what to consume in order to meet certain needs. This is sometimes called the Uses and Gratifications Theory, and it tries to show the different needs that audiences want to satisfy by consuming certain media texts.

Key terms

Disposable income The money someone has left to spend after they have paid for essentials such as housing and food.

Subsidise To reduce the cover price of a media text, such as a magazine or newspaper, by selling advertising space.

The Uses and Gratifications Theory

Media consumers choose texts that fulfil one or more of these needs:

- the need to be INFORMED and EDUCATED about the world in which they live
- the need to IDENTIFY personally with characters and situations in order to learn more about themselves
- the need to be ENTERTAINED by a range and variety of well constructed texts
- the need to use the media as a talking point for SOCIAL INTERACTION or DISCUSSION
- the need to ESCAPE from their 'daily grind' into other worlds and situations.

Grade Studio

Examiner's tip

Understanding audience theory will help improve your grades.

ACTIVITY 5

1. *Choose any television programme you enjoy. Explain how the Uses and Gratifications Theory can be used to explain why you like it. An example has been given to help you.*

I enjoy watching 'Big Brother' because I like to choose which characters are most like me and who act like I would in the house (IDENTIFY). It is really good fun to watch the housemates make such fools of themselves (ENTERTAINED). My friends enjoy 'Big Brother' too, and sometimes we watch together on eviction night to see who is voted out (SOCIAL INTERACTION). I would never go on 'Big Brother' myself, but it takes my mind off my work (ESCAPE)!

2. *Now apply the Uses and Gratifications Theory to a magazine you read regularly.*

Lifestyle magazines

Lifestyle magazines offer a sense of identity, companionship and reassurance, and include titles such as *Cosmopolitan*, *FHM*, *Heat*, *Nuts*, *OK* and *Closer*. They share with their readers the problems and issues of other similar people who also read the magazines. Lifestyle magazines offer guidance and instruction on how to live a particular lifestyle as well as entertainment and escapism. The magazines also challenge readers to respond to advice offered on such matters as relationships, careers and material possessions. It would be interesting to consider how realistic the lifestyle is that is being promoted.

When and how do people consume media texts?

Audiences consume – that is, watch, read or listen to – media products in a range of situations and places. Sometimes they give the text their full attention – primary consumption. At other times they may be watching, reading or listening while doing other things – secondary consumption. This is known as the pattern of **media consumption**. How are the girls in the photos below consuming their texts?

People consume media products in different ways

Key terms

Primary consumer Someone who is focused on watching, listening to or reading a media text.

Secondary consumer Someone watching, listening to or reading a media text while doing something else, such as talking or homework.

Grade Studio

Examiner's tip

Understanding how people 'consume' the media is an essential part of your first Controlled Assessment assignment.

You are going to analyse the media products you consume in one week.

⭐ Keep a diary for one week of all the magazines, television and radio programmes, films, CDs, websites, interactive games, etc. that you consume. This will be your media consumption diary. Remember to:
- note how long you spend on each text
- write down whether you were a **primary consumer** or a **secondary consumer**.

A typical diary entry for one day might start like this:

Friday, 20 March 2009
- Listened to the radio while getting dressed. 45 minutes. Secondary
- Watched C4 while having breakfast. 45 minutes. Secondary
- Listened to Duffy album on my iPod on the way to school. 20 minutes. Primary

⭐ Add up your consumption of each type of media for the week. Choose a way to show your results, e.g. a bar graph, table or pie chart.

⭐ Write a few paragraphs about your media consumption during the week. You may wish to use these headings: **Film, TV, Radio, Magazines and newspapers, Own music, The Internet, Gaming.** *Remember to comment on:*
- *why you chose the texts you consumed*
- *what needs the texts met*
- *what your patterns of consumption are*
- *any media texts you deliberately chose not to consume. If so, why was this?*

Key terms

Ideology A system of values, beliefs or ideas that is common to a specific group of people.

Values and lifestyles

Values and lifestyle – sometimes called **ideology** – may at first glance seem like difficult concepts to grasp, but these are simply terms for the way people think about themselves, about others and about the world in which they live. The only difficult thing about ideology is that it is so instinctive and unspoken that it can be rather invisible. People tend not to know what their values and beliefs are unless they are challenged in some way.

Try this exercise to help you understand ideology and values. Imagine all the students in your class have been stranded on a desert island. No one else is there. Each of you must write down the names of the four students who would best fill these roles:

A: The leader of the group

B: The most trustworthy emotional support for the group

C: The person most likely to fall off the raft you have built into the shark-infested lagoon

D: The person most likely to risk their life to dive in and rescue them.

Count up the votes.

When you count up the votes, you may find a surprising level of agreement amongst your ideal choices for these roles. Since you have similar values or ideologies, you will have similar ideas of who best meets the requirements for each role. For example, the leader may well be the most outspoken, popular member of the group, while the emotional support person is likely to be a mature, cheerful person who happily speaks to everyone, and not just those in their friendship group. The class will have agreed on this because you all understand that, in order to take any of those roles, people need to have demonstrated certain values and standards of behaviour.

Ideology in magazines

Magazines reflect the values and ideologies of their readers because they want readers to feel they can identify with the magazine.

Here are two descriptions of the target readers of two lifestyle magazines as presented on the magazines' websites:

> 'The Elle reader is spirited, stylish, and intelligent; she expects to be successful at everything she does. She takes the lead and breaks the rules.'

> 'The Sight & Sound reader is a true film buff who expects to be given intelligent information on all film releases, not just Hollywood mainstream movies.'

Look at the following web pages showing the online versions of *Elle* and *Sight & Sound* magazines. Read the notes around one of the web pages – these will help you with the activity that follows.

The title of the web page matches the title of the magazine itself

Links to the main areas of interest

Incentive offering free goods in exchange for subscribing

Main image from leading fashion designer catwalk

Links to main fashion items

Opportunity to subscribe to the magazine is built into the page

Feature on fashion 'must-have'

Web page editor gives advice about beauty focus of attention

CD-ROM
Extra!
ElleUK.com
Open the CD in the back of this book and click on the icon below to open a link to the ElleUK.com website.

HTML

The magazine and website are produced by the British Film Institute – an organisation that takes film seriously

The website guide makes site navigation straightforward

The site finder makes it easy for a user to go straight to a specific area

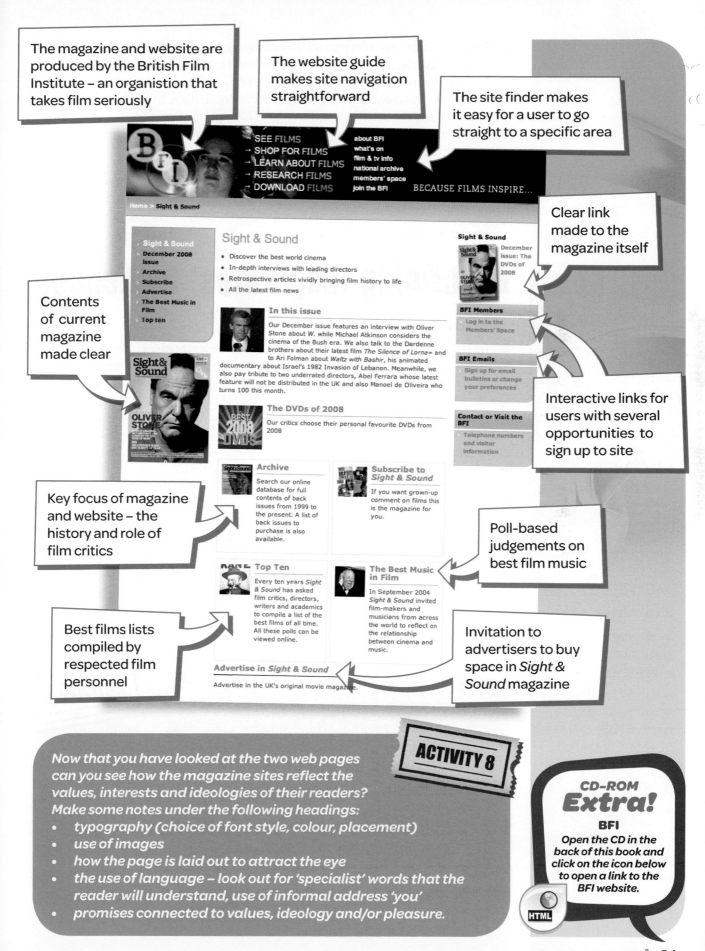

SEE FILMS
SHOP FOR FILMS
LEARN ABOUT FILMS
RESEARCH FILMS
DOWNLOAD FILMS

about BFI
what's on
film & tv info
national archive
members' space
join the BFI

BECAUSE FILMS INSPIRE...

Home > Sight & Sound

Sight & Sound

- Sight & Sound
- December 2008 issue
- Archive
- Subscribe
- Advertise
- The Best Music in Film
- Top ten

Sight & Sound

- Discover the best world cinema
- In-depth interviews with leading directors
- Retrospective articles vividly bringing film history to life
- All the latest film news

In this issue

Our December issue features an interview with Oliver Stone about *W.* while Michael Atkinson considers the cinema of the Bush era. We also talk to the Dardenne brothers about their latest film *The Silence of Lorna* and to Ari Folman about *Waltz with Bashir*, his animated documentary about Israel's 1982 invasion of Lebanon. Meanwhile, we also pay tribute to two underrated directors, Abel Ferrara whose latest feature will not be distributed in the UK and also Manoel de Oliveira who turns 100 this month.

The DVDs of 2008

Our critics choose their personal favourite DVDs from 2008

Archive

Search our online database for full contents of back issues from 1999 to the present. A list of back issues to purchase is also available.

Subscribe to *Sight & Sound*

If you want grown-up comment on films this is the magazine for you.

Top Ten

Every ten years *Sight & Sound* has asked film critics, directors, writers and academics to compile a list of the best films of all time. All these polls can be viewed online.

The Best Music in Film

In September 2004 *Sight & Sound* invited film-makers and musicians from across the world to reflect on the relationship between cinema and music.

Advertise in *Sight & Sound*

Advertise in the UK's original movie magazine.

Sight & Sound
December issue: The DVDs of 2008

BFI Members
Log in to the Members' Space

BFI Emails
Sign up for email bulletins or change your preferences

Contact or Visit the BFI
Telephone numbers and visitor information

Clear link made to the magazine itself

Contents of current magazine made clear

Interactive links for users with several opportunities to sign up to site

Key focus of magazine and website – the history and role of film critics

Poll-based judgements on best film music

Best films lists compiled by respected film personnel

Invitation to advertisers to buy space in *Sight & Sound* magazine

---

ACTIVITY 8

Now that you have looked at the two web pages can you see how the magazine sites reflect the values, interests and ideologies of their readers? Make some notes under the following headings:

- *typography (choice of font style, colour, placement)*
- *use of images*
- *how the page is laid out to attract the eye*
- *the use of language – look out for 'specialist' words that the reader will understand, use of informal address 'you'*
- *promises connected to values, ideology and/or pleasure.*

CD-ROM Extra!
BFI
Open the CD in the back of this book and click on the icon below to open a link to the BFI website.

HTML

Ideologies can be seen on many different levels. Countries have *national ideologies*: if you go on holiday abroad, you will notice patterns of behaviour that would be unusual in the UK. In Japan, for example, people are always extremely polite to each other, and it is considered rude to show anger. Can you think of any things that visitors to the UK might notice about our patterns of behaviour? For example, people often say that the British value patience and love queuing!

Understanding ideology is helpful when it comes to analysing the ways in which magazines and other media texts are constructed to appeal to their target audiences, by offering them material that they will enjoy, understand, value and aspire to.

Describing magazines' audiences

Gender

Some texts have an obvious gender bias. *Action Man* and *Girl Talk* are examples of magazines with a clear male/female bias. Sometimes you can identify if gender is a relevant issue by considering the themes or values at the heart of a text. Look again at the front cover of *Elle* magazine on page 74. A focus on appearance and image is often associated with female audiences. Some people think that magazines can be harmful by reinforcing female stereotypes – for example, girls and women can make themselves ill trying to look like the models in the pictures. What do you think?

Age

Try to avoid making sweeping statements about the age of a target audience, such as: 'this text is aimed at teenagers' or 'the target audience for this magazine is middle-aged people'. You might find the following breakdown helpful because it considers age bands in a more specific way:

Under 5	6–8	9–12	13–15	16–18
19–25	26–40	41–60	Over 60	

TIP

Knowing how to define target audiences is useful in many other Media Studies areas and when analysing media texts.

You will need to be able to describe and pinpoint target audiences throughout your Media Studies course and final External Assessment, so it is worth considering a few ways of defining the audiences for magazines.

Grade Studio

Examiner's tip

Sweeping statements are best avoided as they are not specific and are unlikely to receive high marks in your Controlled or External Assessments.

ACTIVITY 9

Imagine you are a media producer considering the target audience for your new magazine. What do you know about people of different ages?

1. **List and discuss the** probable *lifestyle, likes and dislikes of people in these age groups: 6–8; 16–18; 25–40; over 60.*

2. **Ask yourself about their hobbies, their favourite night out, the television programmes they watch, etc.**

People over 60 are <u>likely</u> to: have low disposable incomes; have similar, non-active lifestyles; not enjoy violence; enjoy films and programmes from the past.

When target audiences are described by their age and probable lifestyle, it is possible that groups can be **stereotyped**. The description of over-60s in Activity 9 may be true of some people, but it is important to remember that many over-60s earn high salaries, run marathons, enjoy thrillers and go to pop concerts!

Ethnicity

Although ethnicity is not always relevant when considering target audience – a text may be aimed at all ethnicities – the racial or religious background of an audience can sometimes be a factor that will influence what a text contains and what messages it will send out. For example, *Asiana* is a magazine that targets Asian women.

ACTIVITY 10

1 *What clues are there on this magazine cover to suggest that the ethnicity of the target audience is important? You might like to consider the words chosen and the presentation of the model, for example.*

2 *Working in groups, find out what magazines are most popular with people in your school. Try to ask students who represent a mix of ages, genders and ethnic backgrounds. What links can you see between these factors and the magazines people enjoy?*

3 *Present your findings in the form of a chart, graph or table and discuss in class.*

FOR THE ASIAN WOMAN WHO WANTS MORE

ASIANA

WINTER 2008 • £4.50

ANNIVERSARY SPECIAL

CELEBRATE

5 Years at the top with the world's best Asian mag

the **style secrets** of **2009**

Ethnicity is a major factor in the audience targeting of *Asiana*

Lifestyle

Being able to discuss the possible lifestyle habits of an audience is important. Try to consider the audience **values and aspirations** (ideology) for the text you are analysing. Media producers research their audiences to find out what kinds of thing are important to them, so that the messages in their texts will appeal to them and make them respond positively. Ask yourself how the text highlights and perhaps reinforces those values.

Look at the front cover of *Shout* magazine below.

- It suggests that the audience might be anxious about their appearance based on the clothes, hair and make-up of the models.

- The audience are obviously very interested in stories about stars and celebrities, and probably use pictures of them to provide role models of beauty, fame and success.

- The magazine assumes that readers will want to know as much about the personal life of celebrities as possible.

In many ways this magazine is a forerunner to magazines aimed at older girls that feature stories about celebrities and their partners.

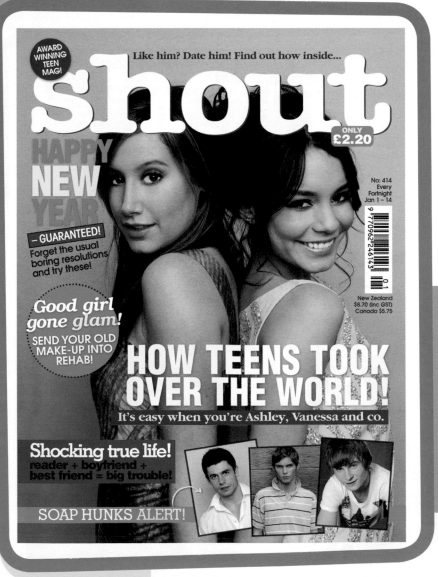

ACTIVITY 11

Look closely at the front cover of Shout. Write bullet-point answers on the following:
- *the likely audience of the magazine*
- *the kinds of feature that might be appealing to this audience.*

In Activity 3 on page 72, you categorised magazines into general interest and specialist groups. Now that you understand how magazine targeting works, and have learned about describing audiences, describe the target audiences of the following magazines:

Sugar   Radio Times   Rugby World   Good Housekeeping   FHM

Lifestyle magazine ideologies

Lifestyle, or general interest, magazines literally offer their readers a 'life style'; or in other words, a model on which to base their lives at this particular moment and advice on what might be needed to get the life they want. To do this successfully, magazines need to be able to make their readers identify with the lifestyle on offer, but at the same time offer them slightly more than they already have. The magazines offer both guidance and **aspiration**: 'You, too, can be like this, if only you do this/buy that, etc.' Successful magazines need to have a clear sense of their target audience and to adopt an appropriate mode of address. The audience for lifestyle magazines is likely to be:

- commercially successful
- aspirational females
- concerned with appearance and image
- the highest spenders on toiletries/cosmetics
- in control of their own lives and living for themselves
- interested in 'ideal' representations of self, home, family, career, relationships and lifestyle
- enjoying their freedom and independence.

Specialist magazine ideologies

Specialist magazines have smaller audiences than lifestyle magazines, as they focus on specific areas of interest, but they are popular with their audiences. Titles include *Total Film*, *NME*, *Angler's Mail* and *Nintendo*. What are your favourite specialist magazines? Why do you like them? It may be because they are more individual in their contents and mode of address than general interest or lifestyle magazines, which can be very 'samey' with an emphasis on fashion, celebrities and health. The following are some of the values of specialist magazines:

- They aim to celebrate the passion and interest of smaller, more individual audiences.
- They are published by and for specialist interest groups.
- They are often written by people with a personal interest in the subject.
- They exist so that people with shared interests can meet and say, 'Hey, I'm into that too!'
- They encourage relationships to form between readers who share the same interests. (See the section on page 93 on online magazines.)

Key terms

Aspiration When an audience sees fashion, accessories, a lifestyle, etc. in a magazine that they wish they could have for themselves.

- They will never sell as many copies as the general interest or lifestyle magazines, but they will always be appreciated by audiences who enjoy the 'alternative' or individual feel of a magazine which does not try to cover too many areas. It is interesting to note that this also applies to other media areas, such as film, when independent, low-budget films appeal to an audience who like quality acting and scripts, and reject big-budget Hollywood films.

Stars and celebrities

Look at the list of stars and celebrities on the previous page.

Magazine producers often feature a **celebrity** or **star** on a front cover in order to increase sales, and therefore profit. Which of these famous people would you classify as stars and which as celebrities?

Keira Knightley   Madonna   Charlotte Church   Ant and Dec   Davina McCall

Matt Damon   Daniel Craig   Samuel L. Jackson   Ian Wright

As a nation, people in the UK are fascinated by the lives of the famous, but how much of this enthusiasm is caused in the first place by the wide coverage of celebrities in the UK media?

Key terms

Celebrity Someone who is popular in one country for appearing in one media field, such as a soap opera.

Star A performer who is famous internationally.

ACTIVITY 13

Look at the list of stars and celebrities on the previous page. Choose one example of a star and one of a celebrity. Write a factfile on each one, indicating:
- *what you know about them already*
- *what they are most famous for*
- *which media areas might represent (or cover) them in some form.*

Example factfile: Charlotte Church
- *First became famous as a child star singing classical music and was referred to as having the 'Voice of an Angel'.*
- *Released her first pop song, 'Crazy Chick' in 2005 and was given a new pop image.*
- *Hosted her first television chat show – The Charlotte Church Show – in 2006 on Channel 4.*
- *Is well known for her marriage to Welsh rugby star Gavin Henson, and has appeared in many lifestyle magazines with him.*

Media producers create texts featuring stars partly to generate audience interest, for example, in a film trailer, and partly to satisfy audience demand for information on stars, for example, magazine spreads showing stars without their make-up. Consider the following:

- Producers make texts which audiences consume and respond to.
- These responses to texts are taken into account by producers when they make more texts.
- Popular formats are repeated so that audiences are given the sorts of text they 'ask for'.

Look at the media triangle diagram, which shows how media producers, texts and audiences are related to each other.

Charlotte Church: Celebrity or star?

MEDIA PRODUCER, e.g. IPC

IPC | MEDIA

MEDIA AUDIENCE, e.g. teenagers aged 15–18 who enjoy a range of non-mainstream music

TIP

It is useful to understand just how much influence the media has in 'making' a star. Consider the range of programmes that do this.

MEDIA TEXT, e.g. NME

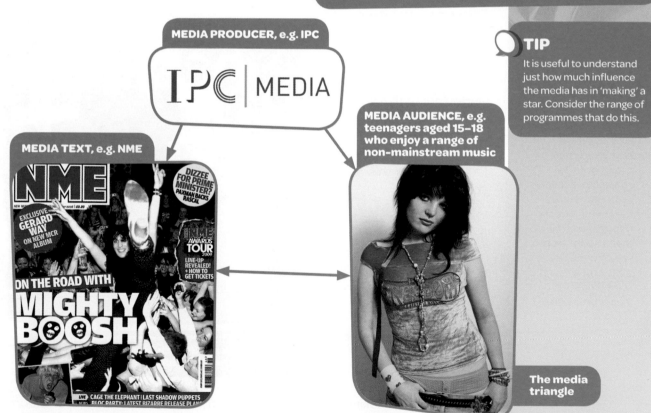

The media triangle

Take a few moments to discuss this triangle and the complex relationship between the maker of a magazine, the magazine itself and its target audience. Who has the most power in this process – the producers who make texts, the texts themselves or the audiences who consume and respond to them?

The media are often criticised for constantly representing stars and celebrities, and possibly even intruding into their private lives. However, famous people need the media to maintain their 'stardom', and we, the audience, are greedy for more information about them. Can you name any people who have become famous very quickly because of constant media attention? Can you think of anyone who has received negative media attention? You might like to think about the star image of Jade Goody, for example. Jade became 'famous' after being in the Big Brother house in 2002, and went on to feature in a series of reality TV shows such as *Celebrity Driving School* in 2003, *Jade's Salon* in 2005 and *Jade's PA* in 2006. She entered the celebrity Big Brother house in 2007 and received overwhelmingly negative media attention when she was seen making racist comments against another housemate, Shilpa Shetty. Since then, Jade has had to work hard to win back media favour.

Talk with a partner about stars and celebrities and their coverage in the media. Try to decide how far you agree with this statement:

Magazines feature too many stories about stars and celebrities.

ACTIVITY 14

How stars are represented

The **representation** of stars and celebrities is worth considering in any media form you are studying. Much has been written about film and television stars, and there are many theories about how and why they achieve fame. Consider this statement:

Stars are people who have become famous in one specialist area of activity and then also often achieve fame in other areas.

The Beckhams have been famous for some time but what are they most famous for *now*? Think about each family member in turn. How has this changed over time?

Another way of looking at stars is to say that they are *'complex representations of real people'*. In other words, they are not completely real, but they are based on someone who *is* real. They are people who have been given some kind of image treatment that will affect how audiences see and respond to them. Even though you may feel you know a lot about David Beckham, could you say that you actually know him?

Catherine Zeta Jones, for example, grew up in Swansea, Wales, and was a little-known television and stage actress until she won roles in Hollywood films in the late 1990s. When she moved to Hollywood and married Michael Douglas, her 'girl next door' image was changed to a more 'A list' look that made her seem more glamorous and unobtainable.

ACTIVITY 15

'Stars are people who have become famous in one specialist area of activity and then also often achieve fame in other areas.'

1. *Discuss this quotation with a partner, then feed back and discuss it as a class. Is this quote helpful when considering star/celebrity coverage in magazines? You may find it useful to have a range of magazines to look at.*

2. *Analyse the representation of one of your favourite stars or celebrities in at least two different magazines. Make a list of similarities and differences. How can the same person be shown differently? You may find it helpful to look at the two images on the right.*

The representation of stars is often linked to 'star image'

Mise-en-scène

The creation of every image, whether still or moving, involves planning and setting up. The careful arrangement of every element in an image to create a particular message or meaning is called the **mise-en-scène**.

Key terms

Mise-en-scène
A French phrase which literally means 'put in shot'.

This mise-en-scène makes the subjects look studious

Exactly the same elements are used here to create a different meaning!

1 The best way to understand how mise-en-scène works is to try it out yourself. Imagine you are the producer of a magazine called . You want the magazine to communicate to its teenage readers that it is cool to be studious and to care about the future, as well as to be popular and trendy. You want to take a picture of a 16-year-old for the front cover. How would you create the mise-en-scène ?

- Choose a suitable setting, for example, a classroom with good displays. Place a desk and a chair in the shot.
- Choose a subject from your class who you think has the right image for the shot.
- Wearing school uniform – how will you make sure the subject looks the part?
- Ask the subject to sit at a desk. How will they position their legs?
- What expression will they adopt?
- Which items of stationery, books, etc. will be on the desk? Why?
- What kind of bag will the subject have?
- Just before you take the shot, how will you ask the subject to pose?

If possible, take the shot!

2 When you have taken the photo, try something else. This time you are the producer of magazine for teenage girls aged 11–14. A photo story needs a shot of a two-timing, school-hating, football-mad teenage boy who is bored in his lesson and desperate for the bell to go. Using only the elements you used in the first mise-en-scène, change their arrangement to create a different meaning.
- What changes might you make to the subject's uniform and general appearance?
- What might happen to the books and pens?
- What pose will you ask for this time?

Using everything you have learned about texts, audiences and producers, as well as about representation and mise-en-scène, you are now going to transform yourself or a friend into a media star. You are going to create a profile of yourself as a star and then take a photograph of yourself as a star to go in a magazine of your choice. Think carefully about the following:

1 Choose an area of specialism, for example, a television celebrity who presents children's programmes.

2 List five bullet points connected to your representation. You could include: a zany sense of humour, a love of animals which is built into your shows, a famous mother.

3 Now create a 'look' for yourself that matches your profile. Think carefully about the mise-en-scène of the magazine page, so that the background is as appropriate as your costume and make-up. Set the shot up and ask someone to take the photograph. Make sure that your facial expression creates an impression of your star personality.

Analysing magazine contents pages

You have already seen that you can find out a lot about what a magazine has to offer by looking at its cover. The next step is to look at the contents page. This will give you an overview of what is inside the magazine you are studying. You can also see how it has been laid out to catch the reader's attention.

The contents page from *Shout*

CONTENTS

what's inside?

PAGE 26

PAGE 21

PAGE 72

free!

THE SHOPPING ISSUE

SUBSCRIPTIONS
If you'd like to have *Shout* delivered to your house, the cost whether you live in the UK or abroad is £57.20 for 1 year (all inclusive of postage). Turn to page 95 for more details.

MOBILE PHONE SERVICES
On occasion, we carry advertisements in *Shout* from companies offering ringtones and graphics for mobile phones. Please be aware that, to order, you must be 16 or over. Before ordering, please read the small print very carefully, check that your phone is compatible and be aware that any mistakes made in ordering are liable to be charged for.

recycle
When you have finished with this magazine please recycle it.

Printed and published by D.C.Thomson & Co., Ltd., 185 Fleet Street, London EC4A 2HS. © D.C.Thomson, 2008. Whilst every reasonable care will be taken neither D.C.Thomson & Co., Ltd., nor its agents accept liability for loss or damage to colour transparencies or any other material submitted to this publication.

Look for:

- the main areas of interest that the magazine covers, for example fashion, celebrities
- the kinds of feature in each area, for example, real life stories and problem solving
- how the reader's attention is drawn to special features, for example, through large-coloured font in eye-catching boxes
- how images and words are combined, for example, the free make-up in the contents page above.

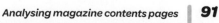

Although every magazine is different, each type of magazine has its own typical features. As an example, look at the typical features of a magazine aimed at teenage girls – *Shout*.

Some of the key features to look out for include:

- **Contents** – (see page 91) tells the reader how to find their way around the magazine. What first impressions do you get about what this magazine considers to be important?

- **Articles on cooking, crafts and make-up** – these encourage girls to take an interest in caring for others and making themselves look beautiful.

- **The 'true story'** – an immediate hook into the reader's own life as she tries to make links between the story and her real-life experiences.

- **The quiz** – a fictional but realistic scenario aims to test readers' potential responses in the real world. Quizzes often promote an 'average' response as the best one. If the girl scores the right number of points, she knows she will not stand out as being too different from her peers. This can directly influence the way that teenage girls see themselves. They are encouraged to conform to certain stereotypes of looks and behaviour, and discouraged from breaking 'out of the mould'.

- **Features about celebrities** – stories about pop, film and television stars help readers to feel they have a relationship with the 'great' and famous. Everyone is interested in the private lives of public figures!

- **Problem pages** – these give a genuine point of contact between the magazine and the reader. Reading about familiar situations or fears is reassuring and removes feelings of abnormality and separation. Look back at the Uses and Gratifications Theory on page 76 – what needs do problem pages satisfy?

- **Advertising for fashion and beauty products** – stereotypical representations of beautiful 'perfect' peers reinforce image and identity and give pre-teenagers a range of products which they can be sure will be acceptable to others.

TIP

Consider the stereotypical image being created here. You might want to create a new contents page that challenges this image.

Why are some magazines blamed for having a bad influence on teenagers? You may like to refer to two or three examples in your explanation.

ACTIVITY 18

Magazines and cross-media

All media areas have relationships with other media areas – in some cases they even depend on each other. Magazines, for example, depend on selling advertising space to keep the cover price cost down for readers.

Advertising

Have you ever noticed how many pages in a magazine are devoted to advertisements? If you carry out a survey of lifestyle or general interest magazines, you may be shocked to find that possibly over half the pages are filled with advertisements. It is estimated that women spend £230 million a year on monthly '**glossies**' and that the magazines themselves then earn another £190 million from advertising.

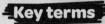
> **ACTIVITY 19**
>
> Watch the 'Making a profit' clip on the CD.
>
> ⭐ **1** *Discuss with a partner what you have learned about how magazines make money.*
>
> ⭐ **2** *Investigate advertising in magazines. Choose two contrasting magazines. Then:*
> - *see how many pages are in each magazine*
> - *decide what the main ideologies/values of each magazine are*
> - *count how many pages are used for advertisements*
> - *decide what kinds of advertisement appear most often.*
>
> ⭐ **3** *In your opinion, what is the relationship between your chosen magazine titles and the adverts they contain?*

CD-ROM
Extra!
Making a profit
Open the CD in the back of this book and click on the icon below to see footage about making a profit in magazine publishing.

The **revenue** that lifestyle magazines get from selling advertising space is far more important than the income they receive from the cover price and individual sales. The amount that they can charge for their advertising space is based on **circulation**. This is why magazines try so hard to be appealing, entertaining and interesting – in order to keep their circulation figures up and charge advertisers more!

Lifestyle magazines are all trying to create an ideology or lifestyle that will end up delivering particular audiences to advertisers, and advertisers in return try to reflect the main interests of the magazine. Advertisers for health, beauty and fashion products will try to buy space in these magazines as they know their target audiences will already be reading the magazine.

Online magazines

With improvements in technology over the last ten years, many media areas such as film and television are crossing over into others. You will notice in the chapter on film, for example, that there is a convergence between film and magazines, the Internet and advertising. In much the same way, magazines have been converging with the Internet.

Here we will consider the cross-media nature of film magazines. Many magazines now have equivalent online versions.

 magazine is the most popular specialist film magazine in the UK. In 2004, the online version of the magazine, called empireonline.co.uk was first posted on the web. It is a successful and popular site, and there is a free subscription for anyone who wants to have the online magazine sent to them each week.

This is what a regular reader of the print version of magazine said about the online version:

'Having read the magazine for a while now, I saw the advert for the site and was amazed. I was shocked to see that there was actually a magazine out there that had a running website that was updated in real time as soon as they had the news. The main features are available to all users with links to the news and reviews section. Their witty reviews and sarcastic news segments live up to the magazine's legend. Your first view of a site is the most important section of any website and Empire doesn't disappoint!'

What the site offers

The site offers:
- trailers and film stills of forthcoming films
- reviews of newly released films
- user polls, voting on favourite categories of films already released
- interviews with actors, directors, producers, etc.
- daily quiz and competitions with prizes
- blogs
- updates on newly released DVDs
- readers' views and opinions and relevant film fan information, for example, National Film Week.

CD-ROM
Extra!
Empireonline
Open the CD in the back of this book and click on the icon below to open a link to the Empireonline website.

HTML

Cross-media aspects

The cross-media nature of the site is important too, and is a good example of how media areas work together. There are links, for example, to:
- advertisements for recording television programmes to PS3 consoles and Play TV
- information on films released to DVD
- links to television sites
- links to magazine offers.

★CASE STUDY★
ACTIVITY

1 Visit the empireonline.co.uk site. Navigate through the news, features, articles and gallery shots. Why do you think the site has proved so popular with users?

2 Look back at the magazine titles mentioned in this chapter. Choose one or two that appeal to you and explore their online version.
- *How are the web pages laid out?*
- *Can you see any similarities or differences between the print and online versions?*
- *What are the most interesting links that the site allows you to explore?*
- *What does the site offer that the print version does not?*

Publishing houses

Magazine publishers are often part of huge, international media companies that also own newspapers, radio and television stations. This is a good example of cross-media. Below is some background information on some of the magazine publishing houses:

IPC has nearly 100 titles, including NME, and sells on average one magazine every 11 seconds throughout the year in the UK.

BAUER (which used to be called EMAP) publishes *Empire* magazine and sells 150 titles in the UK, France and around the world. It is also involved in the marketing of radio, television and music.

FUTURE is a smaller company based in Bath, specialising in film, computing and sports magazines including *Total Film* and *PC Gamer*.

BBC WORLDWIDE is the third largest consumer magazine publisher in the UK. Titles include *The Radio Times* and *Good Food* magazine.

EGMONT publishes 12 titles in the UK aimed at children. Although they refer to their publications as magazines, it is clear that some, such as Thomas and Friends would be referred to by many as comics.

ACTIVITY 20

1. On the CD, watch the clip of the Marketing Director of Egmont publishing house explaining how the Egmont titles are marketed to their audiences. Can you answer these questions?

- How do new titles come about?

- What have you learned about the relationship between magazines and films and television programmes?

- How are audiences encouraged to become loyal readers of titles?

2. Look again at the list of magazines in Activity 3. Choose ten titles. Create a chart like the one below and fill it in. The first title has been completed for you.

Magazine	Publisher	Circulation	Target audience
Empire	EMAP	2,000 per month	Mostly male, aged 18–35

CD-ROM
Extra!
Marketing magazines
Open the CD in the back of this book and click on the icon below to see the Marketing Director of Egmont publishing house explain how the Egmont titles are marketed to their audiences.

ACTIVITY 21

Having read the section on publishing houses, discuss the following issues and questions:

- A recent online survey suggested that there has been a drop in the circulation of music and film magazines. Can you think of any reasons for this?

- What would happen to the choice of magazines available if there were fewer publishing houses?

- How do magazine titles compete with each other? Refer to specific titles if you can.

What have you learned?

In this chapter you have learned about:

Texts

- New terms in relation to analysing magazines
- Conducting a contents analysis to see what is inside any magazine, how it is laid out and the elements on which the magazine places importance
- The values and ideologies of specific magazines
- Creating star profiles for magazine pages

Media language

Genre
- Categorising magazines in a variety of ways
- How to analyse the different features of print and online magazines

Narrative
- The features of magazines that relate to readers' lives
- Telling the stories of stars and celebrities

Representation

- How and why a mise-en-scène is set up
- How to create a mise-en-scène in order to see how many elements in a shot are combined to create meaning
- Representing stars and celebrities

Audiences

- Thinking about and reaching target audiences
- Identifying and describing target audience of specific magazines
- How audiences use magazines and what they get out of them
- Different audiences having different values and beliefs, thus affecting the way they respond to magazines

Institutions

- How design and marketing are directly linked to consumers
- The relationship between producers, texts and audiences
- The profile of some publishing houses
- Generating advertising revenue

Cross-media

- The cross-media nature of magazines, including their important relationship with advertisers and the development of online magazines

Comics, cartoons and animation

Your learning

In this chapter you will learn about:

- comic and cartoon characters, including superheroes
- the codes and conventions of comics, cartoons and animations that are used to communicate meanings for audiences
- attracting target audiences
- types of animation and their effects on audiences
- comics and cross-media.

The popularity of comics, cartoons and animations

Comics, cartoons and **animations** are popular with a huge range of audiences. Comics, for example, are not only enjoyed by young children but (like science fiction) also by older people. This is because they are often used to explore big concepts like human nature, good and evil, and social issues and concerns such as the protection of the environment.

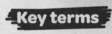

ACTIVITY 1

Name the first example that comes into your head of each of the following. Why did you think of them?

- *Comic*
- *Cartoon*
- *Animation*

Comic and cartoon characters – old favourites

TIP

Use information from family and friends, old comics and videos and the Internet to help you.

People become passionate about the media texts they enjoyed when they were young, partly because they were so involved when they read or watched them. Young children look forward eagerly to their favourite characters coming on television, or to watching the video again and again and joining in with the words and actions. Your childhood favourites become part of your identity. Try talking about your favourite – you may be surprised how much you still care!

ACTIVITY 2

1 Complete a table like the one below to find out as much as you can about each of the characters listed. Try to discover:
- when and where they first appeared
- who created them
- if they were used in more than one media genre, for example, a comic strip that became a television series
- whether they are still featured in comics or television stories today.

Character name	When and where did they first appear?	Who created them?	Are they used in more than one media genre?	Are they still featured in comics or TV stories today?
Scooby Doo	1969 on CBS television, America	Hanna-Barbera productions	Many series on different television channels, plus comics, video games and films	Marvel produce the comic today and there are still re-runs of the TV show in the UK
Desperate Dan				
Care Bears				
Mickey Mouse				
Batman				
Tintin				
Zebedee				

2 Try to build up an information sheet on one of the characters. If you can, include drawings of your chosen character. Discuss your findings with the rest of the class.

Comic and cartoon characters are created deliberately for children to identify with and remember. Many comics and cartoons use 'licensed' characters that readers and viewers are already familiar with. These characters enable comic and cartoon producers to establish business relationships with the creators of the characters. Film studios will sell the rights to popular characters to related media industries.

Winnie the Pooh

Though Disney didn't create Winnie the Pooh, it has the right to license it to be used in a range of media texts as well as Disney films, including a comic, a cartoon series, CD soundtracks and computer games, and also allows Marks and Spencer to sell Winnie the Pooh clothing. This is a good example of the *cross-media* nature of the media, when one media text uses **tie-ins** and **spin-offs** that involve other media industries.

Key terms

Tie-in A media text that uses the characters, and possibly storyline, of a text in another form.

Spin-off Merchandise that uses characters from a media text.

Thomas the Tank Engine

The Reverend W. Awdry first created Thomas the Tank Engine out of a piece of broomstick for his son Christopher. This character ended up being licensed in a series of books, an ITV television series, a film called *Thomas and the Magic Railroad* (2000) and the comic *Thomas and Friends* (published by Egmont Magazines).

ACTIVITY 3

1 *Can you think of any other characters that appear in so many forms as Thomas the Tank Engine?*

2 *Discuss the ways that comic producers create characters and use licensed characters.*

ACTIVITY 4

1 *Choose a character that was important to you as a child. How did you discover the character and why did you enjoy them?*

2 *If possible, undertake some research with young children about the characters they enjoy in comic/magazine form. You will need to create a survey to ask them questions about their favourite comics and characters. Questions could include:*
- *What comics/magazines do you like to read?*
- *What do you like best about comics/magazines?*
- *Can you make a list of your favourite characters from films, comics and television programmes?*
- *Can you draw one of your favourite characters?*
- *Design a new character. What do you like best about your character? The face? Dress? Actions? (You may need to give some help here.)*

3 *Using your knowledge of the kinds of character which are popular with children, create a brand new character for a new comic or cartoon series. Draw the character and label him/her with the main features of interest.*

Character type and function

Vladimir Propp suggested in 1928 that in any story there are only a limited number of character types, each of which have their own purpose in the narrative. Some of these are shown below.

Propp's main character types

Hero

The **central protagonist** of the narrative who drives it forward and has some kind of quest or mission to undertake in return for a reward. Traditionally male, for example, Thomas the Tank Engine, but can be female in modern narratives, for example, Dora the Explorer.

Heroine or Princess

Acts as a reward for the hero for succeeding in the quest. In older, more stereotypical narratives the heroine is a **passive** princess and female, for example, Minnie Mouse. In modern narratives, the heroine can be more active and feisty, for example, Leela in *Futurama*.

Villain

Seeks riches, glory and/or power, and also seeks to stop the hero from succeeding in the quest or mission, while presenting a genuine threat. They sometimes want the heroine for themselves too! They can be male, for example, Mr Burns in *The Simpsons* or female, for example, Mystique in the *X-Men* comics.

Donor or Mentor

Gives the hero important information or equipment to help him or her in the quest. They are often represented as wise or as having special powers, but are not able to do the quest without the hero, for example, Shredder in *Teenage Mutant Hero Turtles*.

Helper

Accompanies the hero for some or most of the journey of the quest, and can even help the hero to succeed, but cannot themselves complete the quest, for example, Jess the cat in *Postman Pat*.

TIP

These character types are relevant in other media areas, such as film and television.

Key terms

Central protagonist Character around whom the text and narrative is centred.

Passive Not helping the narrative to move forward or not helping the hero.

You have to be flexible when you classify characters into these types. Some characters fulfil two, or even more, functions. For example, the heroine could also be the helper – April is the heroine in *Teenage Mutant Hero Turtles*, but she also comes to the aid of the turtles on numerous occasions.

Hero, villain, heroine – but who's who?

ACTIVITY 5

1 *Think up more examples of Propp's character types from stories you know. Create your own chart showing typical characteristics of those types. Were any characters hard to classify? Why?*

2 *Create a character design for a new character, using your chart from the previous part of Activity 5. Label your character to show what type he/she is.*

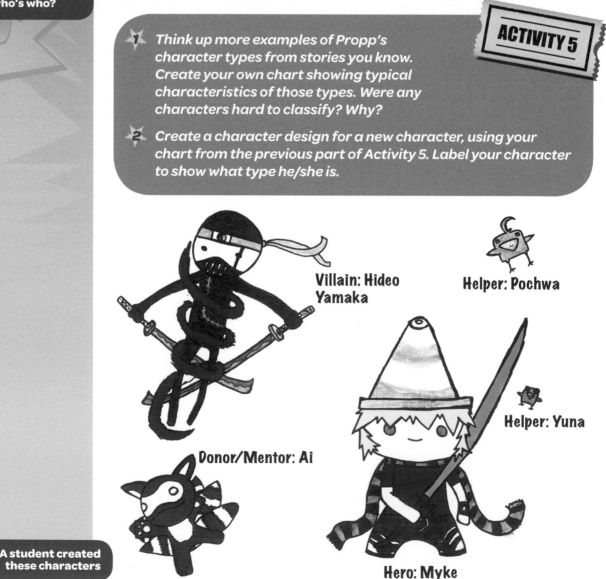

Villain: Hideo Yamaka

Helper: Pochwa

Donor/Mentor: Ai

Helper: Yuna

Hero: Myke

A student created these characters

Comic front covers

ACTIVITY 6

1 *Look at a range of comic front covers. How have they been designed to attract the attention of potential readers? The front cover below has been analysed for you.*

Logo shows quality and authenticity.

Mysterious figure adds reason for the reader to buy the comic and find out more.

Indexical sign of the Eiffel Tower gives sense of place.

Images of heroes using their powers shows action and makes heroes instantly recognisable to the reader.

Villains shown as well as heroes to indicate danger and excitement.

Added feature in the comic is advertised boldly under the main title in an attempt to persuade readers to buy the comic.

Villains fighting heroes shows action and gives the reader a sense of what's to come.

Large image of hero as well as smaller images of other heroes are iconic to the reader and draws the reader to the heroes.

Small amounts of open space so that important figures occupy the most space and make the cover more exciting and attractive.

2 *Choose a different comic and analyse the main features that you think will appeal to its target audience.*

3 *Create the front cover of a brand-new comic that you think will appeal to either boys or girls. Think carefully about your target audience here – look again at the CD-ROM.*

Grade Studio

Examiner's tip

Appropriate use of terminology helps you earn more marks. Remember the terminology of comic deconstruction.

Comic conventions

The main conventions of comics are understood by their audiences and are an important part of the way that comics are read. Although comic strips are not audio-visual texts, they follow many of the same rules of narrative as film or television. They are constructed to be like the frozen frames of moving texts. They are like dynamic **storyboards** which combine words and pictures to create the impression of sound, movement and tension. They rely most of all on complex reading skills on the part of the comic reader – reading comics is far from a waste of time!

Key moments

When you are making a storyboard for a comic strip, it is useful to remember Todorov's Narrative Theory. This suggests five stages in any story:

1 Equilibrium: establish setting, characters and storyline.

2 Disruption of the equilibrium, perhaps by an **oppositional character.**

3 Recognition of the disruption (often the longest part).

4 An attempt to repair the disruption.

5 Reinstatement of the equilibrium.

Your comic storyboard will need at least one frame or panel for each stage.

Key terms

Storyboard The key moments of a story shown using images and notes – see the example on page 107.

Key terms

Oppositional character A character who will play opposite the key central character, either in a relationship (for example, the hero/heroine) or in conflict (for example, the hero/villain).

Richard's skateboard disaster

Richard was fed up with school. One evening, before school the next day, he went to his friend Yousaf's house to watch scary movies. Before they knew it, time had moved on and it was after midnight.

Richard rushed home on his skateboard and fell into bed exhausted.

The next morning, Richard was woken by his Mum shouting to him that he had overslept and his breakfast was ready. He jumped out of bed and hurriedly dressed for school.

Unfortunately, he forgot that he had left his skateboard at the top of the stairs the night before. As he tried to rush downstairs, he trod on the skateboard, which shot out from under him.

Poor Richard fell down the stairs and he ended up at the bottom with a nasty fracture to his leg. His Mum called an ambulance and he was rushed to casualty.

Richard ended up with his leg in traction, and could not go to school for six weeks. Yousaf visited him regularly and Richard was heard to confess to his friend that he actually missed school!

You are going to work in pairs to make a storyboard for Richard's story. You can see an example of a comic storyboard below. You may like to look at the illustrations of comic techniques on page 108 to help you.

⭐1 Decide on the most important details of the story – make a list first. You are going to tell the story in six to eight frames, but you must also remember that the story should control **pace** and **tension** while making sense.

⭐2 Now make a comic storyboard to tell the story. Try to make sure that the meaning is clear. Vary your camera framing so that some frames/panels will be close-ups and some will be from further away.

⭐3 Think about the information you want to add underneath each frame/panel – this should give an idea about the effect of each image.

⭐4 Pass the storyboards around the class so that everyone can see them. Discuss the similarities and differences between the storyboards. Did any pairs use techniques in addition to drawing the key moments? How did these help to improve the impact of the story?

Key terms

Pace The speed at which something happens or a story develops.

Tension The build-up of suspense or anticipation as a story develops.

Example of a comic storyboard written by a student.

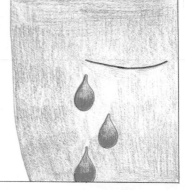

Establishment shot – Castle
Pan wide shot   4 seconds
Harp playing

Full Length shot – princess's window
2 seconds
Harp continues playing
(weeping sound)

Extreme close up
3 seconds
Harp continues playing
(v/o: 'The Mouse princess was very sad')

You will have seen how important it is to choose moments which are rich with meaning and convey a lot of information to the audience. Remember that comic readers are good at reading not only the information in each frame, but also the information implied between frames. For example, if a character is shown in place A in one frame and place B in the next, the audience will understand that the character has travelled there and time has passed between the frames.

ACTIVITY 8

1 Watch the CD clip on making comic stories. Make notes on how comic publishers create comic narratives.

2 Practise creating frames/panels that would show the key moments from fairy tales and well-known stories that you enjoyed as a child.

Examples of comic techniques

The following techniques are often used in comic strips:

Thought bubbles – like speech bubbles, but the words are placed in cloud-shaped bubbles to show what the character is thinking.

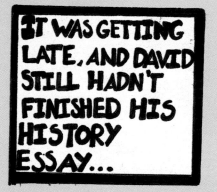

IT WAS GETTING LATE, AND DAVID STILL HADN'T FINISHED HIS HISTORY ESSAY...

Text boxes – small boxes of text which give details that would be hard to show in pictures alone. They are placed at the top or bottom of a frame, or underneath a frame (common in comics aimed at young children).

Speech bubbles – words of speech placed in a bubble pointing towards the mouth of the character who is speaking. Sometimes speech bubbles can point out of a frame to show that a character we can't see is speaking.

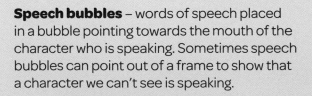

LATER, AT LIZ'S HOUSE ...

Frame links – copy placed between frames to help the reader understand events which may have happened after the last frame and before the next.

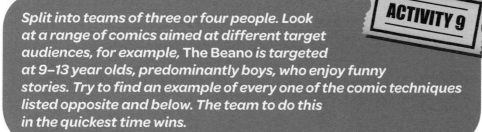
Sound words – comics give the impression of sounds by using inventive onomatopoeic words like 'POW!' and 'ZAPP!!'.

Emotion words – like sound words, comics also use words to show exactly how a character is feeling, for example, 'BOOOOOOOOOOOOORED!!!!'

Facial expressions – simple alterations to a character's face to show emotion.

Movement lines – comic frames give the impression of movement by adding small lines around the edges of characters' bodies and moving objects.

The best way to appreciate how sophisticated comic techniques are is to use them yourself. Follow the steps in the activity below to create a four-to-six-frame photo-comic based on a fairy tale or childhood story you know well. Your aim is to create a text which is eye-catching and easy to understand.

ACTIVITY 10

1 *Start by sketching the frames as a simple storyboard (see page 107). Decide together how to take the shots.*

2 *Take the shots. Elaborate settings or costumes are not necessary, since you can alter the photos using gel pens or correcting pen, by sticking things onto them or by cutting parts of them out. If you use a digital camera you can use a photo-editing package.*

3 *When your photos are ready, create your photo comic. You will need:*

- a large sheet of sugar paper
- mounting paper for each photo
- plain paper for writing or typing out text boxes and speech bubbles
- an assortment of coloured pens, etc. for decoration.

4 *Give a group presentation to the rest of the class: show your photo-comic and explain how you created it and why. Alternatively, make a wall display: label your photo-comic to show how and why you made it as you did.*

ACTIVITY 11

Discuss the process of creating comics. For example, choosing the key moments of a narrative and varying, as much as possible, the size and shape of the frames in which these key moments will be shown.

Superheroes

Many stories in comics, cartoons and animated films are centred on heroic deeds. Yet there is a difference between a hero – who we simply follow throughout the narrative – and a **superhero**, who often has special powers to help him or her save the world! Why do you think that animation is a particularly good media genre for portraying superheroes?

ACTIVITY 12

1. *If you were a superhero, what superpowers would you choose? Why?*

2. *Make notes on, or draw, the superhero you would be.*

3. *Explain how your superhero got their powers.*

4. *If you have time, make notes or draw the **arch-villain** who opposes your superhero.*

Key terms

Arch-villain The character who opposes the superhero and often has special powers too, that are used only for evil. The most memorable arch-villains are those who have a reason for turning to evil, for example, Doctor Octopus in *Spiderman*.

Audiences love superheroes because, through them, they are able to:

- explore beyond the boundaries of human possibility, for example, imagine what it is like to fly like Superman

- engage with the conflict between good and evil, for example, sympathise with Spiderman as he fights against the Sandman

- enjoy exploring the 'dark side' that so many superheroes have, for example, wonder what it is like to give up popularity like Batman.

In recent years, films that are based on comic or cartoon superhero characters have become very popular. This demonstrates the cross-media nature of comics, cartoons and animations.

It is interesting to investigate what has influenced the creation or development of superheroes. For instance, the spread of nuclear weapons or changes presented by radiation are real historical developments that have influenced superheroes.

Superman: comic and film superhero

CASE STUDY

MARVEL COMICS

This case study considers some of the cross-media aspects of Marvel comics.

Your favourite film superheroes will probably come from the gallery created by Marvel comics. Marvel is well known for its colourful and dramatic superheroes, which include Spiderman, The Incredible Hulk, the Fantastic Four and The Silver Surfer.

The first Marvel comic was published in the USA in 1939, introducing the Submariner. Many of the best known Marvel characters were created in the 1960s, starting with the Fantastic Four in 1961. The Incredible Hulk (1962) – influenced by characters from the books *Frankenstein* and *Dr Jekyll and Mr Hyde* – and Spiderman (1963) soon followed. Already Marvel were using **intertextual reference** to create the Marvel universe – characters would guest star in each other's comic strips.

By 1966 Marvel characters had their own animated series on television, showing five different stories featuring Captain America, Iron Man, The Incredible Hulk, Thor and Submariner. In the 1970s not only did Marvel heroes feature in full-length films, but Marvel were asked to create comics based on popular films such as *Star Wars*.

Marvel Enterprises today owns the rights to over 4000 characters, used in comic books, films, television programmes and video games. The success of several blockbuster superhero films in recent years has led to spin-offs such as a Marvel Superhero Top Trumps game.

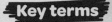

> ### Key terms
>
> **Intertextual reference**
> When one media text mimics or refers to another media text in a way that many consumers will recognise.

Iron Man

A helpful research activity could be to choose one of your favourite superhero characters and find out about their history and development. Iron Man, for example, was first introduced in 1963 by Marvel's designer, Stan Lee: he wanted to make a hero out of a businessman, Tony Stark, who would be 'a rich, glamorous ladies' man but one with a secret that would plague and torment him as well'. Iron Man was a comic character who was first used to explore the fears behind the Cold War, but later to raise awareness of heart problems and alcoholism.

Iron Man was adapted for film in 2008 with Robert Downey Jr playing Tony Stark.

Marvel superheroes

Marvel superheroes often show certain characteristics:

- some kind of tragedy in their past for which they want revenge, for example, The Incredible Hulk
- double identity, for example, Superman
- some kind of change to their genetic make-up that gave them their superpowers, for example, Spiderman.

1 Make factfiles on your favourite Marvel heroes and villains. Include descriptions of:
- their powers
- their personal history
- their greatest adventures.

Use books, comics and a search engine on the Internet. You could also talk to comic fans, or visit a comic supplier such as Forbidden Planet.

2 Now compare the comic and film versions of some well-known superheroes, such as Superman, X-Men and The Incredible Hulk. List and discuss the main similarities and differences between the two treatments. You may find it helpful to read through the information on analysing openings below before you complete this activity.

Analysing openings

The way a cartoon or animation begins is important in setting up its narrative, characters, setting, main themes and general mood. Marvel comics are the basis for many film adaptations. These films usually begin with an *ident* in the form of a comic strip of famous superheroes to show the audience the roots of the film's storyline. The opening sequence that follows may show some of these features:

- establishing shots to set location
- first appearance of the superhero (who may not appear in their superhero form)
- a soundtrack that establishes mood
- graphics that establish the style of the film
- codes and symbols that suggest plot.

1 First read these notes that a student wrote about the opening to Daredevil:

- Opening panning shot of skyscrapers zooms into individual 'braille' style lights which are then 'translated' into title credits. Could the hero be blind?
- The hero wears a dark red lycra outfit with his face hidden. His mask is removed and we are shocked that he is 'revealed'.
- A flashback helps us to understand that he suffered tragedy as a child, but that he also received supersonic sonar hearing as a result of the accident.

2 Watch two or three more openings to films based on Marvel superheroes. Write down the most important points in notes like those above.

3 Share your ideas about the openings you have seen with the class. Make a class list of the important features of openings.

Animation cross-media

The Sony Bravia's animated rabbit campaign has been very successful

We tend to think of animation as being used for cartoon programmes and films, but animation techniques are used right across media areas. Animation is often used in:

- advertising, for example, the Sony Bravia advert with animated plasticine rabbits using stop-frame animation (see image). This advertisement has been used in both print and audio-visual form
- non-animated films as a special effect, for example, the scenes in *The Lord of the Rings* showing Gollum and the Orcs using computer-generated imagery
- openings of non-animated films and television programmes, for example, the award-winning opening film sequence of *Juno* (2008) that cleverly uses a combination of live action and line animation.

Animation techniques

Different techniques can be used to 'animate' still images, each bringing its own unique style to the animation.

Line or cel drawing

This technique was used by the first animators. They drew a figure, framed in a background, many times, each time making tiny adjustments, and filmed each picture for just a frame or two. When the film was shown at normal speed, the figure appeared to move.

These six frames form a simple animation when played continuously

Try creating your own line animation. Think of a simple figure that you can draw, and choose a simple action, for example, raising a hand to wave. You could even copy out the illustrated six-frame animation above and animate it as shown below.

1. *Draw the figure on the first page of a small notebook in the top right-hand corner.*

2. *On the second page, draw the same figure with a slight change to show the beginning of the action.*

3. *On the next page, move the figure further, and so on until the action is completed.*

4. *Holding the notebook firmly in one hand, flick quickly through the pages with the other thumb so that you can see your drawings in rapid succession. Your character will appear to move.*

Model animation or stop-motion

Another successful and easy-to-recognise animation technique is **model animation**. A scale model of a character is moved and filmed in very small stages. This obviously takes a great deal of patience and time, and software that allows the camera to film single frames to create the effect of start–stop motion.

This technique became popular in the 1960s and 1970s, when Ray Harryhausen made model animation his speciality. He created characters such as the skeleton army in *Jason and the Argonauts* (1963), the goddess Kali in *The Golden Voyage of Sinbad* (1974) and Pegasus in *Clash of the Titans* (1980). The latter was his last film and it took Harryhausen a year to create the effects, which used 202 specially constructed shots.

CD-ROM Extra!

Ray Harryhausen
Open the CD in the back of this book and click on the icon below to visit Ray Harryhausen's official website.

HTML

Key terms

Model animation
An animation technique using posable scale models.

The skeleton army in *Jason and the Argonauts*

In 1985, Nick Park joined Aardman Animations in Bristol and a few years later they introduced the world to Wallace and Gromit. Three short films and two full-length films have proved hugely popular with young and old alike. *Chicken Run* (2000) featured the voices of Mel Gibson and Julia Sawalha, while *Wallace and Gromit: Curse of the Were Rabbit* (2005) featured Ralph Fiennes and Helena Bonham Carter. The popularity of Aardman's unique style of model animation is set to last!

ACTIVITY 14

1 Watch one or two scenes from Nick Park's animations. Try to spot how the animators have made the characters and settings as realistic and true to life as possible, for example, Gromit raises an eyebrow to show his feelings; the wallpaper and pictures on the wall.

*2 Explore the official **Curse of the Were Rabbit** website. It is lively, informative ... and animated! Look at the 'behind the scenes' material and discuss what you have discovered about creating model animation characters.*

ACTIVITY 15

If you have access to the right technology, you could create your own simple model animation as a piece of coursework. You can use almost anything for this: Plasticine, yoghurt pots, dolls, Lego, plastic bags ... anything you can imagine coming to life.

1. *Make or draw a simple character.*

2. *Work out a simple series of movements for the character to perform, and film each stage for 1–2 seconds.*

3. *You only need to record about 2 minutes of footage. Ideally you should use animation software such as istopmotion.*

Computer-generated imagery (CGI)

It was obviously very time-consuming to draw so many frames. It took three years, for example, for the animators on Walt Disney's *Snow White* (1937) to complete their drawings. As early as the 1960s, people were working on ways to use computers to make the small adjustments to the original frame.

Since the 1970s, computers have been used in more and more sophisticated ways in animation. The first film to use 3D **computer-generated imagery** (**CGI**) techniques in a significant way was Disney's *Tron* (1983). The film was about a computer programmer (played by Jeff Bridges) who is sucked into his computer and turned into a 'virtual person' who must fight the main programme in order to survive. If you are able to see this film for yourself, you will notice immediately how simple the technology is compared to that of today.

> ### Key terms
>
> **Computer-generated imagery (CGI)** Using computer graphics, especially 3D computer graphics, in special effects.

Tron (1983)

TIP

You might like to explore how **Shrek** uses role reversal and subversion of traditional narratives.

Today CGI allows whole worlds to be created and inhabited – sometimes without any human actors at all. Films entirely animated by computer include *Toy Story* (1995) and the *Shrek* trilogy (2001–2007), while *Beowulf* (2007) uses video-gaming motion-capture computer technology.

What are your own favourite examples of film moments using CGI? Can you think of any moments when the technology works less well?

CGI has changed a great deal since the early days!

ACTIVITY 16

1 *Can you think of any issues that using CGI may raise? Think about CGI being used in celebrity photo-shoots, music videos and advertisements as well as films and cartoons.*

ACTIVITY 17

Watch the film Simone (2002) directed by Andrew Niccol. It explores the whole notion of using computer technology to create perfect computerised people or actors. It also raises some interesting points in relation to audiences and their adoration of stars.

Having watched the film, discuss with your classmates whether 'virtual actors' would work in reality. Support your arguments by referring to moments from the film.

Anime

Anime is a Japanese animation form which combines film-making with Manga comic form. **Manga** comics have been made in Japan for many years, calling on the longstanding tradition of line art and Buddhist scrolls which had to be unrolled to reveal a message. They also used the Western tradition of telling stories in sequence, and the traditions of American comic books.

A manga graphic novel

Anime directors are interested in the effects of technology on society. The link to comics can be seen easily, since the intention of anime is to control the ways in which the viewer's eye looks at the screen. Many of the characters in anime are westernised, and some even look like early Disney characters.

Early anime animation leaned heavily on the idea of big comic frames (which were still) with large painted cels, but gave the impression of movement because the camera panned across them as it would in a film. The result was a semi-frozen animation, which emphasised angles and facial expressions, used tilt-ups and tilt-downs to give the impression of seeing more of a scene, and zoom-ins to draw attention to dramatic detail.

Hayao Miyazaki directed Japanese animation *Spirited Away* (2001)

ACTIVITY 18

1   *Working in a small group or on your own, try using anime techniques. Draw some large comic frames or put together a sequence of photographs to tell a simple story – even the story of your holiday.*

2   *Film the frames or images in close up, then experiment with zooming in on certain details.*

3   *Play the footage back to see how effective this simple animation is.*

4   *You could develop your anime-style work by writing a voice-over commentary to accompany the footage, or adding text boxes, speech bubbles, etc.*

Japanese animation is concerned with meaning and symbolism. It draws attention to important details – since the frozen scene allows more time to look at everything – and gives clues about characters by their appearance. For example, large eyes suggest that characters are heroes or heroines, with good hearts and intentions. Small eyes suggest evil intent and usually belong to characters who are villains or villain's helpers.

Some good examples of anime are *Akira* (1988), *Ghost in the Shell* (1995) and *Howl's Moving Castle* (2004). If you have the chance to see them, or any other anime films or cartoons, you will also notice how music and sound effects are used to create mood and atmosphere.

The *Matrix* trilogy was influenced by manga and anime

Many of you will have seen one or more of the *Matrix* trilogy, directed by the Wachowski brothers, who have admitted to the strong influence of manga and anime on their film-making. They also produced the *Animatrix* series of anime cartoons to accompany the films. This is another good example of cross-media.

ACTIVITY 19

1. *Watch an episode from* **Animatrix**.

2. *Write about the techniques it uses to create mood and tension. Focus on characters' expressions and reactions, music, camera techniques (especially framing, point-of-view shots and panning from one place to another) and sound effects.*

3. *Try to explore the possible meanings and messages in the text.*

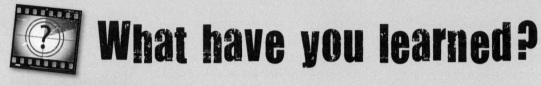

What have you learned?

In this chapter you have learned about:

Texts

- Analysing comics and the openings of cartoons and animations
- Looking at the construction of comic front covers
- Storyboarding and focusing on frames and panels

Media language

Genre
- How comics, cartoons and animations use clear characteristics to allow audiences to engage with, and enjoy, them
- How comic and animation techniques exist in a wide range of genres
- How to include an understanding of comic/animations in coursework

Narrative
- The importance of character types and their function in narratives
- Telling a simple story in key moments
- Codes of realism in comic and animated narratives

Representation

- Representations of the human and non-human
- Ways in which character types are represented
- Superheroes
- How representations are used in anime

Audiences

- Thinking about and attracting target audiences
- Creating surveys and questionnaires
- Exploring audience responses
- Discussing the effect of licensed characters on audiences

Institutions

- How design is directly linked to consumers
- Potentially negative effects of computer-generated imagery
- The history of some publishers
- Use of animated characters as a signature for an animation company

Cross-media

- The cross-media nature of comics, cartoons and animations including their use in advertising, websites, films and television
- Animated websites

6 Pop music

Your learning

In this chapter you will learn about:

- how the music industry is changing in the face of new technology, for example, the Internet
- who decides what music we listen to
- the importance of genre in the music industry
- the importance of the music video in selling music
- what changes are occurring in the way the music press covers the music scene.

Wild things: a brief history of pop music and youth culture

In the decade after the Second World War, teenagers wanted to see themselves as being very different from their parents. Boys dressed in drape suits and ripped up cinema seats when the film *Rock Around the Clock* was shown. Girls combed their hair into 'beehives' and wore high stiletto heels.

Teenagers were often presented by the media as unruly and violent. When Mods fought Rockers on the beach at the seaside town of Margate during the Easter weekend of 1964, many newspapers treated the incident as if war had broken out. The magistrate who tried 44 young people for various offences described them as 'miserable specimens', 'strutting hooligans', 'louts', 'dregs' and 'long-haired, mentally unstable, petty hoodlums'.

But while the press presented a negative view of teenagers, the music and fashion industry soon realised that there was a lot of money to be made from them. They were a new, young audience who had money to spend on enjoying themselves. In 1960 there were 5 million teenagers in the UK, spending £800 million on clothes and entertainment – a tenth of the total of all leisure spending. When it came to records and record players, teenagers made up half the market.

In 1955, British listeners bought just 4 million singles (on record). By 1960 they were buying 52 million singles a year and by 1963, 61 million. This wasn't just due to the popularity of pop stars like Elvis Presley – radio was now broadcasting music and was becoming hugely popular.

Genre became an important part of the record industry. To keep the sales soaring, it was good to have new teenage crazes – different genres – appearing regularly. And if different fashion styles could be linked to music genres, even more money would go through the tills.

This activity will help you investigate the importance of pop music to different generations.

1 Interview someone at least 20 years older than you about their memories of the music they listened to when they were young and how important it was to them. You could use some of the following questions to start you off:

Questions to ask	Response
In which decade were you a teenager (1950s, 1960s, 1970s, 1980s, 1990s)?	
What kind of music did you like when you were a teenager?	
What sort of fashions or style did you dress in? Was this linked with the music?	
How did you buy music – on vinyl? On tape? On CD? Do you have a preference for any of these formats and why?	
What technical equipment did you use to listen to music?	
Which music TV programmes did you watch?	
Which radio stations or programmes did you listen to?	
Did you read music magazines? Which ones?	
What did you like about the music magazines back then?	
Do you think music was better back then?	

2 Now ask yourself the following questions about your own music consumption:

Questions to ask	Response
How do you access or purchase the music you like?	
How much does this cost?	
What format is most of your music in?	
What technology is available to you to listen to music?	
How do you hear new music?	
How do you find out information about music or bands?	
Which music websites are you aware of?	
Which music magazines do you read? Why do you like them?	
Which music websites do you visit? Why do you like them?	
What kind of clothing style is associated with the kind of music you like?	

Music across time

Listening to the same old-school music your parents liked would have been deeply uncool in the 1960s. But some people argue that the constant **re-issuing** and marketing of **back-catalogue** material by the record companies means there is no past, only a continuous present. With an iPod shuffle, the flow of music leaps backwards and forwards across time with every track change.

ACTIVITY 2

In no more than 300 words, compare your experience of music with that of the older person you interviewed in Activity 1.

1. *Do you agree that young people today are listening to a much wider range of music genres? You should give examples of the different genres you and your friends listen to.*

2. *How have technology and the digital revolution altered the way we access and enjoy music? You need to think about the restrictions that affected older people when they only had a vinyl disc and a record player. How do things like the Internet and the MP3 player make a difference for you?*

Examiner's tip

To help you understand the cross-media aspects of the pop industry, create a profile of a rock fan. Focus on a particular music genre and detail things like fashion, lifestyle choices and so on.

Genres in pop music

Look back at the interview you carried out in Activity 1 with an older person about their music listening habits. They will certainly have mentioned individual artists or bands by name. But did they say they listened to a particular genre or type of music? If they were teenagers in the early 1960s, they may have been fans of folk music, listening to artists like Bob Dylan or Joan Baez. If their listening habits developed ten years later, they might have been rock fans devoted to Led Zeppelin or reggae enthusiasts hooked on Bob Marley.

You might be asking why genres are important in music. They are important for the same reasons they are important in any other part of the media:

- They help audiences to recognise things which they think they might like.
- They help the music industry organise the things they want to sell to the audience.

Star power!

The most obvious way to see this in action is to press the genre link on an iPod – iTunes will have given everything a genre. If you want to sample your indie tunes without rock music bursting in, you can listen by genre.

Another way of exploring how the music industry uses genres is to go into any music retail store. The products on sale are arranged into categories. Some of the categories used in big music stores actually cover a variety of different types of music. Jazz is a good example of this. Shops only have limited display space, so it's easier to group Kid Ory (a New Orleans trombonist from the 1920s) with Weather Report (a 70s jazz rock band) in a section labelled 'Jazz'. This leaves much more space for the genres which make the retailers the most money. These are, by definition, 'popular' music – music that sells in large amounts.

ACTIVITY 3

Go into your nearest large music retailer and note down the categories they are using to organise their products.

1. *Does breaking the store down into these sections make the music you want easier or harder to find?*

2. *How often do you now go and buy a CD (or maybe even a vinyl) from a music store?*

3. *Imagine that you are a new artist with your first album to sell. How do you think you could most effectively get your product out to a wide audience? Would you approach a major record label with a demo version of your songs? Would you place an advertisement in the local paper? Or would you use YouTube?*

CASE STUDY

GARY BROLSMA: SUPERSTAR

This case study discusses some of the cross-media aspects of pop music today. It focuses on Gary Brolsma, who became famous through the Internet for his version of a previously-recorded single. At the end you'll be asked in the Activity to discuss the issues that come out of this case study.

Gary Brolsma and the Internet

Have you heard of Gary Brolsma? He could claim to be one of the most successful artists in the history of pop music. His cover version of the song titled *Dragostea din tei*, by the Romanian band O-Zone, was released as *Numa Numa* on 14 August 2006. By March 2008, his song had reached a staggering 700 million people.

Let's put that into perspective. In 1964, The Beatles had the fastest selling vinyl single of all time with *I Want to Hold Your Hand*. The song sold 250,000 copies within three days in the USA and 1 million in two weeks. By October 1972, ten years after they issued their first record, The Beatles' worldwide sales total – that's everything they ever recorded – stood at 545 million units. In other words, Gary's version of *Numa Numa* outstripped the most successful pop band of all time!

Gary Brolsma: global success

Like the Beatles, Gary's success has turned global. Ana Peñalosa is a Mexican Brolsma fan. She first became aware of their global appeal when she arrived in a small village hours from any major city:

'I worked for six months in Bachajón, a town in the state of Chiapas, about 16 hours by bus from Mexico City. The day I arrived in Bachajón there was a market next to the ancient church that spilled over to straddle the one street. Some vendors sold fruit and vegetables, some sold shirts and jeans, others sold music and movie CDs and DVDs. People were sitting and standing in small groups, some were talking, others laughing. A sound system blared music to the crowd. The song was Numa, Numa. '

So where is Gary now? Sipping champagne in a huge villa on a palm-fringed beach? Flying to gigs in his private jet? Preparing to save the planet by dedicating a percentage of the earnings from his next release to combat global warming?

No. Gary never made a cent from *Numa Numa*. He filmed himself **lip-synching** the words of the song on a webcam in his bedroom and uploaded it onto YouTube. He never marketed it. He was never interviewed in the music press. And he certainly never paid O-Zone any royalty for ripping off their song. He just sat down and mimed his cover version, flicked the upload and millions of people saw it for free.

In case you missed out on the *Numa Numa* craze, you should be able to source it on the Internet.

Once you have watched Gary's effort, you can explore the new genre which he created. You'll find a whole galaxy of spin-off music videos dedicated to *Numa Numa*, including one featuring an Osama Bin Laden look-alike, and also Gary's follow-up single *New Numa*.

Key terms

Lip-synching Where a person in a video mimes so that their lip movement matches the words being heard on a soundtrack.

CD-ROM
Extra!

Numa Numa
Open the CD in the back of this book and click on the icon below to open a link to see Numa Numa.

HTML

★ CASE STUDY ★
ACTIVITY

Numa Numa raises a number of the big issues which face the music industry at the moment. Working with a partner or in a small group, discuss the following:

1. Would you say from what you have heard about him that Gary Brolsma is famous and successful? What difference is there between these two things?

2. Why should Gary have offered to pay O-Zone before uploading his version of their track? Or shouldn't he? If not, why not?

3. How might O-Zone have benefited from Gary using their tune?

4. Audiences in 1964 had to go into shops and pay money to hold a Beatles record in their hand. Now anyone can get music free from downloads. Do you think it matters that artists and their record companies don't get paid for their work?

The impact of the Internet

Numa Numa is just one more indication of the phenomenal change the Internet has brought to our lives. It enables an obscure Central European pop song to spread at an extraordinary rate, eventually even making it to a small town in Mexico, without any help from 'big business'.

For the music industry, the *Numa Numa* case study pinpoints the dramatic shift in power. Before the Internet, record companies decided who got to make records, how much we had to pay for them and where we could buy them. Once the Internet was in place, music fans could share their own collections with each other and bands could upload their new albums for free.

This is what the music industry calls its **distribution method**. Put simply, this means how they get things into the hands of people who are prepared, not only to listen, but to pay for the privilege. The Internet has suddenly provided a whole new – and free – distribution method. Like a rabbit in the headlights of the Internet, the music industry has reacted very slowly indeed to the implications of downloads and uploads. As a result, it is in danger of being blown off the road by the juggernaut of Internet technology.

The crisis in the music industry is just a part of the wider impact that the digital revolution has had on the mass media industries. If the music industry is running scared, then so are big film producers, television companies and newspaper magnates.

The following simple communications model can help you to describe how the shift from **producer** to **consumer** works. We need to think of three types of **network**:

Broadcast network This is where there are one or two big producers (like the BBC or ITV) who transmit things like television programmes which an unknown audience can receive individually. They can't respond and they don't know how many others are receiving the same communication.

Metcalfe network The telephone system is the best example of this type of network. There is a greater opportunity to interact with other members of the network as any one individual can call any other individual in the network who has a phone.

Reed network The Internet is an example of a Reed network. It means that not only can any individual communicate with any other, they can also form groups. The number of possible connections is infinite. *Numa Numa* spread around the world because the Internet Reed network meant individuals could send it, in one click, to everyone in their address book. YouTube and Facebook are classic ways in which groups can use a Reed network.

Pre-Internet revolutions

The Internet isn't the first example of a sudden shift in the power balance between those who produce the messages and those who receive them. A much earlier example would be the invention of the printing press in 1450 by Johannes Gutenberg. In those days, the Church was the equivalent of the big media companies. It was the only organisation that could provide information: it was the Broadcast Network of its time. Monks laboriously copied out the gospels by hand, so there were hardly any books in existence at all.

Once Gutenburg had invented the printing press, the genie was out of the bottle. Other people could publish their ideas about religion and a lot of other things. And because books became much more widely available, many more people could be taught to read. People could challenge what we would call the **hegemony** of the Church.

TIP
Consider how you would promote yourself if you were building a website.

Key terms

Hegemony The way people are influenced into accepting the dominance of a power group who impose their views on the rest of the population.

Johannes Gutenberg: inventor of the printing press

Working in a pair or small group, discuss the way that the digital revolution is affecting the following media.

1. **The film industry** – *in the past the only way people could see a film was to pay to go into a cinema. You should think about the many different ways that are now available for you to watch the latest blockbuster, including legally produced DVDs released at the same time as the film print, pirated DVD versions of films and web-streamed versions of films.*

2. **The newspaper industry** – *most newspapers now have an Internet edition. What does this add to a reader's experience?*

3. **The music industry** – *digital downloads are now a common way of buying music (or getting tracks for free). Recording equipment is now widely available. The advantages all seem to be to the consumer of music rather than the producer. Do you agree?*

In each case you should consider the ways in which they started as Broadcast networks and the extent to which they could now be described as Reed networks. What are the effects of this shift on each industry?

Music from the Internet: illegal downloading

The *Numa Numa* case study highlighted the issues of uploading, downloading and file sharing. But why were the record companies so afraid of this new development?

Copyright

The big issue is copyright. Copyright brings in about a third of a record company's profits, so companies are obviously keen to enforce laws that stop people illegally downloading or copying songs.

The battle against copyright infringement goes back as far as the 1980s, when companies became worried about people copying recorded tracks onto blank cassettes. But it has only really begun to hit the industry in the pocket in the last decade.

1968–1998

Record companies earned most of their money from albums in this period. Albums turn 'bands into brands', with the power of spin-offs allowing cash to be made from T-shirts and calendars. Money can also be generated from tie-ins, such as tours or TV shows.

1970s

Copyright infringement issues first arose when people began to record songs onto blank cassettes.

1999

Industry sales have fallen steadily since 1999 because of single file sharing. File sharing has also meant that, for the first time since the 1960s, single tracks have come back into fashion.

2000

The Recording Industry Association of America (RIAA) took the Internet site Napster to court in 2000, over their music file sharing system.

2001

Napster was found guilty, forced to shut down and to invent a new pay-for-download system. Their new site contains the Visa and Mastercard logos! The **media conglomerates**, who had controlled distribution of music before file sharing, kept up their battle to stop it by continuing to use the law. The companies also waged guerrilla warfare on the file sharers. They hired computer experts to dump corrupted files onto sites, so that users had to search around for hours to find the track they were looking for.

2003

Madonna even circulated fake tracks from her 2003 album *American Life*. Fans who tried to download songs were met with silence and an angry message from 'Madge' herself, asking what they thought they were doing!

Key terms

Media conglomerates
Large corporations who own more than one different media company and sometimes a large number of companies.

2004

The RIAA sued 914 Americans for millions of dollars for sharing songs. These people were using software packages KaZaA and BearShare to file-share songs. One of the accused was a 12-year-old girl. Her mother settled out of court by paying the RIAA $2000, and thousands of American families banned their children from using file-sharing sites. (No one knows if the ban worked!) Was the threat killed off? No. Figures from research companies in 2004 suggested that at any given time there were up to 5 million people illegally sharing songs worldwide.

July 2008

The industry claimed they were set to lose £1 billion over the following five years because of illegal downloads.

Record companies are waking up to the fact that digital music is the future and that they must adapt to modern technology or die. In 2007, EMI (one of the biggest record companies in the UK) was bought by a company called Terra Firma. The new owners got rid of people like the former vice-chairman, David Munns, who had likened file sharing to going into a music store and shoplifting CDs. The new owners say they are interested in getting music talent out to as many people as possible using multiple delivery methods and all the digital channels they think their customers might use. They recognise that the future is digital – not selling CDs and suing downloaders.

Marketing in the digital age

If they hadn't been so alarmed, the record companies might have realised more quickly that the Internet provided them with huge possibilities for marketing their products.

A recent trend has been the use of the Internet to launch new albums. Warner launched the new REM record, *Supernatural Superserious*, on Facebook. Radiohead took the unusual step of announcing that their *Rainbow* album was available to download from the Internet and asked fans to pay as much or as little for it as they thought it was worth. The publicity generated meant that it was soon selling in large quantities and it became a big hit. Prince sold 3 million copies of one of his albums through a deal with the *Mail on Sunday*, which gave it away with the paper. Lily Allen, Arctic Monkeys and countless others have launched themselves via email or social networking sites such as Myspace.

Michael Stipe: lead singer of REM

ACTIVITY 5

Working with two or three other people, imagine you are an advertising agency who have been employed by EMI's new owners, Terra Firma. They have asked you to prepare a short report on ways in which you think they should use the Internet to market the material in their catalogue. They are particularly interested in the 12–24-year-old audience.

Think about the way in which you use the Internet to find music, band information and gigs. Which bands have you recently discovered? How did you hear about them? If you heard about an exciting new band from a friend, where would you go to find out more about their music?

Write your report and try to include at least four suggestions for ways in which Terra Firma could market the material of the artists they have in their catalogue.

The rise of the pop music video

A lot of people claim that Queen invented the music video in 1975. But the first use of short clips of film to promote music goes back a lot further.

1940s Films called 'Soundies', made by musicians like Big Joe Turner and Nat 'King' Cole, were shown in bars in the USA.

1956 Films like *Rock Around the Clock* cashed in on the new teenage market for pop music.

1964 The Beatles film *A Hard Day's Night* was released. It became a template for many of the music videos which followed.

1975 Queen made the first music video as we know the genre now.

1981 MTV was launched as a channel, showing only music videos.

1982 Michael Jackson's *Thriller* was launched.

2005 YouTube was founded and quickly became a major site for both amateur and professional musicians to launch their own music videos.

Timeline years: 1940, 1950, 1960, 1970, 1980, 1990, 2000, 2010

Key events during the rise of the pop music video

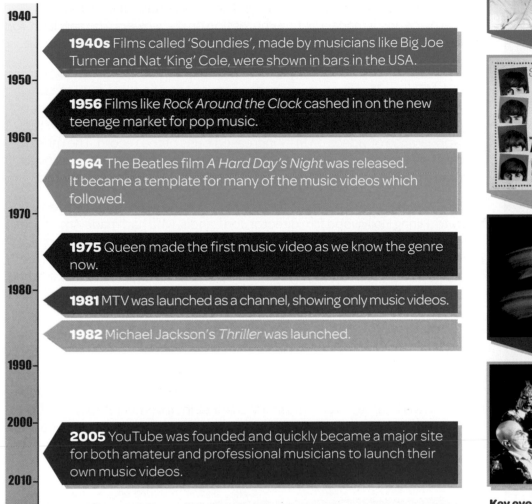

The beginning of rock and roll in the 1950s was the spur for a lot of films which featured the new style of music. These films were made cheaply and quickly to cash in on the latest fashion and so most of them were forgettable. *Rock Around the Clock* (1956) featured Bill Haley's music and swiftly captured the imagination of the new 'teenagers' in Europe and the USA.

By the mid 1960s, The Beatles and The Rolling Stones were major international stars touring all over the world. They began to make promotional films (promos) which could be screened on television while they were touring. Most of these promos were basically filmed performances of a song shot in a simple studio backdrop with the group miming to the record. But The Beatles could lay claim to producing the first music videos as we know them today. *A Hard Day's Night* was a fictional documentary film of the life of the band, directed by Richard Lester in 1964. The film is a mix of songs and comedy, including chases and sequences featuring **jump-cut** editing. It was a **template** for many of the music videos which followed.

Key terms

Jump-cut Where the join between two shots is felt to be abrupt because what follows is something we don't expect to see.

Template A pattern which helps to shape the products that follow.

The big turning point for the music promo came in 1975 when EMI released a 6-minute single by Queen called 'Bohemian Rhapsody'. Releasing a single of this length was quite a risk as many radio stations felt this was too long to fit their type of programming. To help promote the song, the record company commissioned director Bruce Gowers to make a video to accompany the single. This video used trailing images of the band's disembodied heads together with live performance footage. The music press hailed it as a masterpiece and it made a lasting impression on the viewers who saw it on *Top of the Pops*. The video is thought to be one reason why the record stayed at number one in the charts for nine weeks.

In 1981, MTV was launched. It was by no means seen as a surefire success in its early stages – especially since it had less than 200 videos to play out. However, the company commissioned research which seemed to show that the appearance of videos on MTV increased sales of the record. The music industry was convinced, so more videos were made, which in turn improved sales and the connection between music and video was firmly cemented.

In 1982, Michael Jackson's video for 'Thriller' took the genre another step forward. Hiring Hollywood film director Jon Landis, who had made *American Werewolf in London*, Jackson acted out a variety of roles as the video engaged in a parody of the 'horror' genre. It had a lengthy live action sequence before the song actually started, taking the whole production beyond the established conventions and limitations of the music promo of the time, making it almost a short film – with a huge production budget to match. Its uniqueness helped the album to reach sales of over 35 million copies – still one of the biggest selling records of all time.

The importance of the music promo video has continued right through to today. The main change has been the distribution method: you are as likely to view videos on the Internet as on a music TV channel. In November 2005, YouTube was launched and immediately became a main site for musicians of all ages and levels of competence to share their music videos. It has become so successful that major recording artists now use it to launch their own videos.

Michael Jackson's 'Thriller' video

Discuss the following points with a partner:
- *Are promotional videos for songs still important to help sell music?*
- *Are sites like YouTube becoming the place where you watch music video promos, or do you still watch MTV as well? What would be lost if there were no MTV channels?*

Now write a 200-word article to go in a music magazine of your choice, answering the following question:

- *Is the music video an endangered species?*

Analysing music video

Regardless of where you view them, the main purpose of music videos is to promote a song. For those who remember it, it is impossible to hear 'Bohemian Rhapsody' without also recalling the disembodied heads of the Queen band members floating rather awkwardly around the screen. The videos create a 'buzz' around the band and the song which helps to get it noticed and, with luck, purchased.

But some critics, like Andrew Goodwin, have argued that the importance of the music video – and MTV which ensured it was broadcast to a wide audience – goes beyond just selling music. It has altered the way we 'read' moving images. One of the main things about music video is the way in which it moves away from classic linear Hollywood narratives (see Chapter 1: Film, page 9). So, if you try to analyse them as if they used the same 'rules' as film or television, it won't work.

Editing

The biggest difference between most film or television genres and the music video is the way in which they are edited. Some of the technical manuals for people who are training to be film or television editors now talk about 'MTV-style editing'. They point to the ways in which a music video is edited and show how it broke away from the dominant Hollywood style – which is called **continuity editing**.

Continuity editing is based on a number of rules which ensure that when hundreds (or in the case of Hollywood blockbusters, thousands) of separate shots are edited together, they appear to flow naturally. The aim is that the viewer doesn't notice the joins but concentrates on the story being told by the images.

MTV-style editing shouts out at the viewer, drawing attention to the whole process of joining the shots together. In particular, the jump-cut is used a lot in music video. This is where the join between two shots is felt to be abrupt because one shot is followed by something we would not expect to see. It makes the viewer 'jump' and wonder where the narrative storyline has been taken to. The pace of cutting between shots is also much more rapid in MTV-style editing than it is in continuity edits.

TIP

Studying music videos is exciting because they subvert the normal codes and conventions. You might like to deconstruct some music videos and identify how the subversion takes place.

Key terms

Continuity editing
Editing which is designed to make one event follow on naturally from another. Nothing unusual happens to make the viewer notice the fact that an edit has been made.

Andrew Goodwin is Associate Professor of Communication Arts at the University of San Francisco. He is the author of a book on music video called *Dancing in the Distraction Factory* which breaks music videos down into three main categories. These may help you when you are trying to write about them:

- *Illustration* – in this type of video, everything we see in the finished version derives directly from the lyrics of the song. This could be just the artist or band performing the song. If there are other shots, these are easily linked to what is being sung. Goodwin gives the example from The Jam's track, 'That's Entertainment', where the video shows the band performing the song in the studio.

TIP

There are essentially two main types of music video – performance and narrative. However, clearly there are videos that combine the two (hybrids).

The Jam

- *Amplification* – this type of video has sequences which add extra meanings that aren't necessarily in the lyrics themselves. An example would be the video for Garbage's song 'I'm Only Happy When It Rains'. As well as a lot of shots of vocalist Shirley Manson lip-synching the lyrics, there are shots of the other band members drilling holes in their instruments and wearing bizarre costumes and masks.
- *Disjuncture* – this is where the images on the video have no apparent link to the song's lyrics. Often a film-maker has been commissioned to produce what is almost a short film, the soundtrack being the song. An example would be 'There Goes the Fear' by Doves.

Videos which show either amplification or disjuncture are much more interesting to write about than those that just illustrate. The aim of the director will be to take the mood or tone of the song and then develop it in some way. Goodwin suggests that bands who use these approaches want to be seen as more 'arty' and serious about their music.

ACTIVITY 7

This activity will help you to focus on the media language of music videos.

1. *Select an example of a music video which is either an amplification or a disjuncture.*

2. *Write a 300-word analysis of the way the visuals capture the mood or tone of the original song. You should concentrate on:*
   - *shots which are particularly effective for you – what do they make you think of?*
   - *the editing style and how it affects the way the 'story' is told*
   - *the narrative, which probably won't have a conventional 'beginning-middle-end' structure, but what 'story' has been told by the video?*

CASE STUDY

THE MUSIC PRESS

This case study discusses some of the cross-media aspects of pop music today. At the end you'll be asked in the activity to discuss the issues that arise.

All of us find out about our favourite bands from somewhere. Often friends point us in the direction of new things – 'word of mouth', or 'wom' as the music industry calls it. With the rise of the MP3 file, it is now more than just wom – you can send the actual track directly to your friend.

You might think that all this digital activity would have put print-based music magazines out of business. But you'd be wrong. Titles like *Kerrang!* and *Mojo* are selling just as well as ever – although of course they have websites related to their print magazines too.

Thirty years ago, the music press would probably have claimed they were largely responsible for making audiences aware of different bands . So are they still powerful opinion formers?

Here are three different viewpoints from music press 'insiders' on the importance of the music press.

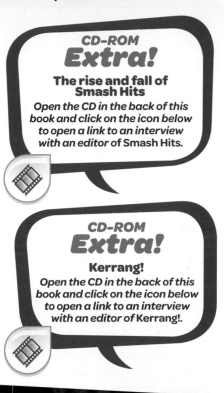

CD-ROM
Extra!
The rise and fall of Smash Hits
Open the CD in the back of this book and click on the icon below to open a link to an interview with an editor of Smash Hits.

CD-ROM
Extra!
Kerrang!
Open the CD in the back of this book and click on the icon below to open a link to an interview with an editor of Kerrang!.

David Hepworth, former editor of Smash Hits and now publishing director of Word and Mixmag:
'The music press don't make bands successful. They're not big enough to do it. People always like to think that there's a plot and that somewhere in a record company boardroom, they're going to force people to like something that people don't like. Well it doesn't work like that.

If you're successful you are lucky, possibly talented, but people like you.

But of course there are bands that the music press like. They tend to be the ones who are groovy, who take good pictures, are a bit sexy and give good copy. But Keane were none of those things, they didn't fulfil any of those criteria at all but Keane found their way out to a huge great fan base.'

Paul Brannigan, editor of Kerrang!:
'The music press is still hugely important. Particularly now in the age of the Internet, there is so much choice out there.

But you still need someone to filter that stuff down. No one has all the time in the world to go checking out every band website, so you look to the music press to tell you where the good stuff is. That's the role of a music magazine.'

Karis Ferguson, founding editor of www.thisisfakediy.co.uk:
'When we first set up thisisfakediy I interviewed a band called Parva from Leeds. We published the interview, but nothing really happened. A few months later I got an email from them. They said they'd changed their name and had a few new MP3s. I downloaded some and it was Kaiser Chiefs.

We had to tell people about them. We uploaded a story instantly: "check out these MP3s!" People got interested. Another indie website, drownedinsound, released their first single. We reviewed it. It was really good underground, everybody talking about it. They signed to Be Unique and now they're touring the world. But they always thank us because we helped them out when nobody else was listening.'

CD-ROM
Extra!
Influence
Open the CD in the back of this book and click on the icon below to open a link to some footage on the influence of the press.

★**CASE STUDY**★
ACTIVITY

From these interviews you can see that not everyone agrees about exactly how influential the music press is in making bands or artists successful.

1. In a small group, discuss how influential you think the music press is today.

2. As a group, write three or four paragraphs setting out your views, giving examples from the actual experience of group members.

3. Share your views with other groups and see if you can come to a whole-class decision about the influence of the music press today.

Representations in the music press

Representation is an important Key Concept in Media Studies. It is about the way the media *represent* people, events or ideas to us. This representation will always involve choices. Any story could have been presented from a different angle or with a different picture.

A part of studying representation involves looking at the use of **stereotypes**. Are media images used so often and so powerfully that they suggest to audiences watching them that whole groups of people or ideas should be viewed in a certain way? Like any other media, the music industry will constantly represent people, places and ideas to its audience in particular ways. For example, look at the cover of *Mixmag* below. Are there any stereotypical features of the way the two men are represented on the cover of this magazine?

Key terms

Representation
How people, places, events or ideas are represented or portrayed to audiences in media texts. Sometimes this is simplistically through stereotypes so the audience can see immediately what is meant, and sometimes the meanings are less obvious.

Key terms

Stereotypes
People grouped together according to simple shared characteristics, without allowing for any individual uniqueness.

THE WORLD'S BIGGEST DANCE MUSIC AND CLUBBING MAGAZINE

mixmag

FREE CD
SVEN VÄTH'S SEXY TECHNO MIX

BESTIVAL
INSIDE BRITAIN'S MOST RIDICULOUS RAVE-UP

outkast
Big movie, bigger tunes ...But are Dre and Big Boi standing together or falling apart?

GIRLS WITH 'TACHES, BLOKES IN DRESSES...
WELCOME TO THE AGE OF WRONG

BIG BOI AND DRE AT THE INTERCONTINENTAL HOTEL, ATLANTA
Photographed by Zach Cordner

Is your CD missing? Then please tell your newsagent "Meine freie CD ist verschwunden"

SANDER VAN DOORN
SAVES TRANCE
GNARLS BARKLEY
CONFESS ALL
DJ SHADOW
CHEATS DEATH

SPOTTERS' DELIGHT!
THE 40 MOST PRICELESS DANCE RECORDS EVER

Plus
DR WHO DAT?
GLOBAL GATHERING
THE AFTERMATH
TOKYO GUIDE
JUANA MOLINA
CONCORD DAWN

EVERY IBIZA CLOSING PARTY!
1,147
CLUB NIGHTS

UK £3.95 SEPTEMBER 2006
OVERSEAS £3.95

In the example below, taken from a 1980s *Smash Hits*, the singer Toyah was presented as someone who might be 'fancied' rather than being discussed as someone having an interesting voice or being an intelligent writer of lyrics. The males 'rate' her in terms of looks rather than musical talent.

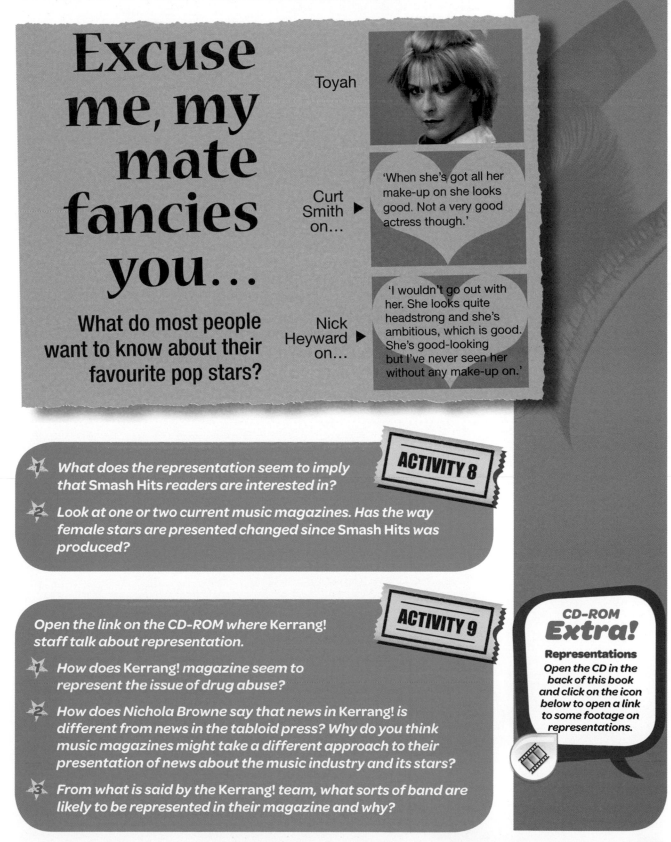

Excuse me, my mate fancies you…

What do most people want to know about their favourite pop stars?

Toyah

Curt Smith on… ▶ 'When she's got all her make-up on she looks good. Not a very good actress though.'

Nick Heyward on… ▶ 'I wouldn't go out with her. She looks quite headstrong and she's ambitious, which is good. She's good-looking but I've never seen her without any make-up on.'

ACTIVITY 8

1 What does the representation seem to imply that *Smash Hits* readers are interested in?

2 Look at one or two current music magazines. Has the way female stars are presented changed since *Smash Hits* was produced?

ACTIVITY 9

Open the link on the CD-ROM where *Kerrang!* staff talk about representation.

1 How does *Kerrang!* magazine seem to represent the issue of drug abuse?

2 How does Nichola Browne say that news in *Kerrang!* is different from news in the tabloid press? Why do you think music magazines might take a different approach to their presentation of news about the music industry and its stars?

3 From what is said by the *Kerrang!* team, what sorts of band are likely to be represented in their magazine and why?

CD-ROM Extra!

Representations
Open the CD in the back of this book and click on the icon below to open a link to some footage on representations.

What have you learned?

In this chapter you have learned about:

Texts
- How the music video has grown in importance
- How the music press has changed to meet new technological developments like the Internet

Media language

Genre
- How music genres are used to classify and sell pop music

Narrative
- The way in which music videos use non-linear narrative to sell songs

Representation
- How the music press represents artists and issues

Audiences
- How audiences consume pop music genres
- How new technologies have altered the way we listen to music

Institutions
- How the Internet has transformed the way the music industry operates
- How the music industry is responding to the threat posed by downloading

Cross-media
- Case study: the strange case of Gary Brolsma 'Superstar' and how the Internet made him famous
- How the music press has responded to new technology and the Internet

7 Advertising and marketing

Your learning

In this chapter you will learn about:

- the three main marketing strategies for selling products, services or ideas:
    - promotional campaigns
    - advertising
    - public relations (PR)
- how patterns of advertising and marketing are changing due to the Internet
- how advertisements communicate their meaning
- how advertisers target particular audience groups
- how stereotyping is used by advertisers.

Marketing

Marketing products and services is big business. The purpose is to encourage us to buy things or to think about things in particular ways. The marketing industry spends billions of pounds every year and employs hundreds of thousands of people.

Researchers believe that we have over 1500 messages aimed at us every day. These messages appear on Internet pages, television screens, the radio, through your letter box, on the pages of magazines and newspapers, on billboards in the streets, on buses and trains, in the supermarket ... to name but a few. The fact that there is so much advertising around means that the marketing industry has to come up with ever more sophisticated ways of grabbing our attention.

Three ways to market your product

If a business wants to communicate with its customers, or **consumers**, it can choose to do this in three main ways:

1. **Sales promotion** – this has the most direct impact on a **brand**'s success because the technique directly affects sales. You will see promotions everywhere every day. Supermarket shelves will have 'buy one get one free' promotions; music magazines will have a free cover-mounted CD; cereal packets will contain a free gift.

2. **Advertising** – this reaches consumers through the creation of a message in a variety of possible forms: a 30-second television advertisement, a page in a magazine, a poster, etc. This is the glamorous part of the marketing industry because it is where all the big money is spent. But for a company or brand, it is also the most expensive way of getting the message out to consumers. Not only will a 30-second television advertisement cost hundreds of thousands of pounds to make, you then have to buy the **media space** to show it.

3. **Public relations (PR)** – by holding an event like a press conference or a launch party, public relations agencies can get a lot of media coverage for a product through articles written in magazines or newspapers, or stories on television or radio news. This isn't 'free' because you will have to pay the PR agent to get the coverage. But it can be a great deal cheaper than advertising.

We will now look in more detail at how these three approaches work.

A newspaper sales promotion

Sienna Miller, Matthew Williamson and Brooke Shields attending the Fragrance Launch party for Williamson's new fragrance.

This case study discusses some of the cross-media aspects of sales promotion.

Print with CD/DVD promotions

A common strategy in newspaper and magazine publishing is to link with CD or DVD producers in joint sales promotion. Some of your music collection may well have come from the front of music magazines which frequently cover mount special edition CDs. David Hepworth, an editor of *MixMag*, says that this practice has now become so common that although magazines with a cover mount don't sell more copies, if you take the CD off, sales drop!

Daily Mirror *example*

In 2004, the Brand Communications Agency, Exposure, brought together two of its clients, the *Daily Mirror* and *Buena Vista Home Entertainment* in the biggest ever DVD promotion in a national newspaper. The campaign ran for a month and readers were offered 'the ultimate movie collection'. It was also supported by a national television and radio campaign.

In one month of continuous coverage, the total space which the *Daily Mirror* devoted to the promotion came to:
- 6 full pages, 3 three-quarter pages, 10 half pages, 16 third pages

- 6 front cover flashes

715,000 DVDs were claimed, meaning there was significant revenue generated for Buena Vista. The *Daily Mirror*'s circulation per day increased by 30,000. All in all, Exposure, the marketing agency who devised the campaign, estimated that the equivalent of £1,300,000 editorial value was delivered to their two clients by the joint promotion.

★CASE STUDY★ ACTIVITY

You have been employed to promote a new men's deodorant. The product is in direct competition to the Lynx brand.

Choose at least two media spaces from the list below and explain how you would select them as a place to promote the brand.
- *Newspapers*
- *Men's special interest sports magazines*
- *The music press*
- *The radio*
- *The Internet*

Advertising

Advertising is about persuading you to behave in a particular way: buy this chocolate bar; go to watch a new movie; give money to a charity, etc.

In the early days of advertising, there was often a simple presentation of the product. The advertisement for the Kodak Bulls-eye camera is a good example of what the industry call the simple **product (or pack) shot**.

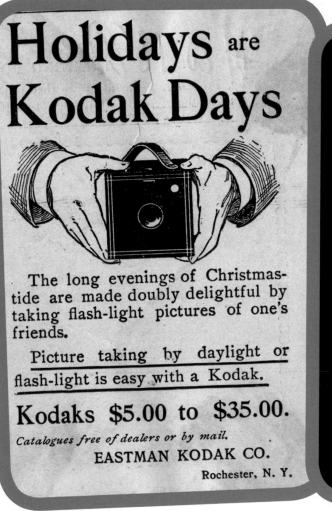

But just showing people things did not persuade them to change their behaviour. Soon advertisers were getting more sophisticated. The Westminster cigarette advertisement shows the beginning of a move towards modern techniques: the cigarette is being smoked by a glamorous woman. The implication is that the cigarette will link those who smoke it to a lifestyle.

Maslow and our needs

Some research in the 1970s by Abraham Maslow is one way of exploring how advertising works. Maslow suggested that human behaviour is focused on satisfying basic human needs. So the most successful advertisements may be the ones which appeal to a combination of the following needs.

Maslow's needs

- **Need to survive**: used by advertisements for food, drink, housing, etc.
- **Need to feel safe**: advertisements for insurance, loans and banks promise security and freedom from threats.
- **Need for affiliation or friendship**: advertisements that focus on lifestyle choices like diet and fashion use people's desire to be popular. They may also threaten them with the failure to be liked or to fit in.
- **Need to nurture or care for something**: advertising which shows cute animals and small children brings this out in the viewer.
- **Need to achieve**: advertisements that are linked with winning, often promoted by sports personalities, tap into the need to succeed at difficult tasks.
- **Need for attention**: advertisements for beauty products often play on the need to be noticed and admired.
- **Need for prominence**: advertisements for expensive furniture and jewellery may use people's need to be respected and to have high social status.
- **Need to dominate**: advertisements for products like fast cars offer the possibility of being in control through the product.
- **Need to find meaning in life**: advertisements for travel or music may appeal to people's need for fulfilment.

ACTIVITY 2

⭐1 *For each of the needs listed above, think of an advertisement that exploits that need, and explain how it does so. You can take your examples from any form of advertising: television, radio, print magazine, Internet or poster. Your teacher could help you find suitable examples.*

⭐2 *What other needs, not mentioned by Maslow, are used to promote products?*

Audience

When Steven Spielberg was asked who he thought was the core audience for his films, he said, 'At this point, it's pretty much everybody...'. Advertising agencies are not so lucky. They have to think hard about how the advertisement will be received by the target audience they are aiming to persuade.

Social class categories

The advertising industry has done a great deal of research into typical lifestyles of various groups in society. In the past, a lot of advertising tried to target people simply on the basis of social class. Six categories were used to parcel people up into particular audience types:

Social class categories

A   High-ranking managers in industry or the professions like law or medicine

B   Middle managers in companies or public services like health or education

C1   Junior managers or supervisors in industry or public services

C2   Skilled manual workers – like carpenters or electricians

D   Unskilled manual workers

E   The unemployed or others on very low incomes from casual work

Advertisers soon found that these broad social class categories were not sophisticated enough to distinguish between the various **niche markets** they needed to target to sell their products.

ITV Sales categories

The next set of categories shown below are those which have been used by ITV Sales to identify potential target audiences, which they call demographics. (The codes in the left-hand column are used by the sales team when they put their data onto computer analysis sheets.)

ITV Sales categories

Code	Explanation
HW	Housewives (these can be men as well as women. A *housewife* is defined as the person who does the major shopping for the household)
HC	Housewives with children
HA	Housewives in the ABC1 socio-economic groups, i.e. those who are more wealthy (as explained in the social class categories list above)
AD	Adults
A3	Adults aged between 16–34
AA	Adults in the ABC1 socio-economic groups
ME	Men
M3	Men aged between 16–34
MA	Men in the ABC1 socio-economic groups
WO	Women
W3	Women aged between 16–34
WA	Women in the ABC1 socio-economic groups
CH	Children

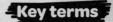

Key terms

Niche markets
Small groups who are targeted because they share the same interests, income, etc.

As you can see, the ITV Sales categories are more sharply defined than the much broader social class categories. This helps the ITV Sales team to target potential consumers in a more sophisticated way.

ACTIVITY 3

1 Choose two programmes on a commercial television channel, such as ITV, that you think would be watched by different types of audience.

2 Watch the advertising breaks in the middle of two programmes.

3 For each advertisement in the break, identify the category (or categories) the sales team would have identified as the target audience, using the codes from the ITV Sales table on page 151.

Lifestyle categories

As consumers have become more sophisticated, advertisers have continued to develop the ways of trying to 'pigeon hole' audiences. The table below shows categories which are sometimes used to define the 16–34 age audience's outlook on life. The industry thinks they are useful where advertisements sell a lifestyle associated with a product.

Lifestyle categories	
Cowboys	People who want to make money quickly and easily.
Cynics	People who always have something to complain about.
Drifters	People who aren't at all sure what they want.
Drop-outs	People who do not want to get committed in any way.
Egoists	People who are mainly concerned to get the most pleasure for themselves out of life.
Groupies	People who want to be accepted by those around them.
Innovators	People who want to make their mark on the world.
Puritans	People who want to feel they have done their duty.
Rebels	People who want the world to fit in with their idea of how it should be.
Traditionalists	People who want everything to remain the same.
Trendies	People who are desperate to have the admiration of their peer group.
Utopians	People who want to make the world a better place.

Advertisers are sharp enough to know that few of us fit only one box. People can change and can also fit more than one category. For example, someone who is an environmental campaigner could be described as a 'Rebel' and also a 'Utopian'. The categories are just helpful to advertisers when they are making distinctions between the various target audiences who might buy the product.

ACTIVITY 4

1. *Find two magazines which you think would be read by different audiences.*

2. *Make a list of the categories from the lifestyle list on page 152 which you think could apply to five advertisements from each magazine.*

3. *What patterns are there in your two lists which might suggest that the magazines themselves are aimed at particular lifestyle categories?*

Grade Studio

Examiner's tip

It is important to consider how audiences are targeted and how representations are used to effectively target those audiences.

Key terms

Denotation This is the understanding of media artefacts – what they look and sound like.

Connotation The hidden meaning behind an image, word or sound that gives it depth.

Deconstruction Looking carefully at how an advertisement communicates its meaning by analysing the connotations of the various parts of the image.

How magazine and newspaper advertisements create desires

As you saw earlier, Maslow suggests that advertising works by satisfying the consumer's needs. However, these needs are not always apparent to the consumer until the advertisement has created a desire.

One way this is done is by offering you an image of yourself, made to look more glamorous, powerful or popular as a result of using the product. This image is designed to make you see yourself transformed by the product.

Denotation and connotation

In trying to unpick how the advertisement is working, it is useful to look at two levels.

1   We can talk about what is *actually there* in the photograph. This is about *fact*. It is straight description which everyone can agree on. We call this level the **denotation** in the photograph.

2   We can move on to consider what the things we can see suggest to us. This might be different from one person to the next. We are moving into the realm of *opinion*. We call this level the **connotation** of the photograph.

Media language and advertising

In the **deconstruction** of any printed advertisement you should think about each of the points in the chart on page 155. They will help you to explore the way media language works in advertising images.

Capture the unexpected

The new Samsung Pixon mobile not only packs an 8 megapixel camera but also has Advanced Shake Reduction, Smile Shot and a dual powered LED – making it the perfect way to capture important moments, day or night. With built-in editing you can put hand-written captions on your favourite shots and share them on the web. So wherever life takes you, take a Pixon and capture the unexpected. samsungmobile.co.uk/pixon

Samsung **Pixon** 8 megapixel camera phone

SAMSUNG

NICE JEANS.

gasoline

Visual feature	Key questions
Facial expression	How would you describe the expression on the model's face? Are the eyes looking directly at the viewer or at something else? What feelings do you think the photographer hoped to conjure up in the viewer through these facial expressions?
Character type	The model will have been chosen to represent a particular type of person. How would you sum up the character type? How does this choice support the message of the advertisement?
Gesture or posture	The model will have been given detailed instructions on exactly how to stand or sit, where to place their hands, the precise way to hold their head, etc. What do the postures and gestures make the viewer think about the model?
Props	All the other objects, or props as they are called, will have been chosen because they support the overall message the photographer hopes to convey. What are the most important props? What connotations do you think each prop was intended to produce in the viewer?
Clothing	Every article of clothing will have been carefully selected. Why do you think the model is dressed in this way?
Setting	Whether the shoot took place on a specially constructed set in a studio or at an outside location, the setting will be used to add further to the overall effect of the advertisement's message. What connotations does the setting in your advertisement summon up in the viewer?

TIP

Try to imagine a totally different model in the advert. Maybe someone from a different age or ethnic group. Would the advert still work? Why/why not?

The following advertisement shows you, using the annotations, how the questions in the table above work in practice. Look at the advertisement, read the annotations, then have a go at the activity that follows.

SJP's long flowing hair is shown off to good effect as it's being blown by a wind machine. This also adds life and movement to the image. Long flowing hair is associated with a certain type of conventional/stereotypical beauty.

The model isn't just anyone – it is Sarah Jessica Parker (SJP). Using a famous actress is an 'endorsement' – and the product actually carries her name on the label too. In a society like our own, which is obsessed with celebrity, associating your product with a celeb is a common advertising technique.

SJP's expression – gazing directly at the viewer, mouth slightly open, the hint of a coy smile – has a sexy edge to it.

The product is displayed prominently – and oversized! It needs to be easily recognisable in the shop.

SJP's posture is very carefully set up. Looking over her shoulder, half turned away from the viewer, she looks like she's being pursued.

The plain white dress given to SJP for the shoot suggests elegance, luxury and purity. The tight bodice emphasises her thin waist (stereotypical 'beautiful' figure). The flowing skirt adds glamour.

The long black gloves reinforce the elegance and sophistication. You only wear these for very special occasions.

The ribbon adds an old-fashioned, feminine touch. It also balances the composition, complementing the product SJP is holding, both in colour and position.

SJP tells us, she 'had to have it'. Carefully chosen words to chime in with the product's name – 'covet', meaning an eager desire for something.

The product label is reproduced here as a gold plaque, linking connotations of richness with the product.

The cool blue colour used for the background provides a good contrast for the warmth of SJP's skin tones and hair colour. It complements the colour of the dress and the ribbon – and especially the product's cap top.

The font used here is 'pre-computer', old fashioned, copperplate writing.

Having looked at the Sarah Jessica-Parker/ Covet advertisement (on page 156), it's your turn to deconstruct an advertisement.

1. Look at the fragrance advertisement below and remind yourself of the key questions in the table on page 155.

2. Using a similar approach to the one used for the Covet advertisement, make notes about the most important denotations in the fragrance advertisement. For each one, explain the connotations for you as a reader of the advertisement.

fantasy
BRITNEY SPEARS™
A new fragrance

fantasybritneyspears.com

3. When you have explored the various connotations, explain who you think the advertisement might have been aimed at and what helped you to make this interpretation.

4. If you were an advertising agency, which magazines would you try to place the advertisement in? Justify your decisions.

Representation in advertising

The images used by advertisers to sell things constantly present us with a particular view of the world. Advertisements do not just sell us products: they constantly sell us a particular version of what is supposed to be desirable.

Stereotypes

Because they have a short time to grab our attention and drive home their message, advertisers often resort to **stereotyping**.

Once stereotypes are established, then advertisers can play around with them.

Like all other areas of advertising and marketing, the use of stereotypes is always evolving to meet changes in society. Recent research identified the following five distinct female stereotypes being used in advertising.

Examples of female stereotypes in advertising

The Beauty Bunny She believes that just because there is science in a beauty product, it will work. She is into every new invention in the beauty industry and reserves her greatest enthusiasm for the latest shampoo or face cream. L'Oreal's 'Because I'm worth it' could be her catchphrase.

The Alpha Female She's a powerful professional whose main focus in life is her career. She's definitely in control, but her entire life is work. She is not shown as a mother, a wife or a lover. She can be seen as rather scary.

The Fashionista She appears in every glossy magazine, such as *Vogue* and *Elle*, and is portrayed as someone who is only interested in the way she looks. She wants to know about the new clothes, the new shoes, the new bags and the new lip colour (but unlike Beauty Bunny is not old enough to worry about skin care). She has neither personality nor, by implication, intelligence.

The Perfect Mum We see her every time a household product or an everyday commodity is advertised. Her biggest concern is her children. She has pushed away every other need in her life. She's a mum, she's not an individual. She's not sexy or ambitious.

The Granny She is the Perfect Mum fast-forwarded 20 years or so. She has few interests outside her grandchildren.

ACTIVITY 6

Look at the five photographs that follow and remind yourself of the five female advertising stereotypes above.

⭐ *Match the five photographs to each of the five female stereotypes.*

⭐ *Write a brief explanation for each photograph to describe how the connotations in the image suggested the stereotype.*

Look at the advertisement for Gasoline below.

1 Which parts of this advertisement do you think present stereotypical gender representations?

2 How have these stereotypes then been played with to create a comic effect?

3 Who do you think the audience for this advertisement was and how do you know?

4 If you were the advertising agency placing it in a magazine, which one would you choose and why?

Advertising: cross-media

This next activity focuses on cross-media aspects of advertising. This is where you are considering how advertising works across different media platforms.

ACTIVITY 8

You are going to carry out a content analysis.

1. *Choose one of the following areas to study:*
   - *gender representations – either male or female*
   - *ethnic representations*
   - *representations of the family.*

2. *Find ten different advertisements which feature representations of the group you are studying. These should be a range of print and moving-image advertisements. For each one, make notes on the types of representation shown.*

3. *Write a 300-word report on the extent to which there was a common pattern in the representations. Or did they offer a diverse view of gender, race or the family?*

4. *Compare your findings with a partner who studied a different area. Discuss whether stereotyped representations can be harmful in any way.*

Intertextuality

Intertextuality is a term used to describe what happens when a producer deliberately makes a reference to another text to add a layer of meaning to the original. For example, to advertise a new cop series, the BBC used a *Radio Times* front cover to link it with a glamorous Hollywood crime movie and its stars. You can compare how similar the images are on page 162.

Internet advertising

As in so many other areas of the media, the Internet has made a dramatic impact on advertising. With the exception of the BBC, which is entirely publicly funded, all other television channels rely on advertising revenue to survive. Commercial television channels can only make the programmes they do if advertisers continue to buy airtime.

Advertisers are spending increasing amounts of money on Internet advertising. This puts commercial television channels under threat. For instance, in 2008 Google received more income from advertising than Channel 4 did. Estimates also suggested that, in 2008, Google took 80 per cent of all new advertising revenue.

One reason why the Internet is threatening traditional television advertising is because there are now a lot of other ways people can entertain themselves. Research shows that, in particular, those under 25 years of age are spending much less time watching television and much more time playing games or surfing the Internet. If the television is on, it is often only on in the background.

Viral advertising

But it isn't just that not so much television is being watched. The Internet can get advertising messages to people much more cheaply. In particular, the use of **viral advertising** has grown very quickly. We are all familiar with the 'viral email' – online joke videos which individuals receive in their inbox and then spread them by sending them on to all the people in their address book.

Viral advertisements latched onto this practice. For instance, third in a recent 'chart' of the most frequently downloaded virals was actually an advertisement for Miller Lite beer. So instead of paying many thousands of pounds to place a slot in the middle of a television programme, an employee in an advertising agency just emailed the advertisement to everyone in his or her email address book. And the message spreads like wildfire.

Buying Internet space

But you can't do it all through virals. Companies will also spend some of their marketing budgets buying space on the Internet. As you will have found out yourself when using a search engine, you will get many thousands of results for any Google search. Research shows that traffic drops by 90 per cent if you are on page 2 of search results – so people pay a lot of money to get themselves in the top three search results.

Key terms

Viral advertising
Spreading advertisements through the use of attachments to emails. It can give very wide coverage at no cost.

Direct hits

Advertisers always want to know that the money they are spending to market their product is hitting the target audience as directly as possible. Sophisticated new software is making it possible for Internet advertising to target niche audiences more directly than a broadcast format like television.

For example, Phorm is a system which tracks the types of site visited by individuals on their own computers. They then redirect advertisements linked to the types of site visited. So if you visit clothing, photography or travel sites, you can expect a lot of related advertisements to pop up in your inbox.

Broadcast to Reed networks

The big change for advertisers is the shift in audience consumption of media from a **Broadcast network** to a **Reed network**.

- **Broadcast network (television)** – this is where one or two big producers (like BBC or ITV) transmit television programmes which an unknown audience can receive individually. They can't respond and they don't know how many others are receiving the same communication.

- **Reed network (the Internet)** – this is where any individual can communicate with any other. In addition, they can also form groups. So YouTube and Facebook, for example, are ready-made interest groups who can be targeted by advertisers.

For the Broadcast networks, like radio and television, the rapid rise of the Internet – a Reed network – is a threat. If they cannot make enough money from advertising, then they will go out of business. For marketing agencies, Reed networks offer a cheap alternative to paying for expensive media space.

Key terms

Social networking site Examples are Facebook and Myspace.

ACTIVITY 10

In this activity you will be exploring Internet networks.

1. *Draw up a list of all the contacts you have on social networking sites, email address books and any other form of computer networking you use.*

2. *Select six other people in your class to work with and add together the total number of contacts held by your group.*

3. *Now go back through your own list.*
   - *Identify all those contacts who you think will not appear in the list of anyone else in your group.*
   - *For every one of those contacts, assume they have the same total number of contacts in their network as you do.*
   - *Add up the total number of potential contacts who are two clicks away from you on the Internet – your secondary contact list. In other words, if you have 50 contacts in your network and you identify 20 of them as being your contact alone, that adds an additional 1000 people to your secondary contact list.*

4. *Now add together all the secondary contacts for the six members of the group.*

You now know the number of people you could potentially reach – at no cost and very quickly. So if you do happen to have anything to sell ... get clicking!

Public relations (PR)

Big advertising and marketing agencies will usually have a department which handles PR for their clients. The purpose of PR is to get the client's brand prominent media coverage by means of events or product placement. In advertising-speak, it is about 'creating brand endorsement and brand visibility' without buying expensive advertising space.

Events

The Events team in an agency will organise anything from a press conference for a football team who have just bought a star player to a major music festival linked to a brand – like the annual Virgin Move! festival in Manchester.

Getting the brief to organise a film premiere can be doubly useful to modern advertising and marketing agencies. It gives them the chance to bring together two clients. As well as working for the film producers who want to launch their latest movie with a blaze of publicity, a beer or soft drink client can link their product to the event by providing the refreshments. With good media coverage, both the film and the drink will get good brand exposure.

Product placement

In the past, film production companies often approached a range of businesses to offer them the chance to have their jeans, drinks, cars, etc. appear in a movie. This was good for the film company as it cut props costs and was good for the clothing or drinks company as it got their product on screen. This was the beginning of **product placement**.

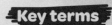

Key terms

Product placement
Giving brands or products to media producers for them to use as props so that the product is seen in a favourable way.

Thanks to effective product placement, James Bond has long been associated with the luxury car maker Aston Martin

Advertising and marketing agencies will have a Product Placement department that will actively seek out placement opportunities for their clients. The people in the department are dedicated to getting the product seen on the right people at the right time and in the right place.

Advertorials

Like product placement, the use of advertorials in print publications are a form of covert marketing. The term comes from a combination of advertisement and editorial copy. It is where a brand which places an advertisement in a magazine also gets an article written about it – usually in a complimentary way.

So, for example, if Apple advertise the iPhone in Q magazine, the deal might also include an interview with a prominent record producer who explains how the iPhone makes his working life so much easier and also provides him with instant access to all sorts of entertainment.

It may not have been just coincidence that the interview with Wayne Rooney in games magazine *Toxic* features a photo of him wearing an EA Sports top, holding a copy of the magazine with the FIFA 09 game on the cover. The references to EA Sports and FIFA 09 will almost certainly have been 'placed' and then the journalist lined up to write the piece.

Working with a partner, imagine you are in the product placement division of an agency. You have been approached by the producers of a new energy drink to link their product with a young, trendy and fit lifestyle.

⭐ List ten people or places you would target to try and get positive exposure for the product. For example, a television chat show or backstage at a music awards ceremony.

⭐ Do you think it is acceptable for agencies to market brands in a covert way? Or should all forms of advertising be made obvious to readers/viewers? (For example, does it matter if Leona Lewis appears on a chat show wearing a t-shirt with a prominent brand logo on it?)

TIP

Consider how many branded items of clothing you and your friends wear.

Interactive advertising and marketing

As consumers become ever more sophisticated in their use of media, the advertising industry develops and refines its methods. The Internet has turned the people formerly known as 'the audience' into participants in and creators of media products and experiences.

The buzzword in the media these days is 'interactivity'. For broadcast television, for example, this translates into programmes which encourage viewers to text or email their opinions. For the advertising and marketing industry, **experiential communication** has become the way ahead.

Key terms

Experiential communication
Where consumers actually interact with the product rather than just look at pictures of it. (See the Nike case study on pages 168 and 169.)

CASE STUDY

NIKE SOLE PROVIDER

This case study discusses some of the cross-media aspects of advertising and marketing. In particular, it considers experiential communication as an advertising and marketing tool.

Experiential communication techniques

One company which has become a big player in experiential communication techniques is Nike. They have used various methods to bring their brand to life for young consumers. Their 'Run London' event provided runs of different lengths to encourage people with different fitness levels to enjoy running. Of course, by taking part in 'Run London', participants were also experiencing the Nike brand.

Nike has a long history of involvement in basketball.

Nike's Sole Provider event

To accompany their book on the history of Nike's involvement in basketball, which was called *Sole Provider*, Nike commissioned their agency to design an experiential event. The brief was to take the information in the book and turn it into a two-week exhibition at the Atlantis gallery in London's Brick Lane. The target audience for the exhibition was split into two distinct demographs:

- trainer fanatics
- basketball players/fans.

In the new experiential approach, the agency hoped that by involving people in the story of Nike's basketball history and interacting with the product, they would experience the brand rather than just being told what to think about it.

The exhibition displayed a lot of old trainers and advertising material, starting with the classic 1972 Blazer shoe right up to the most recent designs. One key problem the agency had to solve was to find an original way of displaying a heap of old trainers which would grab the visitors' attention. The answer they came up with was to put them in glass-fronted fridges!

CD-ROM Extra!

Nike Sole provider

Open the CD in the back of this book and click on the icon below to see footage of the Nike Sole Provider event.

Some Nike classics were given special treatment. The Air Posit from the 1990s had taken some of its design ideas from insects. The agency decided it would be fun to display the 'bugged out shoe', as it was called in New York street culture, in an insect house filled with locusts.

The brief required that the exhibition should involve people in the sport and, by association, become engaged with the brand. So a basketball 'battleground' with two hoops was set up where people could actually play the game as part of the exhibition.

Of course, the experiential communication was supported by all the older techniques:

- The Events department organised an opening night to which important people in the trainer industry and basketball scene were invited. The intention was that they would tell their friends how good the show was, thus becoming 'brand ambassadors', as the industry calls them.

- The PR department secured the main designer of the exhibition an interview on BBC London's *What's On* slot.

- Print advertisements were taken out in the style press to hit the trainer fanatics and also in the basketball magazines to hit that part of the brief.

- A microsite was created to give Internet exposure to the exhibition and emails were sent to individuals within the target demograph to generate an online buzz about the exhibition.

> **TIP**
> Before you begin your planning for this activity, you should research the brief by looking at the Fairtrade website: www.fairtrade.org.uk.

★CASE STUDY★ ACTIVITY

Working with a partner, you are now going to design a digital and experiential campaign for Fairtrade products. The key brand value of Fairtrade is social responsibility to developing countries. Their aim is to promote ethical shopping.

In terms of the lifestyle groupings we looked at earlier in the chapter, the campaign will target:
- *puritans: people who want to feel they have done their duty*
- *utopians: people who want to make the world a better place*
- *innovators: people who want to make their mark on the world.*

Campaign objectives. Fairtrade have asked you to concentrate on:
- *raising awareness and visibility of their logo so that shoppers will recognise products which have been fairly traded*
- *promoting bananas grown on the Caribbean island of St Lucia.*

1. *Storyboard a 30-second viral advertisement which takes a humorous approach to delivering one or both of the campaign objectives.*
2. *Create an experiential stand to be used at music events to enable fans to interact with Fairtrade ideas and meet the objectives of the campaign.*

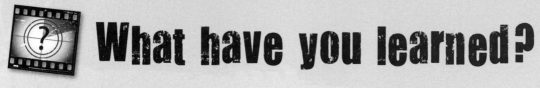

What have you learned?

In this chapter you have learned about:

Texts

- How advertisements in a variety of different forms – printed and digital – communicate meaning

Media language

Genre
- How advertisements use intertextuality

Narrative
- The way stories around lifestyle contribute to advertising

Representation

- How women are often represented stereotypically in advertising

Audiences

- How audiences read advertising imagery
- How advertisers categorise audiences

Institutions

- The three main ways of marketing products or services: promotional campaigns, advertising and public relations events (PR)
- The changes that have taken place in marketing with the arrival of the Internet

Cross-media

- How marketing campaigns often use a range of media forms to promote their brands

8 Radio

Your learning

In this chapter you will learn about:

- how music, speech and sound effects are used by a radio station to create a recognisable house style
- how radio stations research and target their audiences
- how BBC and commercial radio stations are funded, and how this affects their schedules and content.

ACTIVITY 1

Talk about the answers to these questions in a group of three or four. Make notes of the decisions your group has come to.

1 *How important is each of these in your life: TV, newspapers, magazines, radio? Put them into a rank order as a result of your discussion.*

2 *When do you listen to the radio?*
- *In bed at night*
- *While doing homework on a computer*
- *Radio alarm when waking up*
- *While playing video/computer games*
- *At school*
- *Preparing to go to school*
- *Having breakfast*

3 *Where do you listen to the radio?*
- *Bathroom*
- *Kitchen*
- *Car*
- *Other places, such as ...?*
- *Living room*
- *Bedroom*
- *School*

Why do people listen to the radio?

The results of surveys show that people listen to the radio under many different circumstances. Why do people choose to put the radio on? The Uses and Gratifications Theory (see page 76) can be used to show that people consume media texts to satisfy a variety of needs:

- The need to be INFORMED and EDUCATED about the world

- The need to IDENTIFY with characters and situations to learn more about ourselves

- The need to be ENTERTAINED

- The need to use the media as a talking point for SOCIAL INTERACTION

- The need to ESCAPE from our 'daily grind' into other worlds and situations.

ACTIVITY 2

Work in your group again.

1. *Talk about how you use the radio to satisfy the needs listed above.*

2. *Which needs does each radio station you mentioned in your discussion fulfil? Give each one a score between 1 and 10 for each need.*

A short history of radio in the UK

1922 British Broadcasting Corporation licensed to transmit radio programmes.

1928 Radio audience of over 1 million.

1933 First commercial radio – Radio Luxembourg broadcasts popular music programmes on an unauthorised frequency.

1939 Nine million radios in the UK: most people listen to the Prime Minister, Neville Chamberlain, announcing war with Germany.

1947 First portable 'transistor' radios.

1958 Radio audiences dwindle as audiences for TV dramatically increase: BBC Radio's evening audience is down to 3.5 million.

1964 'Pirate' radio stations playing modern pop music start to broadcast to the UK from ships offshore, outside the broadcasting law. They attract large audiences of young people.

1967 Pirate radios closed down by law. The BBC opens pop station Radio 1.

1967 BBC Leicester, first BBC local radio station, opens.

1973 First legal commercial radio stations open: Capital Radio and LBC in London.

1980–2000 An increasing number of radio stations receive licences.

TODAY There are several BBC national network stations, over 40 BBC local radio stations, ten national commercial radio stations, more than 200 local commercial stations and large numbers of community radio stations.

People listened to radios like this in the 1930s

A modern hi-tech radio station

What makes radio stations different?

Funding: Beeb versus the rest

So what is the difference between a BBC radio station and a commercial radio station? The answer is very simple – who pays the bills.

The BBC gets the money to run its radio and television channels from a yearly payment called the *licence fee* (£139.50 in 2008) from everyone who owns a TV. The BBC is called a public service broadcaster because it is funded by the public. Although the BBC makes some money through selling its programmes, books and other merchandise, the public pay the largest part of the bill. So, no licence fee – no BBC.

Commercial radio has to cover its running costs by attracting advertisers who pay to market their products or services on air. No adverts – no commercial radio – or commercial TV!

Talk versus music

Radio stations can also be divided into those that predominantly play music and those whose output is much more speech-based. BBC Radios 1, 2 and 3 and most commercial radio stations base their programmes around music. There is some speech – presenters talk between records, newsreaders give updates and weather forecasts – but the majority of airtime is taken up by music. In contrast, BBC stations like Radio 5 Live and Radio 4 are almost all speech-based, so that if you tune in to them at any time of day or night you are much more likely to hear people talking than music.

Sounding you out

Compared with television, radio is beautifully simple to produce. Although a great deal of thought may have gone into the sounds that come out of your radio and a team of people involved to get them 'on air', there are only three ingredients that programme producers can mix together:

- the human voice
- music
- sound effects.

But those three simple ingredients can be made to sound very different indeed. The look of a big-name trainer is about creating **brand awareness**. The sound of a radio station is also to do with **branding**. How many radio stations can you recognise the instant you hear them? It is vitally important for a station to create their own sound or **house style** because this will be the sound that they know their audience like.

CD-ROM
Extra!

News sources
Open the CD in the back of this book and click on the icon below to see an interview with a radio station news editor discussing news sources.

Key terms

Brand awareness Making the product immediately recognisable to the public.

Branding The distinctive features by which we recognise products.

House style A radio station or publisher's preferred manner of presentation or layout which matches their audience.

The most important feature of a house style is the way the presenters talk to their audience. You know from your own experience that the way you speak to people depends on who they are and what the situation is. If you are caught breaking a school rule, the language and style you use when you tell a friend what happened are very different from those you use to a teacher. Radio presenters adapt the way they speak to suit the audience they think will be listening. Their job is to build up a relationship with each listener, to keep them listening to the station and – vitally important – to get them to tune in on a regular basis.

People who run radio stations often talk about presenters who have a 'good voice for radio'. This is a bit vague, but in his book *Broadcast Journalism: Techniques of Radio and TV News*, writer and broadcaster Andrew Boyd describes a 'good microphone voice' as one that is 'reasonably rich, crisp and resonant and free from obvious impediments'. In contrast, a voice that is 'piping, reedy, nasal, sibilant, indistinct or very young-sounding' would not work so well.

There are other factors that presenters must think about when presenting their programmes. The **tone** they adopt will be crucial. You could use any of the words in the following table to describe the tone of a presenter's voice:

serious	light-hearted	assertive	calm
scathing	soothing	humorous	pompous
aggressive	solemn	mocking	contemptuous
intimate	patronising	chatty	over-excited

ACTIVITY 3

1. *Look up any of the words in Boyd's descriptions that you do not understand. With a partner, discuss the voices of the various teachers you work with. Using Boyd's definition, decide which one you think has the best radio voice and whose voice might work least well on radio.*

2. *Choose which terms in the table above apply to the two voices you have chosen.*

How would you describe the tone of voice used by the radio presenters you listen to most frequently? The tone they use will affect the way they come across to their listeners. Some presenters will want to sound friendly, as if they are talking to their friends. Others will be more formal, providing a 'voice of authority' on whatever it is they are discussing.

Another consideration will be the **pace** at which they talk – is it very slow and measured or is it rapid and quick-fire?

Finally, there will be the **accent** of the presenter's voice. At one time the BBC expected all its presenters to speak in *received pronunciation*, which was seen as a Southern, slightly posh way of speaking. Now it uses presenters who talk in a range of regional accents, reflecting the rich and diverse backgrounds of its listeners across the country.

Key terms

Tone The quality and character of a voice or piece of writing.

Accent The sound of the voice which tells us which part of the country the presenter is from.

Pace How quickly or slowly the presenter speaks.

You are going to research the style and content of these radio stations:

- BBC Radio 1 • BBC Radio 4
- Your local commercial radio station
- A radio station broadcasting in a foreign language.

⭐ Listen to the sound of each station. Use a grid like the one below to make notes of your findings so that you can discuss them with others afterwards:

- Presenters' voices: *use the ideas outlined on the previous page to help you make detailed notes about the style of the presenter's voice.*

- Programme content: *describe the type of music played or the subject being broadcast by speech-based programmes.*

Radio station	Presenter's voice	Programme content
BBC Radio 1		

⭐ Discuss your notes with a partner. Try to decide which type of listener you think each station is targeting with its house style.

TIP
Presenting information as a chart or table will save you time in your exam.

Making the link

Chatting for 30 to 40 seconds and then playing a record may not seem like hard or difficult work, but making it sound that easy is the sign of a good presenter. Remember, most radio goes out live. Presenters try to make it sound as if what they are saying has just popped into their heads, as it would in a conversation with another person.

Some stations follow American research which suggests that presenters prepare their **links** by following these steps:

1. Choose an idea or topic which will interest or amuse your listener.
2. Mind map anything you can think of saying about that topic onto paper.
3. Choose one strong idea from your mind map and write an interesting first sentence which will hook your listeners into the link.
4. Identify two further ideas you will use to develop the topic.
5. Write a really strong sentence to end the piece (sometimes called a *power out*).
6. Make it sound unscripted when you actually do the piece live on air.

Key terms

Link A short piece of speech from the presenter between music or other items

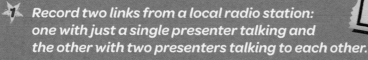
ACTIVITY 5

1. Record two links from a local radio station: one with just a single presenter talking and the other with two presenters talking to each other.

2. Play these back and make a written transcript of exactly what is said.

3. Discuss with a partner whether you think either link seems to have used the American approach.

4. Now try it yourself! Write a script for a 40-second link on any topic of your choice using the six steps. Swap scripts with a partner and edit each other's work to make it as powerful as you can. Practise presenting the link before recording it yourself and discussing the results with a group.

Radio audiences

Radio is no different from any other media form when it comes to thinking about audiences. It needs to know clearly who it is talking to.

Every station wants to get as many people to listen to their output as they possibly can. The BBC Radio stations – local and national – have to prove that enough people listen to them to justify their public funding. Commercial radio stations only exist if they can persuade businesses to buy time to advertise. If no one is listening, advertisers will take their money to a station with big audiences.

So radio stations need listeners, but they cannot all have the same types of listener. What your mum or dad likes is probably a bit different from what you like – whether clothes, music, food or radio programmes. For a radio station, defining its **target audience** is very important.

Take, for example, Gemini FM, which broadcasts to an area of Devon that includes Exeter, Torquay and a lot of small rural towns and villages. This is what they think about their niche audience:

Key terms

Target audience
The types of people who a radio station deliberately tries to attract as listeners

To talk about a 'typical listener' it is easier to refer to a single example. In terms of Gemini FM this is a twenty-five-year-old female who lives in the mainstream of British popular culture, loves eating and drinking and holidays abroad. She is permanently based in the local area and always enjoys a good night out on the town. She loves to spend money – mainly on clothes and fashion, music, magazines, DVDs and other products she's probably seen advertised. This woman is more likely to be a family-driven individual, maybe with young children, and deals with the pressure this brings. She has a passion for television and particularly loves the soaps, celebrity gossip, *This Morning* and *Big Brother*.

It is important to note that Gemini FM is not a female brand. Nothing at the station should alienate our male audience. So why do we specifically target females? Extensive research has proved that men will willingly listen to a station directed at women but it will not work the other way round. In most cases, women tend to be 'rulers' of the household and it is often their choice of station to which the household radio will be tuned! So, by targeting women, we automatically attract the husbands and kids.

So Gemini will use this as a broad guide for what they will call their **audience profile**. But of course it is not as simple as that. They know that at different times of the day there will potentially be different sorts of audience profile. And so they divide their output up into a *clock* to match the things their audience are doing.

The Breakfast slot is an important start to the day, and a station's programming will reflect the fact that all the family are getting ready for work or school. So *survival information* – traffic reports, weather, regular time checks – is a prominent part of the programme content. By mid-morning, listeners will be at work or back home. In Gemini's case, thinking of a typical listener who is 25 and female will guide the type of presenter chosen and the content for that show. The early evening show tends to attract a younger listener, so the musical content and presenter's style will reflect this.

Gemini FM presenters

This broad outline of the types of programme played round the clock is called a *programme schedule*. Deciding on the programme schedule for the station is the responsibility of the *programme controller*.

Is there anybody out there?

Even though radio stations have a clear idea about the types of people they think are listening, they need constantly to check on their **audience share**. They do this by using the information provided by a company called RAJAR (Radio Joint Audience Research).

The sample of data from RAJAR in the following table shows the audience data for just one radio station. The same information is provided for every radio station in the country. Use the notes on page 179 to help you understand the table.

Station	Survey period	Population	Reach (000s)	Reach %	Average hours per head	Average hours per listener	Total hours (000s)	Listening share in TSA %
BBC Radio 1	Q	50,735,000	10,871	21	1.90	9.10	98,786	9.80

RAJAR survey data

Survey period: based on figures from a quarter (Q), half (H) or full (F) year.

Population: the number of people aged 15+ who live within the transmission area of a given station. BBC Radio 1 is a national radio station, so broadcasts to 50,735,000 people.

Reach (000s): the number of people aged 15+ who listen to a radio station for at least 15 minutes over the course of a week. For BBC Radio 1 this was 10,871.

Reach percentage: the weekly reach as a percentage of the population within the transmission area. For BBC Radio 1 this was 21%.

Average hours per head: the average number of hours that a person within the transmission area spends listening to a particular station. For BBC Radio 1 this was 1.90 hours.

Average hours per listener: the average length of time that listeners to a particular station spend with the station. For BBC Radio 1 this was 9.10 hours.

Total hours: the total number of hours that a station is listened to over the course of a week. For BBC Radio 1 this was 98,786 hours.

Listening share in TSA%: the percentage of all radio listening that a station accounts for within its transmission area. For BBC Radio 1 this was 9.80%.

> **ACTIVITY 6**
>
> *Visit the RAJAR website. Look up your own local radio stations, both independent and BBC. Which do you think is the most successful station?*

CD-ROM
Extra!
RAJAR website
Open the CD in the back of this book and click on the icon below to open a link to the RAJAR website.

How do RAJAR find these figures?

Like all statistics of this sort, RAJAR's data is based on the response from a sample of listeners. RAJAR Limited was established in 1992 to operate a single audience measurement system for the radio industry. Results are published quarterly by monitoring a sample selection from every radio station's TSA (Total Survey Area).

- Listening diaries are distributed by RAJAR into selected households in each area of the country. They have to be completed within seven days.

- Diaries are placed with one selected adult over the age of 15 and up to two others in each household.

- The diary's pages are broken down into fifteen-minute intervals each day. The family fill in which radio station they listened to and for how long.

- Every radio station in the family's broadcast area is included in the diary.

- The diaries are collected by RAJAR at the end of the seven-day period. The data is collated and distributed to participating radio stations, and to the public via the RAJAR website.

What have you learned?

In this chapter you have learned about:

Media language

Genre

- How music, speech and sound effects are the common features of any radio station.
- How the ways in which each of those three components is used will give a distinctive house style.

Representation

- The events and ideas reported in radio news will be affected by the sources who provide the information on which the news reports are based (CD-ROM Extra! page 174).

Audiences

- How different radio stations target different audiences.
- How knowing exactly who is listening to a station is essential information for the programme controllers of radio stations.
- How very detailed information is provided to radio stations about their audience share.

Institutions

- Independent commercial radio stations only exist if they can attract enough advertisers – because advertisers pay the bills.
- The BBC is funded from the Licence fee and is able to run stations which might otherwise not exist.

Cross-media

- How radio incorporates a range of media forms such as pop music, news, advertising and so on. See also page 23 on podcasts.

9 External Assessment: investigating the media

What is the External Assessment?

The External Assessment is the part of the course where you will be expected to show what you have learned from your study of the media. It results in a test that lasts for $1^1/_2$ hours and counts for 40 per cent of your GCSE in Media Studies.

The topic and the pre-released brief

You will be given a topic (such as *Comedy films* or *Reality Television*) in advance of taking the External Assessment, so you will have plenty of preparation time. The topic changes every year.

Nearer to the External Assessment time, you will get a pre-released stimulus or brief which will give you a good idea of what you will be expected to do on the examination paper.

The pre-released brief may be a communication setting up a scenario you have to respond to in role. Or it may be an example of an existing item that you will be expected to edit or re-launch. Once you receive the pre-released brief, you will be able to research and plan for the test. Your teacher will be able to advise you, but not formally teach you.

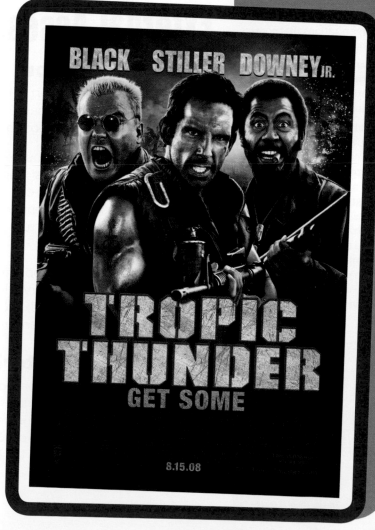

TIP

Timing – you have $1^1/_2$ hours for the External Assessment. Divide your time equally between the two tasks.

Key terms

Media language This is not necessarily written or even spoken language, but the way we 'read' images and sounds and the way things in the media are constructed.

Institutions All media is constructed. 'Institution' is the term given to the organisations that make the media we consume. It could also cover the organisations that control and regulate the media.

Audience People who are reading, looking at, listening to or using a media text.

Representation How people, places, events or ideas are represented or portrayed to audiences in media texts. Sometimes this is simplistically through stereotypes so the audience can see immediately what is meant, and sometimes the meanings are less obvious.

What am I being assessed on?

This part of the course will assess your ability to recall, select and communicate your knowledge of the media topic. So understanding, preparation and research are vital.

You will also be expected to discuss the four Key Concepts of:

- **media language**
- the **institutions** responsible for making the media
- target **audience**
- **representation**.

You will be asked to construct a relevant pre-planning design, including the evaluation of the product.

You will have to answer two unseen questions on the day of the External Assessment, relating to the pre-released information you have already studied. The External Assessment will expect you to cover all four Key Concepts and demonstrate knowledge and understanding of them.

How to succeed in the External Assessment

Topic preparation

The key to success in this part of the course is how much preparation you are prepared to do. The preparation you undertake should involve as much analysis of existing texts as possible.

For example, if the topic of your External Assessment is *Girls' magazines*, you should read as many girls' magazines as possible, including any non-contemporary examples you can get hold of. This will give you a broad basis of the codes and conventions and development of that part of the magazine industry that will in turn give you plenty to discuss and debate in the examination.

If the External Assessment topic appears to favour females over males, or the other way around – don't worry. It is often better to be given a topic that you are not particularly interested in yourself, as this can give you the advantage of being more objective in your analysis.

Pre-released material preparation

When you receive the pre-released material, it is important that you understand exactly what the material says and what clues there are in it relating to the tasks you will be expected to complete. There should be an obvious route to the next step of your planning. Look carefully at what you are expected to focus on and how the key media concepts may be covered.

Your preparation for this External Assessment needs to focus on the four Key Concepts and how you will discuss them and how you will apply the relevant **codes and conventions** to any relevant production task you may be expected to design.

Girls' magazines: an example External Assessment

Imagine the topic is *Girls' magazines*: just as if you were going to create a new magazine for your practical production, you will need to focus on four main things:

- front cover
- contents page
- features and articles
- advertising.

Front cover

Looking at the front cover, you need to establish things such as the style and audience expectations. Don't forget the images – and not just on the front page. What do these represent? What values are demonstrated through these images? For example, the front cover images on girls' magazines rarely depict anyone over a size 8 or without a flawless complexion! This suggests that these are the attributes that the target audience should be aspiring to.

TIP

The External Assessment is unlikely to be on *Girls' magazines*. However, the suggestions here for how to approach it can be applied to most External Assessment topics.

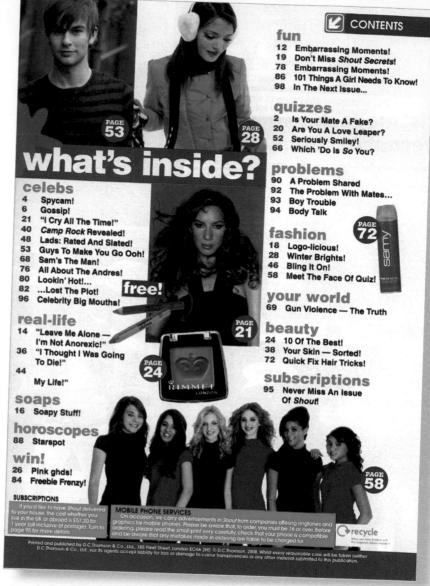

Contents page

A study of the contents page will show the kinds of thing that appear in girls' magazines. By looking at a number of different girls' magazines, it will be possible to see what regular features appear in the majority of the magazines and which features are special and are particular to one or a few. If there are competitions or quizzes, they will also show something about the values the magazine holds. The prizes will reflect the target audience that the magazine appeals to.

Features and articles

The features and articles that appear will demonstrate the style and form of address that the magazine uses. You will also be able to make comments about any issues of bias and representation that appear in the features. You will need to study the tone and language and layout of the articles, which will also give you clues about the intended audience.

Advertising

Advertising gives you clues about the intended audience and the values of the magazine producers. Advertising is also important because it is the main way in which magazines are financed.

Key Concepts

The External Assessment will always expect you to demonstrate understanding of the Key Concepts. Again, taking the example topic of *Girls' magazines*, the table below outlines what you should consider in relation to the Key Concepts:

Key concept	What to consider	What to do
Media language	You will need to show you understand how, for example, girls' magazines are constructed. This will involve careful analysis of as many examples as possible to ensure that you really do understand the media language.	You will already know the media platform that will be the focus of the External Assessment – in this case *Girls' magazines* – so you know what media products to start reading.
Institution	You need to investigate the producers – who is making and financing the magazine.	As the institution is magazines, you know that you need to research publishers and the different roles within the industry and any rules, regulations and controls that might exist in that industry.
Audience	Who is the target audience and how do you know this?	You should have a clue in the pre-released material about the intended target audience, so you will know what kinds of lifestyle you need to be investigating.
Representation	What do the colour schemes, fonts, tone, style, etc. tell you about the values of the magazine producers and their target audience? Are any stereotypes used?	You should have a clear understanding about the issues of representation relevant to the topic from your lessons leading up to the pre-released stimulus.

Sample External Assessment

This sample External Assessment uses the topic of *Girls' magazines*. Remember that, although this is unlikely to be an actual topic, reading the stimulus material and working on the sample paper is excellent practice. You should also read the sample student answer and comments from the Chief Examiner that follow. Can you do better than this student?

Read the following 'brief' (the letter) then complete the tasks that follow.

DREAMCATCHER PUBLISHING
Publishing House
New Street
Newcastle
N79 5SD

27 April 2011

Dear Colleague,

Thanks for responding so quickly! As you know we are hoping to launch our new magazine for young women this autumn. You are joining a prestigious team aiming to produce a magazine that promises to deliver and delivers what it promises!

We want to offer relevant features and interesting articles that will draw in our target audience of 16–20-year-old women, with perhaps some regular features for their boyfriends! We are conscious of the opposition, but feel that this is a niche left for us to fill.

You are going to help us come up with the goods.

At the first planning meeting, come prepared to voice your opinions and present your ideas for this exciting new venture.

Ciao!

Mags Paule
Creative Director

DREAMCATCHER PUBLISHING
Publishing House
New Street
Newcastle
N79 5SD

Thanks for confirming that you are going to make the planning meeting tomorrow. So we can have something to work from, can you complete the following tasks? You need to make sure you include all the research you have already done ready for the meeting. We will make the final decisions after we discuss all the options tomorrow.

Task 1(a)
Who do you consider is our main opposition and what do they offer? You need to be clear about the key features of women's magazines for this age group and give us plenty of examples.

[15 marks]

Task 1(b)
How can we improve upon this? You can use any sketches or diagrams you think might be useful.

[15 marks]

Task 2(a)
Give us your ideas for an enticing title, suggestions for the contents and who we might approach to be on our first front cover. Justify your ideas.

[15 marks]

Task 2(b)
Give us your design for how the first front cover might look. You will also need to annotate your design with the justification for your suggestions.

[15 marks]

Sample student answers

Sample External Assessment – Dreamcatcher publishing

Task 1(a)

Who do you consider is our main opposition and what do they offer? You need to be clear about the key features of women's magazines for this age group and give us plenty of examples.   [15 marks]

Extract from a student's answer

Thank you for offering me this unique opportunity to join you and the team at Dreamcatcher publishing. I am looking forward to the challenge of bringing something new and exciting to young women.

We need to be very aware of our rivals and I have done some research into them:

The main rivals are: *Bella*, *OK*, *Hello*, *Grazia*, *Heat*.

These all deal in celebrity gossip and appeal to our target audience.

Bella: Cost 85p. This magazine is full of fashion advice and style issues.

OK: Cost £1.00. This is full of celebrity news, photographs of the stars, fashion and entertainment.

Hello: Cost £2.00. This also concentrates on celebrity gossip and deals in photo opportunities like celebrity weddings.

Grazia: Cost £1.90. This magazine deals in celebrity news, fashion designs, shopping opportunities, gossip and things like new diets, etc.

Heat: Cost £1.00. This magazine lifts the lid on celebrities. It reveals their secrets and prints unflattering pictures. It has features on films, TV shows, CD releases as well.

It seems that from this research we need to consider taking the following:

- regular features on fashion
- regular features on celebrity gossip including lots of photographs of the stars
- regular features on the latest films, music and television programmes and stars ...

Examiner's comment

This student has produced a good start to the paper. She has responded in role to the task and used the appropriate terminology and written clearly and confidently. She has established many of the appropriate codes and conventions of women's magazines and offered a wide range of examples. She has offered implicit theory in discussing audience appeal.

This is typical of a grade A response.

Task 1(b)

How can we improve upon this? You can use any sketches or diagrams you think might be useful. [15 marks]

To improve on our rivals we need to:

- be cheaper
- offer better prizes for competitions
- include lots of gossip
- include interesting articles
- have problem pages
- include features for the boyfriends
- have pictures of the latest stars of film and pop.

Examiner's comment

This response only shows limited understanding. All she has really done is repeat the brief in a bullet point list. She has implicitly suggested the things that will appeal to a target audience but with no explanation. She has sensibly used bullet points, which avoids the pitfalls of spelling and punctuation, but has failed to offer any explanation of appeal. To improve there needs to be more originality in the ideas and extended explanation. Links to the target audience would also help.

This is typical of a grade E response.

Task 2(a)

Give us your ideas for an enticing title, suggestions for the contents and who we might approach to be on our first front cover. Justify your ideas.   [15 marks]

Title: **Your Voice**

I think this would appeal because it suggests that the reader has a say in what appears in the magazine.

Front cover: There needs to be a celebrity on the front cover. Someone that will appeal to the target audience, someone like Alicia Keys. This is someone that the target audience would like to be like. There would be lots of colour and liveliness on the front cover. There would be some promotional devices on the front cover to attract the target audience, things like splashes to show the price, cover line pictures to attract the readers inside, etc.

Contents: There needs to be a balance of regular features and special articles so that the readers keep interested. There needs to be regular features on gossip and celebrity because most girls in the target audience range like to read about celebrity gossip. I think that there should also be a soap update called 'Soap Suds' which would be a recap of the week's main soaps and any gossip about the stars. There would also be lots of competitions and quizzes with prizes that could be sponsored so that it won't cost us money. We could also have a website which could contain blogs from readers.

Examiner's comment

This student has produced a sound response that fulfils the task. He shows a good understanding of the reader expectations and offers some original ideas for features. The link to the website and reader blogs is a strong point. He also matches the contents to the audience with some obvious appeal. The extract is communicated clearly using some appropriate terminology.

This is typical of a grade C response.

Task 2(b)

Give us your design for how the first front cover might look. You will also need to annotate your design with the justification for your suggestions. [15 marks]

Examiner's comment

This is typical of a grade A response.

Remember this will be done under examination conditions and therefore a 'perfect' finish is not expected. The student has observed all the relevant conventions of magazine covers. The **title** is appropriate and uses lower case letters making it very accessible to the target audience. There are all the appropriate **tag lines** and **coverlines** and the student has not gone mad with the palette, using just two complimentary colours. There is an appropriate **image** in a stance that addresses the reader by looking straight ahead. The lure is in an attractive and noticeable 'call-out' offering the reader something they can aspire to. All the minor points are considered - price, date, even spacing and there is no unnecessary blank spaces. Overall, it is an attractive and appealing front cover.

Controlled Assessment: understanding the media

What is in the Controlled Assessment?

The three types of assignment

The Controlled Assessment is made up of three types of assignment that you will have to complete. These are:

1. Introduction to the media
2. Cross-media study
3. Practical Production and Evaluation

The assignments are designed to build upon each other and develop your media understanding, analysis and skills. They are all selected from banks of assignments.

Each of these assignments includes three tasks. In this chapter we are going to look at the three different assignment types, the tasks that each assignment could include and offer suggestions for areas of study and how you might complete the assignments.

APE: Analysis, Production and Evaluation

You are also going to be introduced to a way of responding to media assignments – APE. This is the method by which you will be expected to tackle all the assignments that you do. APE stands for *Analysis, Production and Evaluation*.

In other words:

- You *analyse* media **texts** in order to understand how they were constructed.
- Then you will be expected to construct or *produce* your own media text, either conforming to or subverting the **codes and conventions** you have analysed.
- Once you have constructed your own media text you will need to *evaluate* it in the light of all your previous analysis.

Assignment 1: Introduction to the media
Platforms and Key Concepts

For this introductory assignment, you are expected to focus on two of the Key Concepts: **media language** and **audience** (see page 186 for more detail on the Key Concepts). So, there will be plenty of opportunity for you to explore your chosen topics and really see how they work.

You will be expected to focus on one **genre** and **platform** in order to analyse existing texts and produce your own media text. Although you need to focus on media language and audiences as the primary concepts in this assignment, you are allowed to mention other Key Concepts if you need to.

Word count

You should only be writing about 500 words for this assignment, so it is important that you plan your response carefully in order to include everything you want to say within the word limit.

Assignment 2: Cross-media study
Platforms and Key Concepts

For this assignment you are going to look at a topic across two different media platforms. You will find another comprehensive 'bank' of assignments offered by the exam board and you will have to choose one of them. All four Key Concepts may be covered, but a particular focus on **representation** and **institutions** is required.

> ### Key terms
>
> **Media language** This is not necessarily written or even spoken language but the way we 'read' images and sounds and the way things in the media are constructed.
>
> **Audience** People who are reading, looking at, listening to or using a media text.
>
> **Genre** A type of media text (programme, film, popular music, etc.) with certain predictable characteristics.
>
> **Platform** This is how the form is delivered – so newspapers and magazines are print platforms and television is a moving image platform.

> ### Key terms
>
> **Representation** How people, places, events or ideas are represented or portrayed to audiences in media texts. Sometimes this is simplistically through stereotypes so the audience can see immediately what is meant, and sometimes the meanings are less obvious.

> ### Key terms
>
> **Institutions** All media is constructed. 'Institution' is the term given to the organisations that make the media we consume. It could also cover the organisations that control and regulate the media.

What is 'cross-media'?

If you think about the world of the media you very rarely see something in just one medium. The news, for example, can be read in newspapers, watched on the television or Internet and listened to on the radio. You can even download a podcast and listen to it on your iPod or mobile phone. Films come out in the cinema and within months you can buy the DVD or even the game.

That is what this assignment expects you to do – take a topic and investigate it across two media platforms. Whatever you choose for your cross-media platform assignment, it will be after some weeks of studying a topic.

Word count

You should only be writing about 800 words for this assignment.

Assignment 3: Practical Production and Evaluation

Key Concepts

Your third Controlled Assessment is the Practical Production. This piece of work is designed to show what you have learned by studying for the first two assignments. You are expected to consider all four Key Concepts: media language, institution, audience and representation, and carry your planning tasks through to completion.

You are going to be tested on Assessment Objectives 3 and 4 (see page 1) so the production planning, the production itself and the evaluation are important!

You are going to be tested on your ability to conform to the appropriate codes and conventions as well as show your creativity and imagination.

Groups or individual?

You can work as part of a small group for this assignment (after all, in the real media world, media texts are rarely created and produced by one person). However, before you begin, you must think very carefully about the make-up of the group and how well you will work together. Your GCSE depends on the success of this production and you have to be able to rely on the rest of your group and they have to be able to rely on you.

All the way through this production you need to keep a careful record of the plans you make and the decisions you take, as the process of completing this assignment is very important.

Research

Once you have decided on your Practical Production topic, you have to begin by completing research into that topic. You will need to show that you have understood the appropriate codes and conventions, the institutions, the audiences and the representation involved in creating the media text. This means the **deconstruction** of at least two texts similar to the one you want to create.

Planning

The research stage is followed by the pre-production, or planning, stage. This is where you make all the plans or mock-ups of the final production piece or storyboards for any moving image work you intend to do. You should keep all relevant planning to include in your folder, but stick to a maximum of 12 planning pages.

Evaluation

When the production is finished, you need to evaluate what you have done in light of the earlier analysis.

Word count

You should only be writing about 1000 words for the evaluation.

> **TIP**
>
> Don't tackle assignments where you need to be really clever with a video camera if you are not confident with a camera or computer editing software. Always work to your strengths.

> **Key terms**
>
> **Deconstruction**
> Taking a media product apart to see how it works and how it is constructed. It is more than just analysis.

> **TIP**
>
> The production itself must keep as closely as possible to the established codes and conventions unless you deliberately decide to subvert them. It is no good establishing that magazines are printed on glossy paper in columns with photographs and colour if you then produce a handwritten piece of writing in continuous prose with a sketch to represent the image.

Sample Controlled Assessment assignments

Read the following assignment tasks then study the sample student answers and examiner comments on pages 196–201.

Note: the sample answers are written by different students and not all of the Tasks are illustrated here.

Sample assignment 1: Introduction to the media - radio

Explore the language of a talk-based community radio extract and how it meets its audience's expectations.

Task 1

Deconstruct a community radio programme of no more than 1 hour. Focus on the careful analysis of a 10-minute extract. You should consider:

- scheduling
- presenters (style and tone)
- output (interviews, chat, topics, advertising, quizzes, etc.)
- audience expectations
- relevant codes and conventions (bedding, jingles, voice-overs, etc.).

Task 2

Create a 1-hour schedule for a community-based radio station meeting the audience's needs.

Task 3

Explain, briefly, the potential success of your schedule in terms of conforming to or subverting the relevant codes and conventions and meeting the audience expectations.

Sample assignment 2: Cross-media study - advertising:

Investigate how healthy eating for children is marketed.

Task 1

Analyse examples of existing advertising of healthy-eating products on the television and in magazines. You need to consider:

- channel or publication including timing if relevant
- dominance of producer
- key slogans or logos
- main image or text – selection of focus
- style and tone.

Remember that you need to draw some conclusions from your findings.

Task 2

Design a storyboard for a television advertisement for a new healthy-eating product and a print-based advertisement for the same product. Explain where and when the television advertisement would appear and where the print advertisement would feature.

Sample student answers

Sample assignment 1: Introduction to the media - radio

Extract from a student's answer:

Task 1

Radio: radio is the medium of sound.

- You can have local radio or national radio or community radio.
- You can listen to radio on the move.
- You have to listen to radio because there are no images.
- People on the radio have to speak clearly.
- Radio has been around since the 1920s.

I am going to investigate community radio. Community radio is radio for a special band of people like shoppers or football fans or people in hospital.

Eastbourne District Hospital has its own radio station for the patients – Radio DGH.

Examiner's comment

This extract is a basic introduction to an assignment. The student has tried to provide some structure by writing an introduction to say what he is doing his assignment on. In this case it is radio and, in particular, community radio.

He is using bullet points, which is a useful way of providing information and evidence of knowledge and understanding. If he had explained the differences between local, national and community radio stations, and given examples of each, this would have shown deeper understanding.

He has stated that you can listen to radio on the move – what exactly does this mean? He also talks about there being no images and having to listen and people on the radio having to speak clearly. These points should have been linked to explain the conventions of radio.

This student answer continues with a fairly solid analysis of the schedule from Radio DGH and the bullet-point introduction shows some evidence of pre-production work and research. What is lacking is the close link with the target audience.

This is typical of a grade C response.

Task 2 and Task 3

I have produced a 1-hour schedule for my community radio station which is designed for Asian teenagers. It is called Asian FM and the programme I have scheduled is the 'Mood Hour'. It will be broadcast between 9.00 p.m. and 10.00 p.m. on Saturday nights. Although a lot of teenagers will be out on Saturday night at the disco, or out with their friends, a lot of Asian teenagers would be expected to be in at this time and this show is for them.

To see this student's schedule, open the CD in the back of this book and click on the icon below.

Task 3

My schedule is right for my target audience. It does say what they want. They want to hear music and stuff so I have given them what they want.

I have included chart music and competitions for them to win a holiday.

Sample assignment 2: Cross-media study – advertising

Task 1
(The storyboard)

Timing: Seconds		Camera: Angle/Distance	Sound: Dialogue/music Lighting: Direction
0.00	Edit cut	Eye level – camera static L. S.	Crowd cheering Announcer: 'the winnner' Natural light Figures runing towards camera
0.02	Edit cut	Camera static M. S.	The winner drinking from can of Webster's The loser miserable in background
0.04	Edit cut	Camera high angle L. S.	Sound of crowds at swimming pool Announcer: 'the winner'
0.06	Edit cut	Camera static M. S.	The winner drinking from can of Webster's The loser looking miserable in background
0.08	zoom in on cans	Camera static M. S.	Disco sounds Disco lighting Chart music The winner with gorgous girl and 2 cans of Websters The loser looking miserable

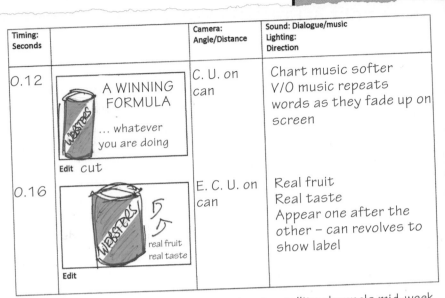

Timing: Seconds		Camera: Angle/Distance	Sound: Dialogue/music Lighting: Direction
0.12	A WINNING FORMULA ... whatever you are doing [Websters can] Edit cut	C. U. on can	Chart music softer V/O music repeats words as they fade up on screen
0.16	[Websters can] real fruit real taste Edit	E. C. U. on can	Real fruit Real taste Appear one after the other – can revolves to show label

To be shown on prime-time terrestrial and satellite channels mid-week and Saturdays before, during and after sports programmes.

Task 2

(The explanation)

The storyboard would have two main characters that would appear in all the adverts. The 'Winner' is easily identifiable just like Fido Dido in the 7UP adverts. He wins all the races on the track and in the pool – there could be more adverts with him scoring goals in football matches. He is then seen drinking from a can of Webster's Fruit Juice which says that if you drink this drink you will improve your skills and get the girls.

The advert for the magazine has the same two characters and these show scenes from the television adverts.

In all the ads they will be black and white like cartoon drawings except for the can which will always be coloured bright green to make it stand out and be noticed.

Examiner's comment

The storyboard shows understanding of the codes, conventions and terminology of storyboarding. It would be improved if he investigated the rules and regulations surrounding advertising and what they can and can't say.

The print advertisement also demonstrates the appropriate conventions. In other words it does what it sets out to do – promote a healthy drink. There is a clear link between the two pieces because the audience would recognise the main character, the logo, the colour scheme and the style.

This is a typical grade C response.

Now read sample assignment 3 below. Then read the sample student response to Task 4, together with the examiner's comments (on page 201).

Sample assignment 3: Practical Production and evaluation

Produce a campaign to promote a new band.

Task 1: pre-production

Select a band or artist you want to base your work on. Research and analyse as much promotional material as possible for that band, including posters, magazine or newspaper articles, television appearances, gig venues, etc. You need to consider:

- different codes and conventions
- appeal to audiences
- producers
- representational issues.

Task 2:

You now need to re-launch an existing band or create a new band in the same style and genre of music as your research. Produce mock-ups of at least four different promotional techniques. These could be selected from: posters or CD design, magazine features, music video extracts, web site home pages, an advertisement for a performance etc. Pay particular attention to how the band will be represented and how they will appeal to their target audience.

Task 3:

Create the final versions of your four selected promotional techniques using appropriate technology.

Task 4: Evaluate your production

- How does your promotional package conform or subvert existing promotional packages?
- How far does your promotional package emulate the work of existing Artist and Repertoire (A and R) divisions within record companies?
- How will the promotional package meet the needs and expectations of the target audience?
- How clear is the representation of your band and how has this been highlighted?
- How have any other necessary considerations been met? E.g. regulations, parental advisory advice etc.

Task 4

Evaluate your production.

Task 4

Extract from a student's answer

I set out to produce a promotional package for a new star, Amber Light, using the knowledge gained from deconstructing the promotional material available for Beyonce.

The promotional package I have designed would attract new and existing audiences for my star. It includes material that fans would expect to see such as CD releases, websites and posters and also offers chances of publicity that would attract new fans, such as the magazine article in a magazine that potential fans might read.

I have produced a promotional package that conforms to the appropriate codes and conventions of CD covers, posters, websites and magazine articles. They would be recognisable to anyone looking at them.

I have tried to make the image of Amber Light look moody and sexy as this is a popular representation for female stars. The background I have chosen suggests a wild side to her character. She is posing in a mass of undergrowth. I would have preferred a jungle background but couldn't make it look realistic. I have used a brown/gold colour for her name and for the writing on the CD cover as this also represents her name.

The target audience for the promotional package is going to be 15–25-year-olds as the music style is popular with them.

Examiner's comment

This is the evaluation part of Assessment Objective 4; her production work would also be considered. The student's evaluation is a little formulaic but she has clearly related her production to the research she has previously undertaken. She is focusing on the concepts and the target audience and highlighting the parts which deal with this.

This extract is typical of a grade A response.

Improving Practical Production work

As well as providing an enjoyable opportunity to get behind a video camera or organise your own fashion shoot, the Practical Production should help you to learn more about the way the media work. You may have written about films, radio programmes or magazines for your coursework. Making a version of one of these for yourself should show you useful things about the way these media texts work.

Whatever type of Practical Production you choose, there are three key words you need to remember: organisation, organisation and organisation! Without a clear plan of attack you will soon get frustrated and your work will not do you justice. This unit will help you to get the most from the Practical Production by making you think like a professional.

When you plan your work, think of the three stages used by the media industry:

1. **Pre-production** – all your research and planning
2. **Production** – using technology to collect the material you need to get your film, magazine or radio programme made
3. **Post-production** – assembling all the photos, recordings and interviews into a finished product and evaluation of the product

What follows are a few lists of useful things for you to do, which should help improve your Practical Production and therefore your marks.

Ten things to improve the analysis and evaluation of your work

The analysis and evaluation form an important part of the work you will do and of your marks. If you are working in a group, it is doubly important because it will show the individual contribution you made towards the work.

The written evaluation *must* include:

1. A clear opening explanation of what you were intending to produce and the target audience at whom you aimed your production.
2. Some evidence that you have thought about, and researched, your target audience and the 'market' for your product.
3. Your own comments on the decisions that were made at each stage of production and why those decisions were made. For example, if you had three video sequences of a particular section of your film and only chose one to include in the final edit, *why* were the other two rejected? These comments on the decision-making process will be important for your teacher when the marks are being given because it shows how much you have learned from doing the production work.
4. In a group production, a clear account of all the things you were responsible for.
5. Links between your product and professionally produced work of a similar nature. How and why is yours different?

6. References to the Key Concepts – make these as often as possible.

7. A final evaluation of the completed production.

8. An appendix to your written piece that includes pre-production work such as storyboards, questionnaires, scripts and work schedules.

   You should *not* include:

9. A string of excuses about your teacher failing to give you the right camera/computer/battery.

10. A minute-by-minute account of every button that was pushed and tripod that was carried – what examiners call the 'dear Diary' approach. You only have 1000 words and this is not enough to waste describing unimportant details.

Ten things to do when making a video

1. Always produce a script or storyboard: never 'make it up as you go along' while out on the shoot.

Unless you have planned what you intend to shoot, you will waste a lot of time and forget things. Pre-planning may not be exciting, but without it you're doomed to produce a half-baked video.

2. Always shoot more than the number of shots which appear on your storyboard.

You will need all sorts of other material to use when it comes to the edit, so make sure you give yourself enough choice. Make sure you have enough 'establishing' long shots to show the location to your viewer. Try shooting the same thing in mid shot and also in close-up so you can see which is most effective later when slipped in between shots on either side in the edit. As a rule of thumb, shoot four times as much material as you will actually use in the edit.

3. At all costs, avoid 'real-time filming'.

Whatever you are filming, it should be broken down into a series of individual shots. Don't try to cover the whole of a chase sequence by running behind the actors with the camera rolling, hoping for the best. Take three or four points along the route of the chase, set up the camera and let your actors run through the shot without the camera moving.

4. Do not use the zoom...

... unless you have a VERY good reason to. Use the zoom to compose the shot. Far too many students have their characters' faces whooshing up into badly framed close-up, making the viewer feel queasy and distracting their attention.

5. Do not use the endless slow pan.

We've all seen (and maybe even taken) that lo-o-o-ng, sl-o-o-ow pan following a character across a scene, sending us slowly to sleep before they finally reach the door and go through it. Don't bother to pan – just frame up on the door, let them walk into shot, open it and cut as they start to close it.

6. Do not 'hosepipe' the camera all over the place.

When they start out, all amateurs use the camera as an extension to their eye. If they have a cathedral in front of them they just waggle the camera up and down and sideways in the hope that we will see the whole building. It's called 'hosepiping' because the end result is about as controlled as a hosepipe not being held when the tap is turned on: it lurches around randomly for no good reason. Decide on some key things in your scene and take individual shots of them with the camera still on the tripod.

7. Do not shoot into the light.

Unless you want a silhouette (and, realistically, most of the time you don't because you can't tell anything about the character), don't stand your actor in front of a window and shoot into the light. Even on the dullest of days, it will be much brighter outside than inside and all the things you don't want the audience to see will be perfectly lit and all the things you do want them to see will be pitch black.

8. Do not forget all about the sound when shooting.

There's a good reason why film crews spend ages waiting for the sound recordist to get the microphones in position and sound levels right. It's because if an actor or presenter is speaking, it is good to hear what they say clearly rather than strain to pick up a tiny voice being drowned out by all sorts of other noises. Video is a two-medium media: pictures and sound. Both are equally important so make sure you use microphones to pick up actors' or presenters' voices.

9. Do not include every visual effect in the editing software package.

Imagine how tedious it would be if every time the shot changed in *Eastenders*, they used a different starburst or tumbling box wipe dissolve. It would interfere with the storytelling. Unless you want the viewer to notice that you are changing shot (and most of the time you don't), just use a simple cut.

10. Do not use the first bit of music from the iTunes library which comes to hand.

The music you use must be just right for the scene because, if it isn't, the audience might laugh at the moment you thought was deeply sad – music is very powerful. Spend time trying out different tracks to see what effect they have on the meaning of the sequence. Do notice the word 'sequence' here. Don't try to add different bits of music to each individual shot.

How to make a success of a photo shoot

If you are making a print-based practical production, the photography will be crucial to the success of the finished product. For a professional fashion/advertisement shoot there will be a number of people involved:

- art director (in overall charge of the shoot)
- photographer (takes the photograph and makes suggestions to the art director)
- two or three photographer's assistants to carry gear and set up lights
- stylist (to supervise costume and make-up)
- the client or their representative (to check they are happy with what is being photographed)
- the model or models.

If the team get three or four really good photos at the end of the shoot, they will be pleased with themselves.

You will probably have a much smaller crew, but you should certainly involve more than one perso n. Above all, you need to look at every single detail of the images that you take to make sure that the photograph is conveying exactly the right message to your audience.

Ten tips on posing your model

When posing any models for each photograph, use the following checklist:

1. **Posture**: how will I pose the model? Lazing on a sofa will give a relaxed feel to the image; sitting upright in an office chair will give a more formal feel.

2. **Facial expression**: do I want to create a moody look or do I want a happy, relaxed feel to the shot?

3. **Costume**: what someone wears tells other people a great deal about them. Make sure that each piece of your model's clothing has been selected to get across the chosen image.

4. **Setting**: think about the message that the setting of your shot will convey. Is the school playing field *really* the best setting for your jeans advertisement – or have you just gone there because it is easy? Make sure there is nothing in the background of your shot you don't want to be there!

5. **Props**: make sure your props fit with the connotations you are trying to set up in the audience's mind. Is your teacher's N-reg Fiesta going to add to the 'cool image' you are trying to create?

Once you have sorted out all of the things on your checklist, your next job is to compose them within the frame of your camera. Although there are no hard and fast rules about what makes a good photograph, the following composition guidelines might offer you a starting point for making interesting images.

6. **Using thirds**: where will you place significant elements in your picture? Research has shown that viewer's look first at the human face – especially the eyes – and any points of high contrast. Photographers often talk about the *principle of thirds*. When looking through the viewfinders of their cameras, they imagine a grid formed by two vertical and two horizontal lines which divide the picture into thirds. They then place key elements of the composition, often using a third to two-thirds proportion. Look at photograph A below and think about the way it has used thirds for its composition.

A

B

7. **Lines of movement**: photographs are often thought to have a stronger composition if the objects in them are seen as 'moving into' the picture (photograph B) or looking into the open space of the picture.

8. **Diagonals and horizontals**: diagonal lines in compositions are said to be more dynamic than horizontal ones. How have lines been used in the composition of photograph C opposite?

9. **Angle**: most photographs are taken at eye level. Taking them from above or below your subject can be another way of creating visual impact. Look at the way this has been used by the photographer of photograph D opposite.

10. **Light**: getting the lighting right can mean more than just making sure there is enough light. The factors mentioned for video production on page 208 apply equally to lighting for a still photograph. Strong sunlight coming through the arches adds to the composition of photograph E opposite.

Five ways to improve page layout

If you are working on a print-based publication like a magazine, or designing a poster, you need to be thinking about the *appropriateness* of your design for your intended audience, as well as how to grab and keep a reader's attention. Graphic design is changing all the time as the creative people who work in advertising agencies constantly try to stay at the cutting edge of fashion.

The following tips should help you produce more effective layouts:

1. Look at a wide range of different publications and make notes of layout features which you think would be good to incorporate in your production.

2. Use a page grid to help you in your page design, even if you decide to break out of it. This is how all page designs in professional publications start out. It gives a starting point onto which the design can be plotted.

3. The various parts of the design do not have to be straight or orderly. Scattered letters can add to the dynamic look of the page. However, if you are using straight lines and columns, make sure they are just that!

4. Use white (or blank) space. It can provide contrast in your design. If everything is spaced out evenly it can look bland and uninteresting.

5. Titles set on a diagonal can add emphasis and look more dynamic.

Assignments you could use

What is in this section?

This section gives you examples of assignments that you could actually complete and submit. To give you some choice, and to show the variety of assignments you might do, there are more assignments here than you would actually use. These are just examples and your teacher will help you decide whether to use these possible assignments or not.

Assignment 1: Introduction to the media – print-based advertising

Investigate how print-based advertising reaches its target audience.

Primary concepts: Media language and Audience
Secondary concepts: Institution and Representation

Task 1   AO2

Analyse two print-based advertisements for a similar product.
You should focus on:

- positioning – image and text
- mise-en-scène
- text – font and size
- target audience.
- colour – lighting and shade

I am all the boys
I've kissed
and the ones I will.

search online for 'I am'

orange

Photographer: John Short Stylist: Chrissie Macdonald

The new Samsung Pixon mobile not only packs an 8 megapixel camera but also has Advanced Shake Reduction, Smile Shot and a dual powered LED – making it the perfect way to capture important moments, day or night. With built-in editing you can put hand-written captions on your favourite shots and share them on the web. So wherever life takes you, take a Pixon and capture the unexpected. **samsungmobile.co.uk/pixon**

Samsung **Pixon** 8 megapixel camera phone

Remember you are analysing, so you need to offer explanations about why and how these things attract the target audience. You could use the two advertisements opposite and above or find two of your own.

Task 2   AO3

Design your own print-based advertisement for a similar product, targeting a specific audience.

Task 3   AO2

Comment briefly on how successfully your advertisement will attract its target audience.

Assignment 1: Introduction to the media – children's comics

Investigate the way children's comics attract an audience.

Primary concepts: Media language and Audience
Secondary concepts: Institution and Representation

Task 1   AO2

Analyse the front covers of two different comics for two different audiences. You need to focus on:

- title, price and publishing schedule (weekly or monthly)
- layout – splash or panel
- content – character or special feature
- colour
- special offers/cover mounts.

What do these things tell you about the intended audience?

You could use the two comic front covers below and opposite or find two of your own.

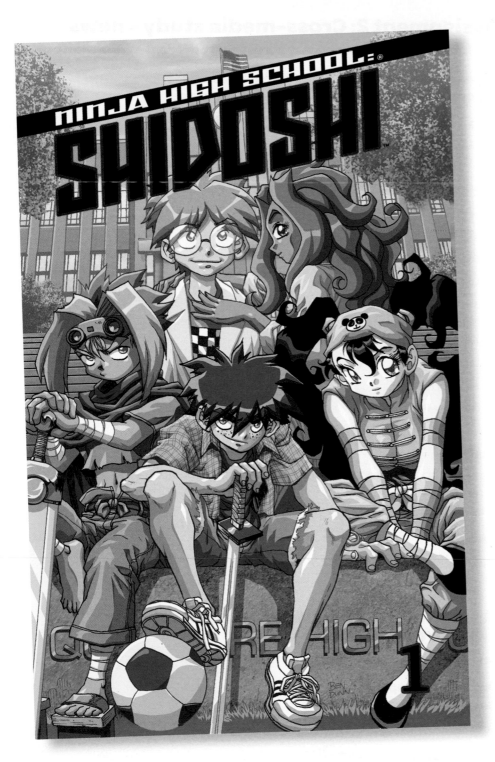

Task 2   AO3

Design the front cover for a new children's comic.

Task 3   AO2

Explain briefly how your comic attracts the intended audience.

Assignment 2: Cross-media study – news

Explore how news is broadcast across two different media platforms.

Primary concepts: Institution and Representation
Secondary concepts: Media language and Audience

Task 1   AO2

Analyse any television news broadcast or radio news broadcast. Focus on the first 5 minutes of the programme. You should consider:

- scheduling
- channel/station
- style and tone
- news selection and sequencing
- use of relevant codes and conventions.

Analyse a newspaper which is published on the same day as your television or radio broadcast. Focus on the front page and at least one other page. You should consider:

- type of newspaper (tabloid/broadsheet, quality/popular, etc.)
- style and tone
- news selection and layout
- use of image/font/juxtaposition.

Task 2   AO3

Design a mock-up front page for a contrasting newspaper and a storyboard/script for a 60-second news bulletin for radio or television for the same day's news.

Task 3   AO2

Justify the news selection for your product in terms of institution and representation.

Assignment 2: Cross-media study – film promotion

Investigate two ways in which a film is promoted.

Primary concepts: Institution and Representation
Secondary concepts: Media language and Audience

Task 1   AO2

Deconstruct a film trailer and film poster for a particular film or genre.

You need to consider:

- the relevant codes and conventions for trailers and posters
- how the film or genre has been represented
- use of colour, lighting, etc.
- camera angles and distance – how these influence representation
- sound where relevant and what it represents

- editing where relevant or selection and cropping of an image and how this influences representation
- how mise-en-scène contributes to the representation
- the industry behind the production.

You could use the film poster below or find one of your own. You could also use the link in the CD (see CD-ROM Extra!) to find possible film trailers. Your teacher can help you with choosing suitable trailers and posters.

Task 2   AO3

Design a DVD case for the release of the film on DVD and a 2-minute interview with one of the stars for a feature on a celebrity news slot. Make suggestions for the kinds of image you want to accompany the interview.

Task 3   AO2

Explain how all of these promotional techniques are used when a new film is released in cinemas or on DVD.

CD-ROM
Extra!
Film trailers
Open the CD in the back of this book and click on the icon below to open a link to possible film trailers.

HTML

Assignment 3: Practical Production – website

Create a four-page website for a celebrity of your choice.

Primary concepts: Media language, Institution, Audience and Representation

Task 1   AO3

Pre-production: research and analyse existing celebrity websites. Focus on the homepage and links to other pages.

Task 2   AO3

Produce either a new site for an existing celebrity or a site for a new fictional celebrity. Clearly identify relevant representational aspects and the intended target audience. Produce mock-up versions of the four relevant web pages, bearing in mind the usual codes and conventions of web design and celebrity promotion.

Task 3   AO4

Create the final versions of the four web pages using appropriate technology.

Task 4   AO4

Evaluate your production:

- How does the website match your original planning?
- How does the website conform to, or subvert, the usual codes and conventions of celebrity websites?
- What is the institutional context and how does this fit in with the career of the celebrity?
- How does the website meet the expectations of the target audience?
- What representations have been highlighted to effectively promote the celebrity?
- What other considerations were taken into account, if any?

Assignment 3: Practical Production – television trailer

Create a 120-second trailer for a new television programme.

Primary concepts: Media language, Institution, Audience and Representation

Task 1   AO3

Pre-production: research and analyse existing television trailers. Focus on the relevant generic conventions of the television programme as well as the institutional context.

Task 2   AO3

Produce a storyboard for the 120-second trailer, bearing in mind the generic conventions of the television programme and the codes and conventions of storyboarding.

Task 3   AO4

Film and edit the 120-second television trailer.

Task 4   AO4

Evaluate your production:

- How far does your production match the codes and conventions of the genre?
- How far does your production match the codes and conventions of trailers?
- Where and when would the trailer be broadcast to have the maximum effect on the target audience?
- How would the trailer appeal to and attract the target audience?
- What representational considerations were made to create the most effect trailer?
- What other considerations need to be taken into account?

GradeStudio

These tips from the Examiner will help you improve your three Controlled Assessment assignments.

Assignment 1: Tips for success
- **Terminology**: use appropriate terminology.
- **Denotation and connotation**: apply these to all your analytical work. It is not enough to just describe what you see. You need to explain why something is constructed the way it is.
- **Genre**: establish the genre of the texts you are analysing and constructing, and establish if any narrative is suggested.
- **Media language and audience** are what this assignment is about. Clearly establish who the audience is meant to be. Marks will be awarded if any relevant secondary audience is established.
- **Presentation**: make your assignment look appealing, effective and easy for *your* audience to read. You can use annotation, charts, diagrams, bullet points or essay format.
- **Research**: keep a note of the publications used for your research and always show what you have learned from the research.

Assignment 2: Tips for success
Ask yourself the following questions as you work on Assignment 2:
- Are the relevant **codes and conventions** of the different media platforms explained clearly?
- How effective is the particular **media platform**?
- How do **audience expectations** differ with the different media platforms?
- How effective are the different **representations**?
- Are the **representations** more suited to a different media platform?
- How are the different **platforms** financed, scheduled, produced and distributed?
- How effective is the **presentation** of the cross-media platforms?
- How clear are the connections between the **cross-media** platforms?

Assignment 3: Tips for success
- **Moving image**: know how to handle the technology. Framing shots and editing are important, as are film language considerations (such as camera angle, distance, sound, lighting and colour, creative editing and mise-en-scène).
- **Sound**: know how to use microphones and mixing equipment effectively. Sound must be clear and appropriate with no unplanned silences! The language, tone and register of the programme need to be appropriate for the target audience and the product.
- **Print**: know how to use appropriate technology. There needs to be appropriate placing of text and image. Also important are language, tone and register of the text for audience and product. Selection and editing of the material need careful consideration.
- **Web-based/new media technologies**: ensure an appropriate mix of text and image and sound. Language, tone and register are all important. Links and interactivity must be appropriate.
- **Codes and conventions** will need to be focused on.
- Use **original images** where possible. Only use found images if you can use them creatively.
- **Cross-media platform study**: there needs to be a balance between the media forms and equal consideration of the relevant codes and conventions.

Glossary

Accent The sound of the voice which tells us which part of the country the presenter is from.

Anchor To pin down a particular meaning of a drawing or photograph often by adding a caption.

Angle The particular point of view a newspaper wants its readers to take on a story.

Animations Audio-visual versions of comics that are used in a variety of media forms such as films and adverts.

Anime A Japanese animation form that combines camera movements with still frames.

Arch-villain The character who opposes the superhero and often has special powers too, that are used only for evil. The most memorable arch-villains are those who have a reason for turning to evil, for example, Doctor Octopus in *Spiderman*.

Aspiration When an audience sees fashion, accessories, a lifestyle, etc. in a magazine that they wish they could have for themselves.

Audience People who are reading, looking at, listening to or using a media text.

Audience profile The types of people who read, watch or listen to a particular media.

Audience share The number of people a particular media attracts compared to its competitors.

Back-catalogue All the previous work recorded by artists or bands.

BBC Charter The official permission from the government for the BBC to charge a licence fee in return for quality programming.

Blockbuster A film that has a huge budget and is expected to be a hit, so-called because of the long queues around the block to see successful films.

Brand A particular type of product, for example, Levi jeans.

Brand awareness Making the product immediately recognisable to the public.

Branding The distinctive features by which we recognise products.

Broadsheets Traditionally, newspapers printed in a large format (pages 37 cm by 58 cm); they are considered to be more serious in content than tabloids.

Caption The descriptive words next to a picture.

Categorising Ordering or grouping similar texts, for example, magazines, according to the features they have in common.

Celebrity Someone who is popular in one country for appearing in one media field, such as a soap opera.

Central protagonists Key characters around whom the text and narrative are centred.

Circulation The number of copies of a newspaper or magazine which are sold.

Codes and conventions The things that make a piece of media what it is, i.e. the things that define it. For example, we associate horses, spurs, saloons and tumbleweed with Westerns and flashing lights, actors in shiny suits and lack of gravity with science fiction. Likewise, we associate a red-topped masthead, banner headlines and celebrity gossip with the popular tabloids.

Commercial broadcaster A channel funded by money from advertising, for example, ITV.

Computer generated imagery (CGI) Using computer graphics, especially 3D computer graphics, in special effects.

Connotation The hidden meaning behind an image, word or sound that gives it depth.

Continuity editing Editing which is designed to make one event follow on naturally from another. Nothing unusual happens to make the viewer notice the fact that an edit has been made.

Consumers The people who buy, read, watch or listen to media products.

Conventions The typical characteristics of a particular type of text.

Copy Material for articles that appear in newspapers or magazines.

Cover price The price charged for the magazine that is displayed on the front cover.

Cross-media When more than one media area come together, often in a business relationship – for example, comics and television.

Cross-plot A way of tracking different storylines through a single episode of a TV drama series.

Deconstruction Taking a media product apart to see how it works and how it is constructed. It is more than just analysis.

Demograph The type of audience watching or reading a media product.

Demographics Another word for audience categories.

Denotation This is the understanding of media artefacts – what they look and sound like.

Disposable income The money someone has left to spend after they have paid for essentials such as housing and food.

Distribution method The way the music industry distributes music tracks to its audience.

Download Any file that is available on a remote server to be downloaded to a home computer. YouTube is an example of a file-sharing website.

Downmarket People who have smaller incomes and less money to spend on anything beyond the basic living requirements.

Endorsement Giving approval to something.

Experiential communication Where consumers actually interact with the product rather than just look at pictures of it.

Film pitch An idea for a new film which is presented to film producers. This usually involves ideas for a plot, possible actors, promotion and marketing.

Form When we talk about a media form we mean the method used to mediate meaning, i.e. print and electronic texts, moving image, television, film, etc. and sound.

Gatekeeping Where reporters or editors block certain issues but allow others through into newspapers or news broadcasts.

Genre A type of media text (programme, film, popular music, etc.) with certain predictable characteristics.

Glossies Magazines with thick, 'glossy' paper, expensive advertisements and a high cover price.

Hegemony The way people are influenced into accepting the dominance of a power group who impose their views on the rest of the population.

House style A radio station or publisher's preferred manner of presentation or layout which matches their audience.

Hybrid When at least two genres are brought together to create a new genre, for example, the superhero movie combines the genres of superhero comics and action films.

Ident Like a logo, an instantly recognisable feature of a film, character or company, for example, the Hulk's green fists.

Ideology A system of values, beliefs or ideas that is common to a specific group of people.

Institutions All media is constructed. 'Institution' is the term given to the organisations that make the media we consume. It could also cover the organisations that control and regulate the media.

Intertextual reference
When one media text refers to another media text in a way that many consumers will recognise.

Jump-cut Where the join between two shots is felt to be abrupt because what follows is something we don't expect to see.

Lifestyle magazines Magazines dealing with lots of topics and issues to appeal to a wide audience.

Link A shot piece of speech from the presenter between music or other items.

Lip-synching Where a person in a video mimes so that their lip movement matches the words being heard on a soundtrack.

Manga Popular Japanese comics that have influenced anime films.

Marketing The process of making customers aware of products, services and ideas in the hope that they will buy into them.

Market research Finding out what audiences like or dislike about aspects of the media through interviews, surveys and focus groups.

Masthead The title of the newspaper which appears in large type at the top of the front page.

Media conglomerates Large corporations who own more than one different media company and sometimes a large number of companies.

Media consumption The media texts you watch, listen to or read.

Media language This is not necessarily written or even spoken language, but the way we 'read' images and sounds and the way things in the media are constructed.

Media space Any space in newspapers, magazines, on the radio or television where advertising can be placed.

Mise-en-scène A French phrase which literally means 'put in shot'.

Model animation An animation technique using posable scale models.

Mode of address The ways that a text creates a relationship with its audience.

Multi-stranded narrative When a television drama follows more than one storyline and also interweaves them.

Narrative A story or account.

Narrative structure The way a story is organised and shaped in terms of time and events.

Network An interconnected group or system.

News values Things that help a story get into the news.

Niche markets Small groups who are targeted because they share the same interests, income, etc.

Opening (or title) sequence A series of shots and music or graphics that appear at the start of a programme or film.

Oppositional characters Characters who will play opposite the key central character, either in a relationship (for example, the hero/heroine) or in conflict (for example, the hero/villain).

Pace The speed at which something happens or a story develops.

Passive Not helping the narrative to move forward or not helping the hero.

Peak time The hours between 6.00 p.m. and 10.30 p.m. when most people are watching television and viewing figures are at their highest.

Picture editor The person responsible for choosing the photographs that go into a newspaper.

Platform This is how the form is delivered – so newspapers and magazines are print platforms and television is a moving image platform.

Post-production Activities at the end of the production process, e.g. editing, sound dubbing, credits, marketing and promotion, focus groups, trailers, articles and features.

Pre-production Activities at the beginning of the production process, eg. ideas, bids for finance, storyboards, scriptwriting, planning and designing, set construction, casting and rehearsals.

Primary consumer Someone who is focused on watching, listening to or reading a media text.

Producer The person who makes a product.

Production Shooting in purpose-built sets or in outside locations.

Product (or pack) shot A picture of the actual product, for example, a packet of Corn Flakes.

Product placement Giving brands or products to media producers for them to use as props so that the product is seen in a favourable way.

Public service broadcaster A channel funded by a licence fee that has to provide a choice of programmes to appeal to all social groups, for example, BBC1.

Readership The number of people who read a newspaper or magazine. This is usually higher than circulation, as several people can read the same paper/magazine.

Red tops Tabloid newspapers with red mastheads.

Re-issuing When a record company releases songs recorded some time before and which have probably already sold well.

Representation How people, places, events or ideas are represented or portrayed to audiences in media texts. Sometimes this is simplistically through stereotypes so the audience can see immediately what is meant, and sometimes the meanings are less obvious.

Revenue The money generated by selling advertising space in a magazine or newspaper, on television, websites etc.

Secondary consumer Someone watching, listening to or reading a media text while doing something else, such as talking or homework.

Social networking site Examples are Facebook and Myspace.

Special effects Exciting and dynamic visual or sound effects used to create impact in films.

Specialist magazines Magazines focusing on a particular area of interest to appeal to a narrow or niche audience.

Spin-off Merchandise that uses characters from a media text.

Star A performer who is famous internationally.

Stereotypical Showing groups of people in terms of certain widely held but over-simplified characteristics, for example, showing women as nagging housewives.

Stereotypes People grouped together according to simple shared characteristics, without allowing for any individual uniqueness.

Stock character A supporting character who is often quite stereotypical and whose job it is to help the lead characters, to be saved by them or to die!

Stock footage Material held in a library which shows something relevant to the news story.

Storyboard The key moments of a story shown using images and notes.

Sub-editor The person responsible for the layout of a newspaper.

Sub-genre Genres can be divided into sub-genres, for example, teen comedies are a sub-genre of comedy.

Subsidise To reduce the cover price of a media text, such as a magazine or newspaper, by selling advertising space.

Subversion When a technique is used which does not fit a theory or the usual way of doing something (for example, when a twist takes the narrative in a new direction).

Superhero A heroic character with special powers and a lifelong mission.

Tabloids Traditionally, newspapers with pages half the size of broadsheets; they are usually more highly illustrated and can be less serious in their tone and content than broadsheets.

Target audience The specific group of people that a media text is aimed at.

Template A pattern which helps to shape the products that follow.

Tension The build-up of suspense or anticipation as a story develops.

Text This is not just the written word but a film text, radio text, etc.

Tie-in A media text that uses the characters, and possibly storyline, of a text in another form.

Tone The qualilty and character of a voice or piece of writing.

Typography The choice of font style and size, graphic design and layout.

Upmarket People who are comfortably off with a reasonable income.

Values and aspirations
The ideas and goals that are important to people.

Viral advertising Spreading advertisements through the use of attachments to emails. It can give very wide coverage at no cost.

Watershed An agreement between terrestrial channels not to show explicit material until after 9 p.m.

Heinemann is an imprint of Pearson Education Limited, a company incorporated in England and Wales, having its registered office at Edinburgh Gate, Harlow, Essex, CM20 2JE. Registered company number: 872828

www.heinemann.co.uk

Heinemann is a registered trademark of Pearson Education Limited

Text © Pearson Education Limited 2009

First published 2009

12 11 10 09
10 9 8 7 6 5 4 3 2 1

British Library Cataloguing in Publication Data
A catalogue record for this book is available from the British Library.

ISBN 978 0 435404 00 0

Designed and produced by Kamae Design, Oxford
Original illustrations © Pearson Education Limited 2009
Illustrated by Tony Forbes
Cover design by Pete Stratton
Picture research by Ginny Stroud-Lewis
Cover photo © Garry Black/Masterfile
Printed in the UK by Scotprint

Acknowledgements
The author and publisher would like to thank the following individuals and organisations for permission to reproduce photographs:
© The Advertising Archives p114, 149 (right), 156, 157, 159 (all photos); ©Alamy/Alex Segre p71; © Alamy/AllOver Photography p77 (top); © Alamy/Chris Fredriksson p127; © Alamy/Coaster p43 (bottom); © Alamy/DEK C p124 (middle); © Alamy/Frances Roberts p12 (bottom); © Alamy/INTERFOTO Pressebildagentur p124 (middle left); © Alamy/Jon Arnold Images Ltd p145; © Alamy/Jon Challicom p32 (bottom); © Alamy/Roberto Herrett p18; © Alamy/WoodyStock p77 (middle); © Art Directors and Trip/Helene Rogers p11 (bottom three photos); © Bettmann/CORBIS p128 (bottom); © Channel 4 pp36, 48; © Colin Jones/Topfoto 124 (top); © Corbis pp 3 (bottom), 87 (top),121; © Corbis/Angelo Hornak p14 (top); © Corbis/Bettmann pp15 (top), 124 (far left),149 (left); © Corbis/Challenge Roddie p104 (middle); © Corbis/Denis O'Regan p138; © Corbis/Neal Preston p124 (second from left); © Corbis/Reuters/Ray Stubblebine p24; © Corbis/Rune Hellestad p133 (bottom); © Corbis/Saba/Louise Gubb p58; © Corbis/Sygma p6; © Corbis/Wally McNamee p168; © Corbis/Walter Rawlings/Robert Harding World Imagery p207 (middle); © Daniel Attia/zefa/Corbis p68; © David James/Warner Bros/ZUMA/Corbis p111; ©Getty Images p104 (right), 124 (second from right), 147, 153; © Getty Images/AFP p22; © Getty Images/Felbert+Eickenberg p32 (top); © Getty Images/Film Magic pp 88, 89 (middle left); © Getty Images/Lichfield Archive p135 (second from bottom), 139; © Getty Images/Lonely Planet p59 (top); © Getty Images/Michael Ochs Archives p124 (third from left, third from right); © Getty Images/Photodisc p59 (bottom); © Getty Images/Popperfoto p124 (middle right); © Getty Images/WireImage pp124 (far right), 126; © Ian West/PA Wire/PA Photos p43 (top); © The Illustrated London News Photo Library p52; © Image Source Pink/ Alamy p28; © INTERFOTO Pressebildagentur / Alamy p47; © ITV p38; © ITV Granada p42; © JHP Teen / Alamy p205 (left); © The Kobal Collection pp135 (bottom), 136; © The Kobal Collection/ABC-Tv/Danny Feld p44 (bottom); © The Kobal Collection/ABC-TV/Moshe Brakha p41; © The Kobal Collection/Allied Artists p4; © The Kobal Collection/Columbia pp115,135 (top); © The Kobal Collection/Destination Films/Gullane Pics p102; © The Kobal Collection/Dreamworks/Aardman Animations p116; © The Kobal Collection/Dreamworks LLC p185; © The Kobal Collection/Focus Features p17 (top right); © The Kobal Collection/Focus Features/Greg Williams p33; © The Kobal Collection/Marvel Enterprises p17 (top left), 213; © The Kobal Collection/MGM/United Artists/Sony p165; © The Kobal Collection/Monarchy/Regency p162; © The Kobal Collection/Polygram/Suzanne Hanover p11 (top); © The Kobal Collecton/STUDIO GHIBLI p120; © The Kobal Collection/20th Century Fox p104 (left); © The Kobal Collection/20th Century Fox-film corporation p5 (right) © The Kobal Collection/20th Century Fox/Marvel p112; © The Kobal Collection/United Artists p135 (second from top); © The Kobal Collection/Walt Disney Pictures p117; © The Kobal Collection/Warner Bros Pictures pp5 (left), 15 (bottom),17 (bottom right), 118; © The Kobal Collection/Warner Bros/Castle Rock Ent. P17 (bottom left); © Mandy Esseen p89 (bottom left, bottom right); © Martin Phillips p173 (left and right), 178 (left and right); © Matthew Birchall / Alamy p87 (bottom right); © Michael Germana/Starmax/EMPICS Entertainment/PA Photos p89 (top right); © NASA/HSTI; © PAPhotos p44 (top) © Paul Kane/Getty Images p134; © Pearson Education/Tudor Photography p172; © Photoshot/UPPA p35; © Rex Features p49; © Raymond Press Agency p65; © Rex Features p69; © Rex Features/FremantleMedia Ltd p143; © Samantha Scott / Alamy p205 (right); © Shutterstock p133 (top); © Shutterstock/Andriy Doriy p12 (top); © Shutterstock/Andriy Rovenko p206 (bottom); © Shutterstock/Cristian Alexandru Ciobanu p207 (top); © Shutterstock/foto.fritz p30 (bottom); © Shutterstock/ifong p77 (bottom); © Shutterstock/LesPalenik p29 (left); © Science Photo Library/Sheila Terry p30 (top); © Shutterstock/Liv Friis-Larsen p206 (top); © Shutterstock/Ljupco Smokovski p29 (right); © Shutterstock/rook76 p14 (bottom); © Shutterstock/St. Nick p207 (bottom); © 2006 TopFoto/Ken Russell p123; © Wikipedia p131.

Every effort has been made to contact copyright holders of material reproduced in this book. Any omissions will be rectified in subsequent printings if notice is given to the publishers.

Chapter 1: Cover of *Empire* magazine © Empire, used with permission; BBFC logos: These classification symbols are the property of the British Board of Film Classification and are both trademark and copyright protected. Used with permission of BBFC; **Chapter 2**: Quote from the BBC charter is used with permission of the BBC; Ofcom Logo is used with permission of Ofcom; BBC 1 and BBC 2 TV listings used with the kind permission of the *Radio Times*; Peter Fincham quote is used with permission of the BBC; E4 TV listings used with the kind permission of the *Radio Times* magazine; **Chapter 3**: Edward R. Murrow quote © Edward R. Murrow used with kind permission of the estate; Masthead from the *Sun* used with permission of NI Syndication Ltd.; Front page of the *Sun* ('It's the Sun wot won it') used with permission of NI Syndication Ltd.; Front page of *The Times* ('Major plans reshuffle today') used with permission of NI Syndication Ltd.; Front page of *The Times* ('When war came to America') used with permission of NI Syndication Ltd.; Extract and front page of the *Daily Mail* ('Time's up for happy hour') used with permission from the *Daily Mail*; 'You're Spuddy Clever Walter' from *Hold Ye Front Page: 2000 years of History on the Front Page of the 'Sun'* by John Perry & Neil Roberts, © 1999. Used by permission of HarperCollins Publishers; 'Monkey Nutter' from *Hold Ye Front Page: 2000 years of History on the Front Page of the 'Sun'* by John Perry & Neil Roberts, © 1999. Used by permission of HarperCollins Publishers; Extract from the *Daily Mail* ('Shameless') used with permission from the *Daily Mail*; **Chapter 4**: Cover of *Elle* magazine used by kind permission of *Elle*, Paris; Screen grab from ElleUK.com used by kind permission of Elle, Paris; Screen Grab from the BFI website used by kind permission of the British Film Institute; Cover of *Asiana* magazine used by kind permission of I & I Media Limited; Cover and contents page of *Shout* magazine used by kind permission of D.C. Thomson; Cover of *Anglers Mail* used by kind permission of IPC Media; Screen grab of *empireonline.com* used with the kind permission of *Empire* magazine. www.empireonline.com; Film review from empireonline.com used with the kind permission of *Empire* magazine. www.empireonline.com; Cover of *Empire* magazine used with the kind permission of *Empire* magazine. www.empireonline.com; Cover of *NME* magazine used by kind permission of IPC Media, a Time Warner company; Cover the *Radio Times* used with the kind permission of the *Radio Times* magazine; Cover of *Thomas and Friends* magazine used by permission of Egmont; IPC Media logo used by permission of IPC Media; Cover of *PC Gamer* magazine used by permission of Future Publishing Ltd.; **Chapter 5**: Cover of *Dandy* used by kind permission of D.C. Thomson; Cover of *Beano* used by kind permission of D.C. Thomson; Cover of the *Fantastic Four*: TM & © 2009 Marvel Characters Inc. Used with permission; Cover of *Shidoshi* magazine used by kind permission of Antarctic Press; **Chapter 6**: *Numa Numa* article used by kind permission of The Salzburg Academy on Media & Global Change; Two covers of *Mixmag* magazine, used by kind permission of Development Hell Ltd.; David Hepworth extract from *Mixmag* magazine used by permission of Development Hell; Keris Ferguson extract used by kind permission of This is Fake DIY; **Chapter 7**: Extract from the *Daily Mail* ('Free DVD inside') used with permission from the *Daily Mail*; Cover of the *Radio Times* used with the kind permission of the *Radio Times* magazine; Wayne Rooney article and photograph from *Toxic* magazine used with permission of Egmont; **Chapter 8**: BBC Radio 1 audience data for period ending September 2008 from Radio Joint Audience Research website: www.rajar.co.uk; **Chapter 9**: Cover and contents page of *Shout* magazine used by kind permission of D.C. Thomson; **Chapter 10**: Samsung advertisement used by permission of Samsung; Orange advertisement used by permission of Orange; Cover of *Beano Max* used by kind permission of D.C. Thomson; Cover of *Shidoshi* magazine used by kind permission of Antarctic Press.

Single User Licence Agreement: AQA GCSE Media Studies ActiveBook CD-ROM

Warning:

This is a legally binding agreement between You (the user or purchasing institution) and Pearson Education Limited of Edinburgh Gate, Harlow, Essex, CM20 2JE, United Kingdom ('PEL').

By retaining this Licence, any software media or accompanying written materials or carrying out any of the permitted activities You are agreeing to be bound by the terms and conditions of this Licence. If You do not agree to the terms and conditions of this Licence, do not continue to use the AQA GCSE Media Studies ActiveBook CD-ROM and promptly return the entire publication (this Licence and all software, written materials, packaging and any other component received with it) with Your sales receipt to Your supplier for a full refund.

Intellectual Property Rights:

This AQA GCSE Media Studies ActiveBook CD-ROM consists of copyright software and data. All intellectual property rights, including the copyright is owned by PEL or its licensors and shall remain vested in them at all times. You only own the disk on which the software is supplied. If You do not continue to do only what You are allowed to do as contained in this Licence you will be in breach of the Licence and PEL shall have the right to terminate this Licence by written notice and take action to recover from you any damages suffered by PEL as a result of your breach.

The PEL name, PEL logo and all other trademarks appearing on the software and AQA GCSE Media Studies ActiveBook CD-ROM are trademarks of PEL. You shall not utilise any such trademarks for any purpose whatsoever other than as they appear on the software and AQA GCSE Media Studies ActiveBook CD-ROM.

Yes, You can:

1. use this AQA GCSE Media Studies ActiveBook CD-ROM on Your own personal computer as a single individual user. You may make a copy of the AQA GCSE Media Studies ActiveBook CD-ROM in machine readable form for backup purposes only. The backup copy must include all copyright information contained in the original.

No, You cannot:

1. copy this AQA GCSE Media Studies ActiveBook CD-ROM (other than making one copy for back-up purposes as set out in the Yes, You can table above);

2. alter, disassemble, or modify this AQA GCSE Media Studies ActiveBook CD-ROM, or in any way reverse engineer, decompile or create a derivative product from the contents of the database or any software included in it:

3. include any materials or software data from the AQA GCSE Media Studies ActiveBook CD-ROM in any other product or software materials;

4. rent, hire, lend, sub-licence or sell the AQA GCSE Media Studies ActiveBook CD-ROM;

5. copy any part of the documentation except where specifically indicated otherwise;

6. use the software in any way not specified above without the prior written consent of PEL;

7. Subject the software, AQA GCSE Media Studies ActiveBook CD-ROM or any PEL content to any derogatory treatment or use them in such a way that would bring PEL into disrepute or cause PEL to incur liability to any third party.

Grant of Licence:

PEL grants You, provided You only do what is allowed under the 'Yes, You can' table above, and do nothing under the 'No, You cannot' table above, a non-exclusive, non-transferable Licence to use this AQA GCSE Media Studies ActiveBook CD-ROM.

The terms and conditions of this Licence become operative when using this AQA GCSE Media Studies ActiveBook CD-ROM.

Limited Warranty:

PEL warrants that the disk or CD-ROM on which the software is supplied is free from defects in material and workmanship in normal use for ninety (90) days from the date You receive it. This warranty is limited to You and is not transferable.

This limited warranty is void if any damage has resulted from accident, abuse, misapplication, service or modification by someone other than PEL. In no event shall PEL be liable for any damages whatsoever arising out of installation of the software, even if advised of the possibility of such damages. PEL will not be liable for any loss or damage of any nature suffered by any party as a result of reliance upon or reproduction of any errors in the content of the publication.

PEL does not warrant that the functions of the software meet Your requirements or that the media is compatible with any computer system on which it is used or that the operation of the software will be unlimited or error free. You assume responsibility for selecting the software to achieve Your intended results and for the installation of, the use of and the results obtained from the software.

PEL shall not be liable for any loss or damage of any kind (except for personal injury or death) arising from the use of this AQA GCSE Media Studies ActiveBook CD-ROM or from errors, deficiencies or faults therein, whether such loss or damage is caused by negligence or otherwise.

The entire liability of PEL and your only remedy shall be replacement free of charge of the components that do not meet this warranty.

No information or advice (oral, written or otherwise) given by PEL or PEL's agents shall create a warranty or in any way increase the scope of this warranty.

To the extent the law permits, PEL disclaims all other warranties, either express or implied, including by way of example and not limitation, warranties of merchantability and fitness for a particular purpose in respect of this AQA GCSE Media Studies ActiveBook CD-ROM.

Termination:

This Licence shall automatically terminate without notice from PEL if You fail to comply with any of its provisions or the purchasing institution becomes insolvent or subject to receivership, liquidation or similar external administration. PEL may also terminate this Licence by notice in writing. Upon termination for whatever reason You agree to destroy the AQA GCSE Media Studies ActiveBook CD-ROM and any back-up copies and delete any part of the AQA GCSE Media Studies ActiveBook CD-ROM stored on your computer.

Governing Law:

This Licence will be governed by and construed in accordance with English law.

© Pearson Education Limited 2009

Toys and Games

TIME-LIFE BOOKS

Alexandria, Virginia

Toys and Games

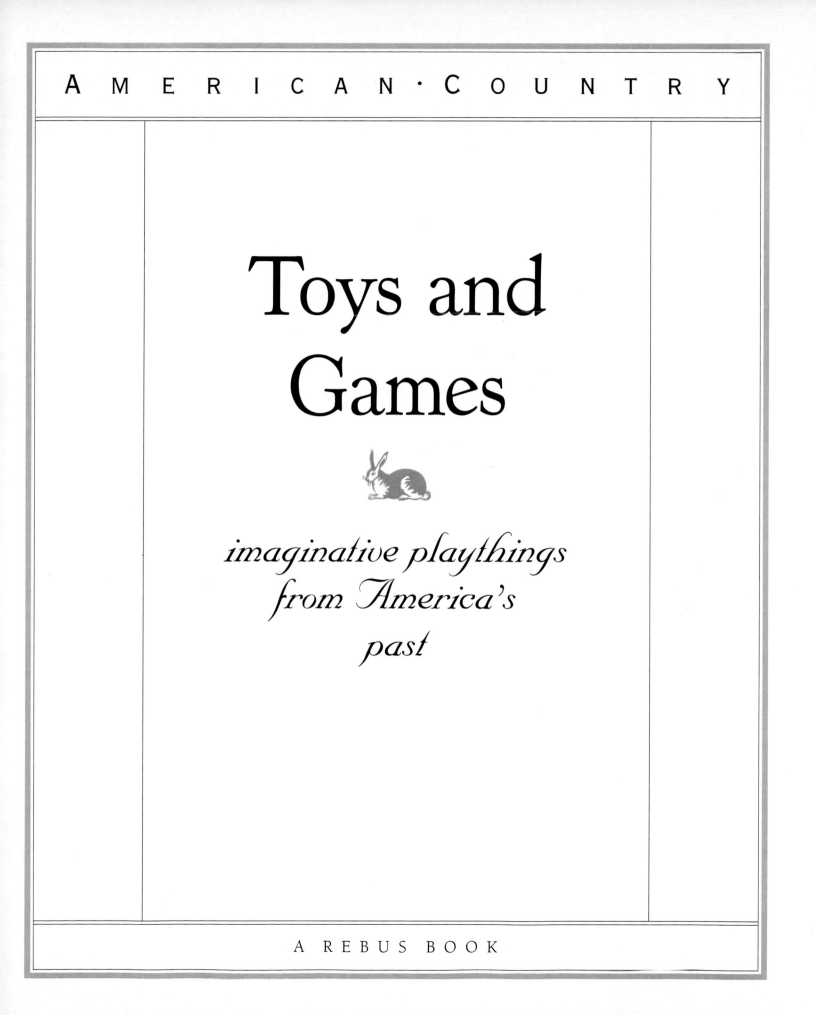

*imaginative playthings
from America's
past*

A R E B U S B O O K

CONTENTS

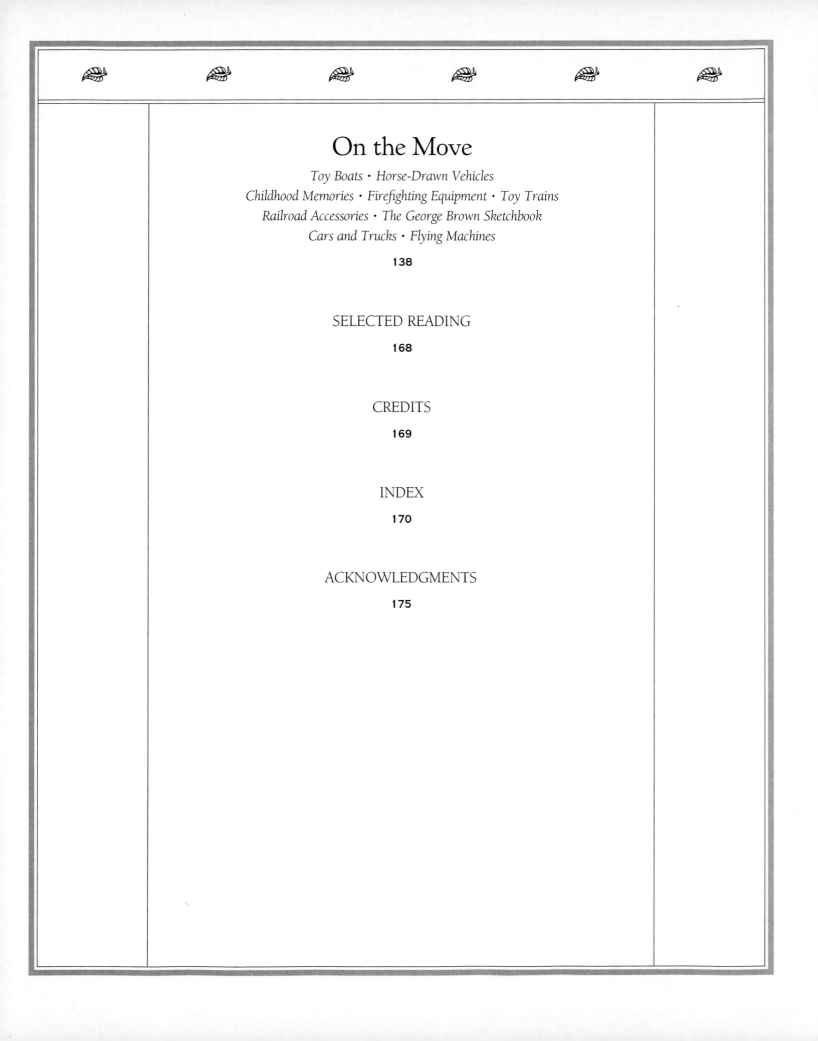

On the Move

*Toy Boats · Horse-Drawn Vehicles
Childhood Memories · Firefighting Equipment · Toy Trains
Railroad Accessories · The George Brown Sketchbook
Cars and Trucks · Flying Machines*

138

Remarkable for both their inventiveness and their quality of craftsmanship, the toys and games presented in this volume provide an overview of the vast range of commercially made playthings available to American children from the colonial period into the 1900s. Homemade rag dolls and other folk toys also had an important place in American childhood, but those that could be bought off the shelf were especially coveted, and have their own particular story to tell.

That story stretches surprisingly far back in time, given the hardships of colonial life and a long-lived Puritan sentiment equating play with sin. Shipments of toys are known to have arrived in Boston Harbor at least as early as 1712, and manufactured playthings were widespread among prosperous families by the middle of the century. Most were imported, and probably included treats like the "neat dress'd Wax Baby," "Grocers Shop," and "Tunbridge Tea Sett" that appeared on a Christmas list George Washington made up for his stepchildren in 1759.

The "Tunbridge" in Washington's tea set referred to the Royal Tunbridge Fair in England, one of the many trade fairs held for centuries throughout Europe. At these noisy, colorful bazaars, toy sellers filled their stalls with dolls, carved animals, hobbyhorses, and a host of captivating trinkets, such as whistles and pinwheels. Celebrated for their goods, some of the fairs lasted into the 1900s, eventually attracting buyers from around the world. The founder of F. A. O. Schwarz, established in New York City in 1862 (and now the oldest existing toy store in America), traveled to the Leipzig Fair in Germany each spring to make his selections, and the practice was common among American merchants up until World War I.

That is not to say that there were no toymakers in America, where small workshops were in fact crafting playthings by the 1700s. It was not until after the Civil War, however, that any large-scale production occurred. At that time, technological advances, most notably in color lithography and in the manufacture of cast iron and tinplate, began to revolutionize the toy industry, enabling Americans to compete with European trade. Business boomed as small companies grew bigger, turning out dozens of toys—often with interchangeable parts—in a single day; in the 1870s, the annual output of some major American firms is believed to have numbered between forty and fifty million items.

In a never-ending quest for novelty, toymakers raced to outdo one another, caught up in the excitement of inventing and patenting devices that would make their dolls walk better, their trolleys clang louder, or their horses gallop faster than those of their competitors. Enlightened ideas on the nature of appropriate childhood behavior also brought more diversions into the American household, as playing with dolls, toys, games, and puzzles was increasingly regarded as good for the character. A broader price range opened up the market as well. By the early 1900s, some kind of commercially made plaything—be it a top-of-the-line special, an inexpensive copy, or at the very least, a tin penny toy—would find a place in virtually every American nursery.

Small Friends

*favorite dolls and
stuffed animals*

By the Victorian era, playing with dolls was considered not only a pleasurable pastime, but also valuable preparation for parenthood. While dreaming and prattling with her doll, "the child becomes a girl, the girl becomes a maiden, and the maiden a woman," asserted an 1869 article in *Godey's Lady's Book and Magazine,* adding that "a little girl without a doll is nearly as unhappy and quite as impossible as a wife without children."

The store-bought dolls owned by American children came primarily from Europe, which remained the center of doll manufacturing into the 1900s. While some, such as fine wax dolls, were affordable only to wealthy families, mass production eventually made most types, including those of porcelain, bisque, papier-mâché, cloth, and paper, widely available to a growing middle class. Their popularity as "small friends" was rivaled only by that of stuffed animals, most notably those produced by the German maker Margarete Steiff; while Steiff produced hundreds of different animals, she is best known for an American favorite, the stuffed bear, which she began exporting to America in 1904.

The detailed garments worn by early dolls might be stitched at home or tailored by professionals who specialized in making such clothing.

Wooden Dolls

Owned by an English convent student, the rare William and Mary nun doll above left dates to around 1690 (it was later taken to Korea); the English Queen Anne doll above right is from the early 1700s.

Readily available and easily worked, wood was one of the earliest materials to be used in manufacturing dolls. The main areas for European woodcarving were in the forests of the Austrian Tyrol and what is now Germany, most notably in and around such towns as Sonneberg and Nuremberg, which were well known for their toys by the early 1700s. Peddled at markets, lathe-turned wooden dolls were produced as part of a well-organized cottage industry involving entire villages. In a system still influenced by medieval guild rules, there was a distinct division of labor: members of one family would do the carving, while members of another specialized in painting the dolls.

Somewhat similar in appearance to the German versions, English wooden dolls of that time were also lathe-turned and hand-finished. Early English wooden dolls are generally classified by the period in which they were made: William and Mary (1688-1702), Queen Anne (1702-1714), and Georgian (1714-circa 1800). While there are

Continued

The circa 1735 carved Georgian doll opposite, with characteristic spade-shaped hands and dotted eyelashes, wears her original silk dress and shoes adorned with tiny metal buckles.

Made with plaster mask faces, the English dolls at right date to the early 19th century. Although such dolls were crafted rather crudely, they might still be elegantly dressed. The twins in the foreground, for example, wear silk-lined and embroidered net gowns in the fashionable Empire style.

subtle variations, the dolls from these periods were quite similar in design, with placid, rosy-cheeked faces distinguished by high foreheads, wide, almond-shaped eyes, and tiny lips pressed into rather prim expressions. Featuring finely carved faces, jointed limbs, and scooplike hands with individual fingers, these figures displayed a high level of craftsmanship.

By the early 1800s, however, English toymakers were producing cheaper dolls that showed far less attention to detail. Instead of carved wooden limbs, the toys were fitted with arms and legs of rolled linen, which ended in stubby hands and feet. The once intricately carved faces, in turn,

were replaced by plaster "masks" quickly applied to wooden knob heads.

These mask-faced dolls were produced to compete with the inexpensive dolls imported from Bavaria and Austria that were popular during the 1800s. The less expensive Germanic dolls, which were also shipped throughout the Continent and to America, are known as peg woodens since they were jointed with tiny pegs. Peg woodens resembled the 18th-century English dolls in body and limb, but had smaller, sweeter faces. Their carved or painted hair was fashionably coiffed, sometimes with decorative combs that earned the dolls the name "tuck combs."

Only six inches tall, the early-19th-century German "peg woodens" above were used in a dollhouse. These "tuck combs" all have carved hair and decorative combs— even the three figures wearing silk floss wigs.

Papier-Mâché Dolls

Dating from the second half of the 1800s, the papier-mâché dolls at right were all made with cloth bodies. The largest figure in the group, measuring over two feet tall, was manufactured around 1875 by Ludwig Greiner of Philadelphia. The two smallest dolls, both with glass eyes, were produced around 1855 in Germany; the others are also thought to be German.

Moderately priced, the pert, round-faced papier-mâché dolls that were made both here and abroad were a favorite among 19th-century children. An economical material made from paper pulp, papier-mâché was ideal for doll heads since it could be easily molded into detailed facial features, yet dried with a durable surface. The early papier-mâché dolls, dating to the 1820s and 1830s, were sold as complete dolls, with kidskin bodies and wooden legs and arms. Ready-made dolls from the 1850s onward were more likely to have cloth bodies; by this time, however, it was also common for the heads to be sold separately to buyers, who would craft the bodies at home.

While Germany was the center of European papier-mâché doll manufacturing, there was some production in France and England. In America, the most notable maker was Ludwig Greiner, a German immigrant who in 1858 obtained the first U.S. patent ever issued for a doll's head. With their pleasant faces and wavy, center-parted hair, Greiner's dolls were close cousins to their European counterparts.

The papier-mâché dolls above were made in Europe around 1835. The central figure, 7¾ inches tall,
has wooden limbs and a kidskin body; all three dolls wear their original dresses.

Wax Dolls

Naturalistic coloring and glass eyes give these wax dolls a particularly realistic look. The dipped-wax girl above left dates to about 1845, while the poured-wax baby above right was made around 1900, probably by the Pierotti family of London; each strand of its human hair was inserted individually.

Perhaps the greatest pleasure for a little girl of days past was to possess a luxurious wax doll imported from Europe. Although fragile, wax had a translucence that yielded an especially realistic look; used mostly for the doll heads and limbs, it was well-suited to modeling the details—tiny, perfect fingernails, soft dimples, delicately arched eyebrows—that made these dolls look so lifelike.

The properties of wax were turned to great advantage by two families of Italian dollmakers living in London—the Pierottis, who made dolls from the 1790s to the 1930s, and the Montanaris, who worked between the 1850s and 1880s. Both firms excelled in the exacting poured-wax technique, which involved building up layers of wax in molds. However, manufacturers in Sonneberg, Germany—the other primary production center for wax dolls—preferred the less costly method of dipping papier-mâché or wooden forms into liquid wax.

While some wax dolls had molded tresses or wigs, the finest were made with strands of human hair or mohair actually rooted into their heads. In the ultimate quest for realism, the Pierotti firm took commissions for portrait dolls: "Likenesses modell'd and casts taken," they advertised, adding that "by sending in their own hair," girls could have it used for their dolls' stylish coiffures.

The clothing of wax dolls like those at left ranged from simple outfits to elaborate, professionally tailored ensembles. The circa 1880 cloth-bodied Victorian bride, who stands twenty-six inches tall, is dressed in a nine-piece wedding outfit complete with red ribbon garters. The other two wax figures, from Germany, are garbed more modestly and have painted shoes, an inexpensive alternative to those stitched of fabric or leather.

China Dolls

Dolls with china heads and limbs were produced in Europe as early as the 1750s, but did not become popular until around the 1840s, when costs had been reduced enough to make the toys widely affordable. While some dolls were made as a sideline by such established porcelain firms as Meissen and Royal Copenhagen, the majority were turned out by women and children in thriving workshops, most notably in the German doll-making centers of Sonneberg and Nuremburg.

Painted and fired to a high gloss, porcelain heads were produced by the thousands and marketed all over the world. In the 1870s, one New York importer advertised china heads in eighteen different sizes, ranging from 2¾ inches to 8¾ inches and costing from sixty-three cents to fifteen dollars a dozen wholesale. Heads could be purchased separately or already attached to a body of wood, cloth, or kid; it was also possible for a buyer to choose both a head and a body in a store and to sew them together at home. In any event, if a head were to break, as frequently happened during play, it could be easily replaced.

China dolls, often distinguished by a delicate pinkish complexion and rosy cheeks, are particularly notable for their coiffures, which followed the fashions of the day. In general, dolls from the 1830s and 1840s had their hair pulled into a bun, or done in the twist said to have been favored by the young Queen Victoria. Those made in the 1850s wore it with a center part, often with a snood; a wrapped braid was popular later in the century.

The mid-19th-century dolls at left all feature china heads that were made in Germany. The small doll in the foreground, 7½ inches tall, is especially fancy; she has porcelain legs and arms, and her coiffure is ornamented with a gilded bandeau. Black hair was the rule; china dolls seldom appeared as blondes before the last quarter of the 19th century.

A GIFT FROM PARIS

This "lady doll," shown with her trunk of clothes, was brought from France to America in the 1860s.

Among the loveliest playthings little girls could dream of owning in the mid-1800s were French "lady dolls"—delicate bisque or glazed porcelain figures dressed in the latest fashions. While such fancy dolls were imported here for sale, many were also brought directly from France by travelers. At the time, Paris represented the epitome of fashion and culture, and wealthy Americans making the Grand Tour were eager to carry home stylish French clothes and furnishings for themselves, as well as stylish playthings for their children.

The porcelain lady doll above, which features blue glass eyes and a wig of real hair, was one such present, given to Emily Woolsey Soutter of New York City by her godmother in the 1860s. The doll, measuring seventeen inches tall, is accompanied by a little paper-lined wooden trunk that still bears the label of the dollmaker's exclusive shop where both items were bought: Maison Huret, 22 Boulevard Montmartre, Paris. As was the custom, the wardrobe and accessories were added to over many years, and now number forty pieces. Some were purchased at Huret and other toy stores, and some were homemade. All are miniature replicas of the sort of finery a young lady would herself have enjoyed, including a dressing kit, elegant silk dresses, beribbonned hats and bonnets, a fur muff, a fan, lace-trimmed pantaloons, and leather shoes.

Bisque dolls like the European examples at right, dating from the late 1800s to the early 1900s, came outfitted with an array of clothes and accessories that were miniature versions of those a real child might have. The circa 1889 German Simon & Halbig doll in the sleigh is warmed by bunting and a plush hat. The little girl in the blue plaid dress, circa 1895, is a classic French "bébé" made in Paris by the Jumeau firm.

Bisque Dolls

P roduced primarily in Europe, bisque dolls, made of translucent, matte-surfaced porcelain tinted a delicate pink, were popular by the 1860s. The early craze was for well-dressed "lady dolls," but by the late 1870s a new doll had begun to appear in shop windows: the famous French "bébé." This appealing child doll featured a new body type: the composition limbs and head were crafted with ball joints and strung together with elastic, which allowed the doll to be posed in a number of lifelike positions. Later in the century, the dolls were also detailed with mechanized "sleep eyes" that blinked closed, or "flirted" from side to side, enhancing the naturalistic effect.

The chief bisque doll producer of the period was the Parisian firm founded by Pierre-François Jumeau, which was active until 1899. Jumeau dolls are noted for their pretty faces, with big eyes, heavily fringed lashes, and delicate mouths. The dolls were elegantly turned out in coiffed wigs, and boasted stylish wardrobes. Other noted French dollmakers of the period included Casimir Bru and Jules Steiner, whose bisque bébés rivaled Jumeau dolls in quality and beauty.

Many German firms also began crafting bisque dolls in the late 1800s, overshadowing the French market by the early 1900s with high-quality wares at lower prices. Because Germany was already home to well-established doll and porcelain industries, the resources were available for well-known companies such as Simon & Halbig, Kämmer & Reinhardt, and Armand Marseille to become leading bisque doll producers.

The five German bisque dolls at right were purchased around 1925 at the F.A.O. Schwarz toy store in New York City, where they had been dressed as a contemporary bridal party and used for display. Their costumes, including handkerchief-hemmed dresses and gold lamé bandeaux, were professionally hand-tailored and reflect the fashions of the day.

The cloth dolls above, molded with glue-stiffened stockinet and detailed with oil paint, are the work of two of the earliest doll manufacturers in America. The little girl was made by Izannah Walker around 1870 and features the painted shoes and hair typical of her dolls. The little boy was crafted at the turn of the century by Martha Chase.

Put together with a few fabric scraps and a lot of imagination, homemade rag dolls have been friends to children for centuries. It was only logical for professional dollmakers to capitalize on the appeal of these soft toys, which, unlike more fragile wax and porcelain dolls, could be squeezed and loved without being broken. Recalling old-fashioned rag dolls, commercial cloth dolls also drew their success from a market for nostalgia, and many were modeled on the homemade toys "grandma used to make."

Among the earliest professionally made dolls in America were those produced by Izannah Walker, a somewhat eccentric Yankee entrepreneur from Central Falls, Rhode Island. Walker dabbled in carpentry and real estate, tinkered with various inventions, and was

crafting dolls for sale by the 1850s. In 1873, she secured a patent for a press-molded doll made of stockinet, an elastic knitted fabric. "My doll is inexpensive, easily kept clean, and not apt to injure a young child which may fall on it," boasted her patent papers. Walker dolls were also double-stuffed to yield a flexible surface that helped prevent the oil-painted features and hair from cracking off.

Inspired by a Walker doll she had owned as a child, another American dollmaker, Martha Chase, began producing her own stockinet dolls in the 1880s. Her "unbreakable" dolls were so successful that she eventually built a small factory behind her house in Pawtucket, Rhode Island. With their jointed knees, hips, shoulders, and elbows, Chase dolls were generally more natural-looking than the Walker toys. By 1922, they were

Continued

Cloth Dolls

Among the cloth dolls at left is the large, thirty-inch-tall figure, sewn and painted by hand in the 1870s. It was such classic rag dolls that inspired the designs for commercially made versions like the three small Babyland Rag Dolls also shown here, manufactured by the E. I. Horsman Company of New York City. The two Babyland girls, made around 1917, have painted faces, while the features of the Dutch boy are lithographed; the company started using the printing technique in 1907.

27

The dolls at right were crafted in the 1920s and 1930s by the Italian firm of Enrico and Elena Scavini, under the trademark name Lenci. In addition to their appealing faces, these felt dolls are notable for their handsome costumes. Many Lenci toys, like the little tennis player shown here, were dressed in sporting outfits.

available in nineteen models, including half a dozen based on the characters in *Alice in Wonderland*. The best sellers, however, were Chase's pudgy-faced children, which came in four sizes, from newborn to toddler.

As the 20th century progressed, more and more American cloth doll makers tried their hand in the business. Providing competition to Chase dolls, for example, were the well-known Kamkins dolls, designed by Louise Kampes. Crafted in her Atlantic City, New Jersey, studio, the Kamkins dolls were sold on the boardwalk between 1919 and 1925. Featuring bright blue eyes and gentle faces, these dolls were characterized by an appealing simplicity.

European cloth dolls, on the other hand, could be quite sophisticated. Those by the Italian firm of Enrico and Elena Scavini, for instance—which began turning out pressed felt dolls in the 1920s under the name Lenci—were designed by professional artists and intended to expose children to "good taste." Expensive from the start, Lencis were distinguished by finely painted faces, which often featured side-glancing eyes, and exquisitely designed garments. Also known for the quality of their clothing were dolls by the English maker Norah Wellings, who started a soft-toy factory in England in 1926 and sold distinctive playthings made of felt, plush, and velvet.

Another noted European maker was the German artist Käthe Kruse, whose dolls were designed to give children "an education toward motherliness." The all-cloth Kruse dolls produced from 1910 through World War II looked and felt especially lifelike, and were crafted with waterproofed muslin so that they could be given baths; their sweet, emotive faces made them especially easy for a young mother to love.

The 1920s cloth dolls above include, from left to right, a Buckingham Palace guard and a South Sea islander by Norah Wellings of England; two sweet-faced children by German toymaker Käthe Kruse; and a Kamkins boy doll from the Louise Kampes workshop in Atlantic City, New Jersey.

THE RAGGEDY ANN STORY

One of the most beloved, and certainly best-selling, cloth dolls ever made is Raggedy Ann. With her big black eyes, tousled yarn hair, and striped leggings, she has charmed children for most of this century—as have her younger brother, Raggedy Andy, and other dolls modeled after characters in a series of "Raggedy" children's books by Johnny Gruelle.

A cartoonist and illustrator from Norwalk, Connecticut, Gruelle also dabbled in toymaking, and patented his design for Raggedy Ann in 1915. The doll's name was inspired by two poems penned by family friend James Whitcomb Riley: "The Raggedy Man" and "Little Orphant Annie." Gruelle's idea was to sell the doll along with children's books that would feature Raggedy Ann as the central character. As the entrepreneur went to work writing and illustrating the first book, his wife and sister began sewing the dolls.

Complete with a sugary preface detailing his daughter Marcella's discovery of Raggedy Ann in an attic, *Raggedy Ann Stories* was published by the P. F. Volland Company in 1918. Both the book and the doll were an instant success. Demand soon overwhelmed the production capability of the Gruelle women, so Volland found a factory to take over the doll-

making that same year. After the publisher went out of business in 1935, the licensing rights were disputed, and passed on successively through several different companies. The dolls were so popular that many people also sewed their own at home.

As a result, Raggedy Ann's appearance changed over the years. The earliest commercially made dolls featured brown yarn hair and black shoe-button eyes, and the so-called "candy heart" (actually of brass or plastic) inserted in the chest. In time, Raggedy Ann became a redhead and her button eyes were often replaced with those of tin or plastic—or were printed right on her cloth face. Sometimes the doll's upturned mouth was marked with red lips and her triangle nose outlined in black; her "I Love You" heart was printed in red on her chest.

By the time Gruelle died in 1938, he had written more than twenty Raggedy Ann and Andy books, and as many as ten million copies had been sold. The Raggedy doll family, in turn, expanded as companions from the storybooks inspired other dolls. In 1920 Raggedy Ann was joined by Raggedy Andy, who usually wore a round hat and a plaid shirt. Ann's mammy, Beloved Belindy, and the long-faced Percy Policeman were other favorites.

The Raggedy family at left includes Anns, Andys, Beloved Belindy, and Percy Policeman, made through the 1940s. The apron-clad doll seated in the black chair dates from 1918, the year the first Raggedy Ann book came out.

Printed Cloth Dolls

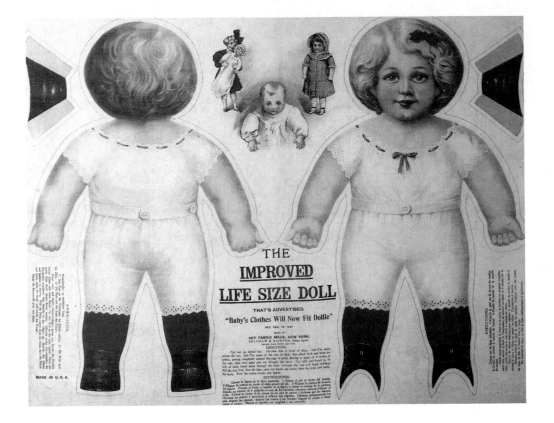

Introduced in the 1880s and popular into the 1940s, printed cloth dolls were made possible by improvements in color lithography, which provided an inexpensive way to transfer patterns onto fabric. Widely affordable, most of the dolls were designed to be cut and stitched at home, and were made from printed fabric sheets sold at fabric shops and general stores; some kits could also be mail-ordered.

Among the best-known American firms to make use of the four-color lithography process was the Arnold Print Works, a North Adams, Massachusetts, textile manufacturer that produced a range of animals and storybook characters. Also active was the Art Fabric Mills of New York City, which specialized in figures such as Buster Brown and Punch and Judy, and advertised a life-size doll that could wear the clothes of a two-year-old. In this century, printed cloth dolls were also used by food manufacturers as advertising premiums. In 1925, for example, the Kellogg Company offered Goldilocks and the Three Bears in exchange for four cereal box tops and thirty cents.

The 1900 Art Fabric Mills pattern above, for a life-size doll, was printed with directions in several different languages. The dolls at right include a Skye terrier named "Tatters," a rooster, Red Riding Hood, and a cat, all from Arnold Print Works; a bear by the Saalfield Publishing Company in Ohio; an English rag doll; and a 1920s Cream of Wheat chef offered as a premium for ten cents and a box top.

Stuffed Bears

The most familiar of all stuffed animals is probably the bear, which made its formal debut in the early 1900s, soon after President Teddy Roosevelt's much-publicized refusal to kill a tethered bear cub while on a hunting trip. A Brooklyn novelty store owner named Morris Michtom capitalized on the to-do surrounding the 1902 incident by having his wife make two bears out of mohair. Displayed in his shop, the toys created a sensation, and Michtom produced more bears for sale; with written permission from the White House, he called them "Teddy's Bears." (Michtom's business eventually evolved into the Ideal Toy Company.)

At about the same time, Margarete Steiff, a German seamstress who had founded a toy business in 1880, began crafting her own bears, with sweet, personable faces. The Steiff stuffed animals were spotted at the 1903 Leipzig toy fair by an American buyer who arranged to ship them across the Atlantic.

Soft, lovable bears, all generally referred to by the public as teddies, were soon being manufactured in quantity in England, America, and Germany (Steiff manufactured 974,000 bears in 1907 alone). Usually made of plush or mohair, with black button or glass eyes, each had an irresistibly befuddled expression, and its own beguiling personality.

Stuffed with sawdust, straw, or excelsior, the teddy bears at left were made in Germany and America from 1905 to the 1940s.

Paper
Dolls

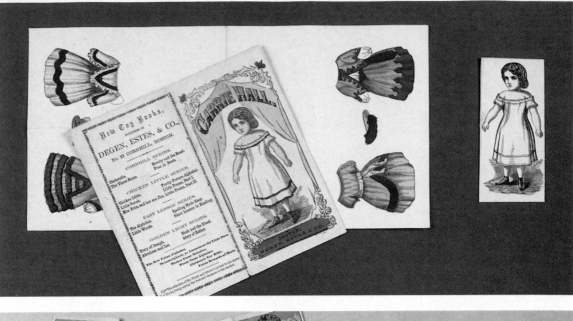

Dating from the second half of the 1800s, the American-made paper dolls at right—which were never cut out—reveal the remarkable detail with which the printed figures and costumes of these inexpensive toys were rendered. They were made by Degen Estes of Boston, Peter G. Thomson of Cincinnati, and Clark Austin & Smith and McLoughlin Brothers, both of New York City.

Opening worlds of possibilities to any child with imagination and a little pocket money, paper dolls were one of the great successes of the toy world, developing hand in hand with the printing industry. Engraved and hand-tinted, the first known paper doll set commercially produced in America, which chronicled "The History and Adventures of Little Henry," was published in 1812 by J. Belcher of Boston.

Paper dolls, however, appear to have been relatively scarce before the mid-1800s, when the lithography process came into use. While a number of companies began printing paper dolls at this time, the leader in the field was the New York City firm of McLoughlin Brothers, who published their first dolls around 1857. The McLoughlins kept close pace with refinements in printing technology, moving from hand-tinting to full-color printing as developments allowed. With each new advance, the paper toys produced by their firm, as well as by other companies here and abroad, became more widely available and less expensive. They were sold in sheets, booklets, and boxes, published in magazines, and packaged with children's books so that young readers could use the paper characters to act out favorite stories; individual sheets could cost as little as a penny apiece.

In addition to their reasonable price, paper dolls were appealing for their vast variety. The dolls represented all manner of figures, from his-

Continued

The Fanny Gray set above, published in Boston in 1854, is among the earliest known commercially made paper doll toys produced in this country. Fanny's five costumes were not mere changes of clothing, but "action costumes" designed to show her engaged in various activities, such as selling matches or walking her dog.

The paper doll above was modeled on the world-famous Italian ballerina Maria Taglioni, and came with costumes drawn from the roles she created; the set was produced around 1840, probably in France. The boxed sets of paper dolls at right, manufactured in France around 1830, included hand-colored costumes depicting both high-style Parisian fashions and traditional provincial dress. Hats, wigs, and headdresses were among the accessories provided.

A "puppet" paper doll, the little dancer above was designed to shift her eyes from side to side when her legs were moved. She had several costumes and was probably printed in Germany in the 1870s for sale abroad. The boxed set of dolls at left, possibly made as early as 1830, included a boy and a girl figure, as well as twelve costumes for each— one for every month of the year.

Dating to the mid-1800s, the rare German mechanical paper toy above was lithographed and hand-colored. It featured a figure that could "walk" when its base was rolled, eight character changes, and background scenery.

torical and mythological characters to contemporary personalities. Many of the dolls had identities and lives all their own, detailed in booklets that came boxed along with them. The character of Fanny Gray, for example, a paper doll created by Crosby Nichols & Company of Boston in 1854, was an orphan who was rescued from a pitiful existence selling matches on the street by a long-lost uncle. The beautifully lithographed Fanny Gray set came not only with five different costumes, but also with a background scene showing "The Cottage Where Fanny Lived."

While most paper dolls were enjoyable for their detailed outfits, some offered more sophisticated fun, with designs that went far beyond the simple notion of changing clothes. One animated paper figure, for example, made in 19th-century Germany, was attached to a mechanical base, which, when moved, shuffled the feet to make it walk. The paper toys known as puppet dolls, in turn, were made with moving joints so that the figures could "dance." Still other dolls came equipped with elaborate paper tableaux to provide a colorful background setting.

The two paper figures above could be dressed as sixteen different gods and goddesses from classical mythology, and came with a text printed in French and German; the set was published in Vienna in 1841. The English firm of S. J. Fuller produced the dolls at left in the early 1800s. The books that came with them told moralizing tales, which were illustrated with the costumed figures.

Dollhouse albums—homemade books of colorful scenes used as backdrops for playing with paper dolls—were an offshoot of the craze for scrapbook art that swept America during the second half of the 19th century. At the time, it was fashionable among the middle class to collect and paste down the inexpensive fancy paper goods that new printing technology was making increasingly available.

In addition to greeting cards and box labels, albums were filled with colorful die-cut images made specifically for scrapbook projects and known, fittingly, as scraps. From a dollhouse album made around the 1870s, the pages above show just how much of an artistic exercise a scrapbook could be. Especially elaborate, the volume opens to reveal some twenty different interiors, including everything from baroni-

DOLLHOUSE ALBUM

al halls to a well-stocked kitchen.

In creating the rooms on the blank pages of this scrapbook, the maker incorporated an imaginative range of printed pieces, including magazine illustrations, trade cards, scraps, and bits of fancy craft paper. There are also elements cut from the min-

iature paper theater sets and room scenes popular in the Victorian era.

Characterized by the fantastical look that often typified such scrapbook scenes, the interiors were not meant to be terribly realistic. They do, however, reflect the prevailing decorating styles of the day, and

are particularly remarkable for their rich color and for the sense of perspective—if sometimes skewed— that they manage to convey. The attention to detail is also a visual delight: fireplaces blaze with flames, flowers sprout from vases, and windows open to reveal distant vistas.

44

Small Worlds

a child's fantasies in miniature

Among the most common diversions once found in the American nursery were miniatures, perhaps the ultimate playthings for letting young imaginations run free. Ranging from arks, zoos, and circuses to dollhouses and their myriad furnishings, such toys have a long history—dating in some cases to medieval times. Their golden age, however, was the 19th century, when they were marketed by toymakers not only for their potential to amuse, but also for their ability to prepare children for responsible adulthood.

A little girl could practice for her future years as a housewife, for example, by holding a tea party with toy china, overseeing a household for her dolls, shopping at a miniature grocery, or preparing an imaginary meal in a doll-size kitchen. Colorfully printed paper theaters and scenes, in turn, provided exposure to drama and history, while zoos, arks, and circuses introduced children to exotic animal species. Whatever their theme, such toys had a universal appeal, as children delighted in playthings that gave them an opportunity to re-create the world around them.

Introduced around the 1870s, dollhouses covered with lithographed paper offered
an inexpensive alternative to finely crafted wooden versions.

Animal Toys

Animals, both familiar barnyard species and exotic types exhibited in zoos and traveling menageries, were once a part of nearly every child's life. Toymakers, of course, were quick to capitalize on their appeal, and produced figures that represented the animal kingdom in all its endless variety. Germany especially, with its numerous family enterprises and tradition of handcraftsmanship, was a man-

ufacturing center for animal toys. These were made primarily in the regions of Bavaria and Thuringia for Nuremburg merchants who exported them by the thousands throughout Europe and to America.

Among the most popular animal toys of the 19th and early 20th centuries—indeed, among the most popular of all toys—were Noah's arks. Commonly referred to as Sunday toys because

their biblical theme made them suitable for play on the Sabbath, they came in several styles. The simplest were no more than little wooden huts perched on flat-bottomed rafts, whereas more elaborate arks might feature deep hulls, interior rooms, and fancy architectural details. Many of the toys were fitted with hinged roofs, making them convenient storage boxes for the passengers: Noah and his family, and all manner of ani-mals—sometimes hundreds of them—ranging from tiny ladybugs to lumbering elephants.

Arks were not the only toys that incorporated animals. Domestic creatures, such as cows, sheep, and horses, for example, might be combined with barns, stables, fences, and trees to create a farm, while more exotic species were ideal for a menagerie or zoo complete with cages or pavilions.   *Continued*

Looking more like houses than boats, the Noah's arks at left, all dating from the second half of the 19th century, reflect the varied details of vernacular German architecture. The whimsically scaled figures represent Noah and his family, the pairs of beasts that were saved from the deluge, and, on each rooftop, the dove that brought an olive branch to the ark when the storm was over.

Whatever their use, the animals were generally either molded from a composition substance or crafted in a process that involved lathe-turning a ring of wood to form the profile of a particular figure. The ring would be sawed into numerous slices, each bearing the same profile; these were then detailed with carving, paint, and perhaps flocking. As a result, most of the wooden animals had a somewhat flattened appearance. That the craftspeople had never actually seen a good many of the creatures they were re-creating in miniature also contributed to the stylized look of the toys.

To speed production, toymaking families frequently specialized in just a few different types of animals. One traveler to Germany in 1879 noted visiting a craftswoman who had learned from her mother how to make only goats, elephants, dogs, wolves, and sheep—and who was teaching her children to do the exact same figures. The efficiency of such toymakers was difficult to compete with. Carvers could turn their few animals out in vast quantities, and as the playthings were exported very cheaply, there was little manufacture of animal toys outside Germany before the 20th century.

The colorful painted detail and individual, sometimes befuddled, expressions of the animals made toys like these irresistible to children. For a realistic touch, the manger in the stable above could be filled with actual hay, while the various beasts in the two menageries at right were made with flocked coats. All three animal sets were crafted in Germany and date from the 1860s or 1870s.

The Humpty Dumpty Circus at right, made by the A. Schoenhut Company of Philadelphia, captured all the gaiety and excitement of the big top. Schoenhut's animated figures were exceptional for their clever detailing. The hand-painted animals featured leather ears, and the performers wore realistic cloth costumes.

Circus Toys

🍃

From the late 1700s onward, the circus provided popular entertainment across America. Both small traveling circuses and the three-ring spectacles made famous by Barnum and Bailey drew crowds eager to see performing animals and acrobatic acts. Reflecting the fascination for such attractions, circus toys abounded, and included everything from individual wooden acrobats to entire big top scenes printed on paper. Mechanical hippodromes made with figures that revolved on a platform were especially popular, as were windup clowns. "Parades" of horse-drawn circus wagons filled with animals also evoked the excitement of the circus coming to town.

One of the most elaborate circus toys was the Humpty Dumpty Circus, made by the A. Schoenhut Company of Philadelphia. Produced from 1903 until the 1930s, Schoenhut's circus expanded from the few pieces originally manufactured to include cages, parade wagons, and some sixty painted wooden animals and performers that could be set up in their own ring under a cloth tent. Both the animals and the human figures were especially remarkable because, made with elastics and ball joints, they took on realistic poses. Moreover, the performers, including acrobats, clowns, and ringmaster, were designed with notches in their hands and feet enabling them to swing from a trapeze, perhaps, or snap a whip at snarling lions and tigers. With all its possibilities for fun, Schoenhut's circus was a coveted plaything, and one of the few American toys of the day to be exported to Europe in any quantity.

THE SCHOENHUT LEGACY

In 1872, Albert Schoenhut, a young German immigrant descended from a long line of toy-makers, began a small business in Philadelphia that made toy pianos. By the time of Schoenhut's death in 1912, his six sons had joined the firm, and his single-room workshop had grown into a five-acre complex producing not only pianos, but also hundreds of other amusements.

The toys at right are a sampling of the playthings the A. Schoenhut Company designed before the firm stopped production in 1935. The company is most famous for its Humpty Dumpty Circus, but it introduced other toy sets as well, such as Teddy's [Roosevelt's] Adventures in Africa, and Mary Had a Little Lamb. Other offerings included blocks, balls, and a line of round-bottomed Rolly-Dolly Toys, promoted as "the first toy for the baby." There were also dolls, dollhouses and doll furniture, toy guns and cannons, and wooden boats. And as comic strips captured the public's imagination in the teens and 1920s, the firm introduced toy versions of such characters as Felix the Cat and Bonzo the Pup.

The Schoenhut company prided itself on its fine craftsmanship and its ability to compete with European toymakers. One advertisement that ran during World War I read: "Did you think that all toys came from Germany? You're wrong. One of the largest toy factories is right here in the United States."

Paper Scenes

Produced primarily in Europe, intricate scenes ranging from the ever-popular menagerie and circus to famous battles and other historical events were among the many successful paper toys to emerge in the 1800s. Designed as sets, these imaginary worlds came complete with backdrops, figures, separate scenery—either precut or in ready-to-cut sheets—and instructions for the assembly of the components, which could be quite numerous. The circa 1890 zoological garden at top left, for example, included forty-seven cutout cards, each mounted on a wooden block, representing visitors, entry gates, cages, and nearly one hundred different species of animals. And among the many parts of the complicated seascape at bottom left were boats that "sailed" along slots in the roiling surf; on shore were houses, as well as townsfolk engaged in such activities as fishing and chopping wood.

Paper was a versatile material for these toys, since it could easily be fashioned into an infinite variety of shapes. It was also inexpensive, offering an economical way for toymakers to mass-produce playthings with multiple pieces. The cheapest of the toys were unprinted, intended to be colored in at home; hand-tinted and lithographed paper scenes cost more. "Penny plain," advertised one prominent English toymaker, "twopence coloured."

The circa 1890 paper zoo above and the seacoast
scene at left, dating from around 1865, were made
in Germany. The seascape was color-lithographed,
while the zoo was hand-tinted.

Paper Theaters

The brilliantly colored paper toy at right, entitled Grand Theater of Metamorphoses, *in serious and grotesque representations, was printed in Germany around 1860. Each pair of legs was fitted with two torsos, whose positions could be switched by rotating a wooden pin. The pin could also slide along a horizontal slot in the scenery, allowing a child to move the characters about the stage while changing their identities.*

Playing with the paper theaters that were popular in the 19th century was an ideal way for children to experience the magic of stage life. Given the long-standing passion for drama in England, it is not surprising that the country was a major producer of the toys. One of the earliest and most prolific publishers was the English firm of William West, who introduced some one hundred and forty different versions between 1811 and 1831. Theaters were also produced beginning in the early part of the century in Germany and France; American makers did not offer them until the 1870s.

Paper theaters typically came with a stage, plus all the pieces required for a particular play: scenery, actors, props, script, and often stage directions for manipulating the figures and creating sound effects such as thunder and cannon shots. Many of the toys were modeled on current plays, and publishers of the paper sets sometimes sent artists to live productions so that they could copy the scenery, as well as the actors' costumes and dramatic poses, to ensure accurate renderings. In addition to sets for specific plays, extra ready-to-cut sheets depicting various characters, costumes, and backdrops were available, making it easy for young producers to expand their repertoire.

The two late-19th-century German-made theaters at left came with numerous characters, which could be maneuvered via wire handles. Since the scripts that originally accompanied these theaters have been lost, it is no longer known what dramas the players were meant to perform.

The New York City firm of McLoughlin Brothers issued the American Theatre *above* in the early 20th century. The lithographed paper set was equipped with a grooved wooden stage, on which figures from fairy tales could stand and be moved into different positions; Little Red Riding Hood is enacted here. The late-19th-century shadow theater at right, from Germany, features silhouetted figures with movable limbs.

*Produced by the Milton
Bradley Company of
Springfield, Massachusetts,
in the 1870s, the theater
above measures only 10
inches wide and 7½ inches
high. In addition to this river
view, the hand-tinted
lithographed toy could be
set up with forest and street
scenery. The colorfully lithographed* Theater Imperial
*at left was published by
J. H. Singer of New York
City around 1885. On stage
is the final scene from* The
Battle of Bunker Hill.

Intended for export to English-speaking countries, the two toy grocery stores at right were made in Germany in the second half of the 19th century. Their realistic interiors feature counters and tiny labeled spice drawers, and are filled with goods of the type purveyed in food shops of that era. Scales, pickle barrels, canisters, and foodstuffs could all be purchased individually at toy stores to stock such miniature shops.

Shops and Rooms

The fascination with "playing store" or "playing house" was the inspiration behind miniature shops and rooms, which were manufactured in the second half of the 19th century, primarily in Germany, England, and America. Such toys appealed to children's curiosity about the world around them and to their natural desire to imitate adults. The playthings were also welcomed by parents for their educational value.

Generally of wood or paper, toy shops—descendants of the models of market stalls that were known in Europe as early as the 1600s—were usually made as three-sided interiors that might also feature partial storefronts. The interiors were often amazingly detailed, with carved counters, labeled drawers, and glazed display cases all presided over by a doll "proprietor." The store shelves were invariably well stocked with appropriate wares, which came with the shop or could be purchased and added separately, piece by piece. Grocery stores, for example, might be equipped with everything from grain sacks to bottles of patent medicines, while butcher shops displayed joints of meat hanging from tiny hooks. Food shops were the most common, but toymakers also produced facsimiles of basket, glassware, and millinery shops, as well as apothecaries.

Equally elaborate were miniature house interiors, made of wood, paper, or tinplate. The first toy rooms were the intricate Nuremberg

Continued

The German-made general store above dates from the mid-19th century, and is especially elaborate, with a carved wooden counter and leaded windows. The lady shopkeeper presides over an emporium filled with period wares, including tobacco boxes, baskets of fruits and vegetables, and sewing utensils.

The two-story miniature room setting above, handcrafted in New England from a crate, dates from the mid-1800s.

kitchens, crafted in that German city beginning in the 1600s. Extensively exported to the States, such kitchens were popular well into the 20th century, partly because there was virtually no limit to the miniature utensils and cookwares that could be used to outfit them.

Scaled-down versions of many other rooms of a household, made both commercially and by doting parents, were also favored. Children found it just as much fun to own a fancy drawing room or a bedroom, for instance, and decorate it with the stylish furnishings of the day, as they did to cook up an imaginary meal in a toy kitchen.

The circa 1900 two-room interior at top, from Pennsylvania, is a homemade version of the manufactured rooms available at the time. Made in Germany around 1860, the high-style parlor, middle, retains its original wall detailing and brocade-covered chairs and sofa "gilded" with embossed paper. The interior at bottom was decorated to reflect a middle-class German drawing room of the mid-1800s with all its accessories; the yarn winder on the table is a rare piece.

The origins of the dollhouse date back to the 1500s and 1600s. At that time, it was fashionable among German and Dutch aristocrats to collect miniatures and exhibit them in little houses, or in rooms built into display cabinets. "Baby houses" for children appeared in England in the next century, but these elegant architectural objects, crafted by cabinet-makers, were affordable only by the wealthy. Not until the mid-1800s were dollhouses mass-produced in Europe and America, giving middle-class children the chance to become heads of their own miniature households.

As microcosms of the adult world, dollhouses reflected recognizable architectural styles and could resemble colonial manors, urban brown-

Continued

The sophisticated wooden dollhouse above, with glass windows and handsome moldings, was handcrafted around 1850 to replicate a brownstone once owned by a prominent New York City family.

Antique Dollhouses

The brownstone interior, left, retains its original cornice moldings, wallpaper, scenic painting, and faux marbre fireplace. The furniture, dating from the mid-19th century, includes a miniature set of white "Biedermeier" pieces made in Waltershausen, Germany.

stones, or Victorian cottages; some were modeled on specific buildings, including the homes of the children for whom they were made. On elaborate examples, no detail was overlooked. Glass windows, gingerbread trim, and turned railings appeared on the exteriors, and inside there might be hand-printed wallpapers, and even working plumbing and electricity.

Most dollhouses were made of wood embellished with carving and painting. By the 1870s, wooden houses covered with colorful lithographed paper were also produced by manufacturers both here and abroad. Many other buildings, including barns, churches, stores, stables, and firehouses, were offered as well.

Each room of the Lines dollhouse features a different wallpaper, and lace-curtained windows.

G. & J. Lines, the British manufacturer of the dollhouse above, called this circa 1895 model a "splendid mansion." The finely constructed wooden house features glass windows, paper-covered "brick" chimneys, and gold-painted trim. A cistern on the roof provided the top-floor bathtub with water.

The lithographed buildings at left include a firehouse complete with a horse-drawn pumper, made in 1895 by the R. Bliss Manufacturing Company of Pawtucket, Rhode Island, and an 1890 stable from the W. S. Reed Toy Company of Leominster, Massachusetts. The bungalow with turned wooden posts and the red brick house are from the Converse Toy and Woodware Company of Winchendon, Massachusetts. The large two-and-a-half-story house at center was made in Germany around 1905. The entire front opens, and the interior features electric lights.

Dollhouse Accessories

*Most of the dollhouse carpets
at right were crafted at
home; the little velveteen
"Oriental" and "Navajo"
throw rugs are advertising
giveaways from the
early 1900s.*

For a child, much of the appeal of playing with a dollhouse came from adding continually to the contents, and toymakers helped make it possible to fit out a miniature interior by producing every imaginable household furnishing in a tiny scale. Wooden and metal furnishings from Germany were imported to America in quantity, and domestic manufacturers also turned out their share. By the late 1800s, companies such as Stevens & Brown of Cromwell, Connecticut, and Althof, Bergmann of New York City were offering a broad range of tinplate accessories on the market. It was not uncommon for parents, and children themselves, to contribute their own items to a miniature household as well, crafting little furnishings from whatever materials they might find on hand.

Dollhouse accessories were designed to look as much like their full-size counterparts as possible, and virtually anything found in a real-life household might also be found in miniature. Children could have their dolls roll out cookie dough with a tiny rolling pin, tidy their carpets with little sweepers, and undertake the tasks of washday with a complete line of laundry equipment, including irons and wringers.

There were also pewter utensils and porcelain dinner sets, old-fashioned candlesticks and "modern" gas lamps, potted plants, clocks, ashtrays, fans, watering cans, and umbrella stands. Of course, every manner of stylish furniture was available, including elaborate bedroom, dining room, and kitchen sets, "upholstered" parlor suites, and even chairs and tables for the dollhouse garden.

There was virtually no end to the possibilities for outfitting a dollhouse. Accessories could include workaday items such as the cleaning utensils above left, as well as decorative pieces and accessories like the dishware, clocks, and houseplants above right.

Miniature Dishware

The set of pottery doll dishes above was probably crafted in Germany around 1880. Each piece is decorated with a transfer print of a little girl; manufacturers often used such images of children to attract a young buyer's eye.

Playing hostess at a party for friends or dolls has long been a favored childhood pastime. Tea, coffee, and dinner sets, produced primarily by English potteries and made specifically for this purpose, began to appear around the mid-18th century. Available only to the affluent, such early miniatures were simply copies of full-size dishes, and came in many of the same styles. With them, children could set little tables with everything from soup tureens to candy dishes in creamware, salt-glazed stoneware, and fine porcelain, just like those adults used. There were even miniature versions of the Chinese export wares that were fashionable in the late 1700s.

In the 19th century, the market for toy dishes

broadened, and more goods—many at lower prices—became available. Sets in such materials as enamelware, tin, and britannia, a pewterlike alloy, were introduced. One britannia tea service, made by a Boston silversmith, was promoted around Christmas of 1875, in a publication called *The Youth's Companion,* for six dollars. "Best of Britannia, formed by hand," read the advertisement. "A most beautiful present for a little girl." Pottery pieces, decorated with transfer prints, spattering, or luster, however, continued to be the most common miniature tableware. Toy dishes featuring such designs as nursery rhyme characters, animals, and mother-and-child scenes, intended to appeal to young people, were also increasingly prevalent.

The dishware at left would have made any child proud to host a party for her dolls or friends. The pieces are typical of the pottery, britannia, and enamelware miniatures made from the late 1800s to the 1930s.

THREE

Moving Amusements

action toys designed to surprise and delight

For as long as they have been producing toys, manufacturers—well aware of children's natural fascination with anything that moves—have made playthings that "perform" by popping up, bobbing, ringing bells, rolling on wheels, walking, or going through a clever series of actions when some mechanism (preferably hidden) is set into motion. The heyday of most mass-produced action toys came after the 1850s, during a period of rapid industrialization in America. Made of lithographed tinplate or cast iron, an enormous variety of playthings, ranging from simple pull toys to complex clockwork devices, rolled off assembly lines at affordable prices.

In the 1880s, however, when European firms began inundating the American market with huge numbers of simple spring-driven tin windup toys that cost only pennies, American manufacturers found it difficult to compete. By 1900, tin clockwork toys had become obsolete; by 1930, most cast-iron toys had also begun to be replaced by cheaper tin playthings made both here and abroad.

Push and pull toys that featured prancing horses were manufactured by the millions during the second half of the 19th century.

Jack-in-the-Boxes

Designed to startle an unsuspecting child, the Jack-in-the-Box—in which a scary or funny-faced figure propelled by a coiled spring pops from a box when the lid is unlatched—is one of the oldest types of mechanical toys. Made in Europe as early as the 16th century, and originally called a Punch Box, the toy usually concealed a grimacing, hooknosed clown with a jaunty cap, who was modeled after the puppet character Punch or, when dressed in a gown, his wife Judy. Another early variation—known as the Snake-in-the-Box—opened to reveal a springing reptile.

The name "Jack-in-the-Box" was probably not given to the toy until the 17th century. It is thought to derive from the term used for the sharpers and peddlers (known as Jacks) who sat in portable booths on the street and sold quack

The Jack-in-the-Boxes shown here, made from around 1880 until the turn of the century, all feature paper-covered wooden boxes and pop-up clown figures. From left to right: a jolly, single-toothed clown with a tiny topknot; a German-made Punch character with a plaster head; a papier-mâché-head clown with crêpe paper clothes; and a scary-faced fellow with white wool whiskers, made in Germany.

medicines and gimcracks to a gullible public.

By the mid-1800s toymakers in both Germany and America had begun manufacturing Jack-in-the-Boxes, and the toy quickly became a favorite in Victorian nurseries. The boxes themselves were generally made of lightweight wood, then covered with a colorful printed paper; sometimes lithographs depicting fanciful scenes of childhood were pasted onto the boxes as well.

The pop-up figure, which had come to be known as Jack whether it was a clown or not, would have a molded plaster or papier-mâché head, facial features highlighted in bright paint colors, clothes of cloth or crêpe paper to hide the spring, and sometimes hands made of wood. Because few early Jack-in-the-Boxes were labeled by their makers, the provenance of many of these toys remains unknown.

Sand Toys

Made in America around 1870, the sand toy above left features a dancing girl whose arms and legs move when the sand mechanism is activated. Similarly, the blades on the circa 1870 German windmill, above right, are set into motion when the sand trickles down.

Sand toys—inexpensive glass-fronted wood or cardboard boxes featuring paper figures or scenes that were set into action by the movement of trickling sand—were popular throughout the 1800s. Children spent hours watching the little dramas that took place in these miniature "theaters": an organ grinder's arm moved up and down as he played for a cavorting monkey, a ballerina danced upon a stage, the blades of a windmill turned as though propelled by the wind.

Produced early in the century by competing French and German firms, and later in America, sand toys were activated by an ingenious mech-

anism hidden in a rear compartment of the box. To work the toy, a child would turn the box either clockwise or counterclockwise a few times, causing the sand to drift down through a funnel-like aperture. As it did so, it would fall onto the blades of a tiny paddle wheel, which would move wires that, in turn, set the figures into motion—often for as long as two or three minutes.

While most sand toys had only a single figure, some were more complex, with two or three characters that moved simultaneously. One particularly elaborate example featured a group of cats dressed as acrobats dazzling spectators in a circus tableau of trapeze and cycle acts.

The sand-driven mechanism in the back of the mid-19th-century German toy, above, has four separate wires, which simultaneously move the fiddler's arm, the leaping dog, the banjo player, and the dancing man. The French toy at left, made around 1850, has only one wire, which moves the mother's arm up and down to bounce the baby.

Push and Pull Toys

The simplest of all moving toys were those that were merely pushed or pulled. A specialty of many well-known American firms, such playthings were manufactured in countless variations, with animals and vehicles the most common forms. Many of these toys featured tin figures mounted on cast-iron wheels; companies specializing in tin toys purchased the wheels by the ton from other firms. After the Civil War, however, when vast resources of iron ore were discovered, cast-iron was often used to make the entire toy.

Continued

Nineteenth-century American tin hoop toys like those above often featured horses or circus animals at their centers.

When the early-20th-century American stick toys opposite were pushed, the racehorse galloped, the donkey tried to buck off his rider, and the lithographed wooden rooster strutted and pecked.

As the circa 1870 American tin toy above is pulled along, the animals and trainers move in full circles.

Among the most popular push toys were wheeled stick toys, propelled by a long handle. Elaborate examples often had figures that moved up and down as the toy was raced around a room. Also favored, especially by very young children, were hoops, which could be set rolling with the simple tap of a hand.

Pull toys were sometimes equipped with gears or weights that allowed the figures to turn, bob, or perform tricks. The most common inspiration for such toys was the horse, which was often depicted with a rider, but could also be found pulling elaborate carriages, and all manner of other vehicles used for pleasure or commerce.

The fifteen-inch-high American tin pull-toy horse opposite, made in the 1870s by Hull & Stafford of Clinton, Connecticut, was the largest of three available models. Balanced solely by the small red weight, the horse bobs when the toy rolls on its wheels.

Of the many creatures that appeared as pull toys, horses were by far the favorites. The 19th-century examples at left are all of painted tin. The riderless lead horse, patented in 1876 by William Harwood, a New York City entrepreneur, was mounted on a tall base, making it appear larger than its 8½ inches.

Victorian Childhood

The children in this c. 1845 portrait were shown with their hobbyhorse, an expensive toy made with real horsehair and animal hide.

By the mid-1800s the American marketplace was bursting with products made both here and abroad. For the first time, children were recognized as a consumer group, and toymakers competed to fill nursery shelves with an ever-widening selection of shiny new playthings.

The toy business owed its health to an expanding economy, but growth was also fueled by shifting attitudes about childhood. Gone was the Puritan notion that parents would lose their offspring to Satan if they did not keep them industriously employed at all times; the concept of play for play's sake had firmly taken hold. Young people still had to measure up to stiff codes of conduct, but ideas about what sort of behavior could be considered acceptable relaxed considerably. Running after a hoop, beating noisily on a drum, or galloping on a hobbyhorse was actually deemed good for little children.

While they enhanced a child's life, toys also became status symbols for the parents who could afford to purchase them. Smallfolk were often posed for their portraits with the popular playthings of the day—either their own, or those kept on hand as props by professional artists. Nothing, after all, indicated a happy home better than a happy child with the latest commercially made toy.

When he painted their 1841 portrait, the artist Edwin Weyburn Goodwin posed his children with the toys they had received for Christmas.

This little boy, painted around 1854, showed off his toy horse and wagon.

Hoops were popular portrait props when this little girl was painted around 1850.

Tin Windup Toys

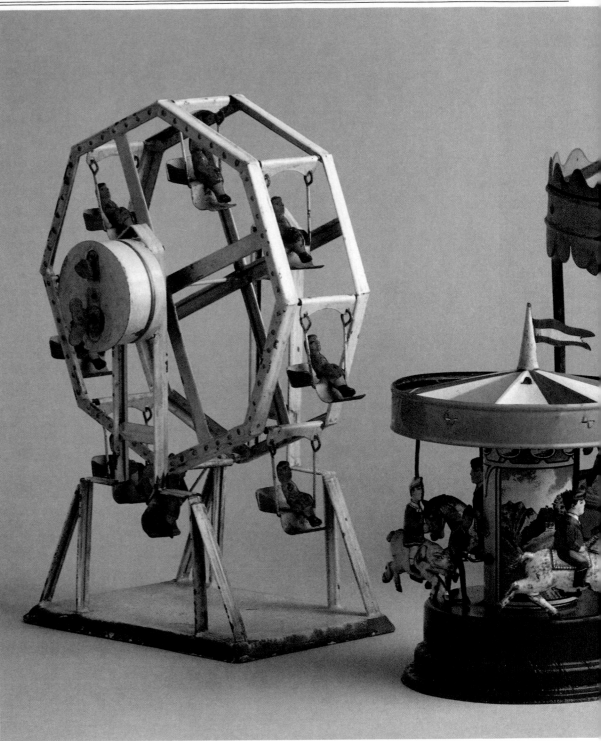

Tin toys activated by a lightweight spring were first assembled and painted by hand in Germany in the 1850s. By the 1880s, a new lithographic process had been developed that made it possible to mechanically color-print tinplate, and it was not long before companies in Germany, France, and England were producing hundreds of thousands of these inexpensive spring-driven tin toys for worldwide distribution. The most famous manufacturer was Ernst Paul Lehmann of Brandenburg, Germany, whose company, founded in 1881, is known

When he painted their 1841 portrait, the artist Edwin Weyburn Goodwin posed his children with the toys they had received for Christmas.

This little boy, painted around 1854, showed off his toy horse and wagon.

Hoops were popular portrait props when this little girl was painted around 1850.

Bell Toys

Patented in 1872 by Stevens & Brown, the bell toy above was known as The Chime until 1874, when the boy was added and it was repatented as Hoop and Boy.

Push and pull toys that jingled and clanged with the sound of bells were first manufactured in the 1860s. Perhaps not coincidentally, nurseries in Victorian houses were often on the second floor, where children could play without disturbing the household.

The earliest bell toys were produced in tin-plate, and by the 1870s they were also being made of cast iron. As in other types of push and pull toys, the forms these toys took were often inspired by the things that children found most exciting in life, such as Santa Claus and circus caravans. Some of the playthings had mechanisms that activated amusing bell-ringing fig-

ures—a monkey might swing around on a pedestal to strike a bell, a dog would catapult back and forth through a hoop to ring two different chimes, or, in the case of one toy known as The Waddler Bell Ringer, a goose waddled along ringing a bell in its beak.

Many of the leading toymakers of the day, such as Stevens & Brown of Cromwell, Connecticut, and Althof, Bergmann in New York City, manufactured these playthings. The toys were also made as a sideline by companies such as Gong Bell Manufacturing and J. L. Watrous, both of East Hampton, Connecticut, which specialized in hand bells and bells for houses and carriages.

The tin and cast-iron bell toy above was made by Althof, Bergmann in 1874. The front wheels are set off center, which makes the camel bob when pulled.

Clockwork Toys

[leaf ornament]

Tin mechanical toys that operated on clockworks were invented by American toymakers in the mid-19th century. The idea for these playthings may have been sparked by European *automata*—extremely elaborate and costly mechanical toys that had been made since the mid-1700s. Yet, while *automata* were offered as one-of-a-kind pieces, or in limited editions, mainly for the pleasure of adults, American clockwork toys were mass-produced and intended specifically for children.

As the name suggests, the mechanical parts of the American toys were actual clockworks, made with heavy brass gears and a powerful steel spring that, when wound with a key, could run for up to an hour. Credit for the first American clockwork toy is given to George W. Brown of Forestville, Connecticut, a clockmaker who started his own toy company in 1856. Over the next two decades, Brown would produce dozens of designs for tin clockwork toys, ranging from walking dolls to a seventeen-inch-long horse-drawn chariot that carried a driver and an eight-man band.

Although Brown's company is known to have been making clockwork toys in the late 1850s, the first patent for such a toy was not issued in the United States until 1862. It was for a walking doll with the decidedly unchildlike name of Autoperipatetikos, from the Greek *auto*, meaning

Continued

The patent for America's first registered clockwork toy, Autoperipatetikos, at right, was issued in 1862. The walking doll came in a number of variations; this one has a papier-mâché head.

Clockwork toys often depicted children at play. A youth rides a tricycle in the example above, patented by George W. Hawkins of New York City in 1870. The toy at left, produced by Stevens & Brown of Connecticut in the 1870s, features a girl pushing a baby carriage (actually the girl walks when she is pulled along by the clockwork carriage).

Many late-19th-century clockwork toys, like those shown here, display great ingenuity. The rare doll above left, made in France, moves her head and arms as a music box plays in the base she stands on. The other toys, all produced in America, include a knife sharpener, a cigar-puffing Ulysses S. Grant, and a boy acrobat who jumps up and down as his horse gallops.

self-propelled, and *peripatetikos*, to walk around. Patented by its designer, Enoch Rice Morrison, the doll was manufactured by the Martin & Runyon Company of New York City and soon appeared in a number of variations both in America and abroad.

By the turn of the century clockwork toys had become common in Europe and America, and patents for more than one hundred different models had been issued to dozens of American designers. In addition to dolls and animals that walked or crawled across the floor and vehicles that "motored" around the room, there were more complicated clockwork playthings, such as the fourteen-inch-high General Grant Smoker, patented by A. H. Dean of Bridgeport, Connecticut, in 1877 When wound, the General would raise his arm to put an actual lit cigar into his mouth; as he did so, a mechanism inside the toy caused him to inhale, and then exhale perfect smoke rings.

While American clockwork toys met with great success on the market, their heyday was brief. By 1900, European toymakers were exporting scores of spring-driven tin windup toys that children could purchase for only pennies.

Few clockwork toys were as elegantly dressed as the unusual circa 1870 French fashion doll above. When wound, she moved across the floor, taking her dogs for a walk.

93

George W. Brown of Connecticut patented the patriotic clockwork hoop toy at right in 1872 under the name Man in Two Wheels. One of the hoops is slightly smaller than the other, which made the toy run in circles instead of in a straight line.

The two clockwork toys shown here were both made by the Ives Manufacturing Company of Bridgeport, Connecticut, in the 1870s. The boy above drives his horses, which gallop up and down pulling the wagon. The boat at left, known as The Double Oarsman, has a movable rudder and was designed to be used in the water. Only four boats of this type are known to exist.

Tin Windup Toys

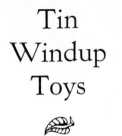

Tin toys activated by a lightweight spring were first assembled and painted by hand in Germany in the 1850s. By the 1880s, a new lithographic process had been developed that made it possible to mechanically color-print tinplate, and it was not long before companies in Germany, France, and England were producing hundreds of thousands of these inexpensive spring-driven tin toys for worldwide distribution. The most famous manufacturer was Ernst Paul Lehmann of Brandenburg, Germany, whose company, founded in 1881, is known

The whirling motions of carousels and other amusement park rides were easily duplicated by in-expensive spring-driven windup toys. All of those at left were made in Germany between 1895 and 1915; the two carousels play music as they turn.

to have exported ninety percent of his toys.

American toymakers scrambled to catch up. One of the first to do so was Leo Schlesinger of New York City, a producer of clockwork toys who made the switch to the cheaper spring mechanism by the turn of the century. His firm

was followed by such companies as the Acme Toy Works of Chicago, founded in 1904, and Ferdinand Strauss of New York City, established in 1914. But it was not until after World War I, when anti-German sentiment and a new demand for home-produced goods created impor-

Continued

tant changes in the toy market, that America began to make major gains on its European rivals.

Indeed, by the 1920s American manufacturers had more than overtaken the competition. The giant in the tin windup toy field from the twenties through the 1960s was the New York City firm of Louis Marx & Company, which prided itself on producing quality playthings at reasonable prices. Louis Marx himself kept close watch on children's interests in an effort to ensure that his designs stayed current. Some of his most popular items were inspired by comic-strip, film, radio, and television characters; others chronicled every new type of vehicle that flew, traveled on land, or floated on water.

The natty little mouse band above, called the Marx Merrymakers, was one of Louis Marx & Company's most popular toys. When the spring was wound, the piano player banged on the keyboard, and the other mice variously directed, drummed, or danced along. The toy first appeared in Marx's 1931 catalog, where it was priced at ninety-eight cents.

In the 1890s European manufacturers began exporting a wide variety of lithographed tin windups. The toys at left, made in France, England, and Germany, date from 1905 onward.

HONEYMOON
EXPRESS

One of the most enduring tin windup toys ever produced was the Honeymoon Express, introduced in 1926 by Louis Marx & Company of New York City, and sold by the firm in more than forty variations over the next four decades. While the basic form of the toy—a vehicle that carried passengers around a circular track—never changed, the design was updated periodically, and the theme occasionally deviated from the original idea of a honeymoon trip.

Introduced in 1926, the first Honeymoon Express was pulled by a steam locomotive that chugged along through a picturesque landscape on its way to a station called Richmond. It is thought that Marx may have derived his idea for this toy from an early German-made tin train set like the octagonal one included at right. By 1928 the honeymoon site was New York City, and, in addition to the train, the toy also sported a circling airplane. In the 1930s the steam locomotive gave way to a streamlined passenger train and the plane was modernized as well.

Among the first of the Marx toys to vary from the honeymoon theme was the 1927 Pinched, which featured a speeding car being stopped by policemen. In 1936 the Popeye Express had the familiar comic-strip character flying an airplane over the circling train. And, in 1954, the Subway Express carried commuters through a plastic tunnel from 42nd to 52nd Street in New York City.

Mechanical Banks

Mechanical banks were toys that taught children to save money by making the process fun. No child, for example, could resist putting a penny into a bank like the remarkable Eagle & Eaglets, shown at top right above. When a coin was placed in the beak of the mother eagle and the lever was pressed, the bird tilted forward and dropped the money into the nest. Simultaneously, her eaglets rose up, opened their beaks, and actually made a chirping sound, which was produced by a bellows inside the bank's base.

Continued

All of the cast-iron mechanical banks above were patented in the United States between 1873 and 1920. In the center is the popular Tammany Bank, made by the Connecticut firm of J. & E. Stevens; it features a greedy figure that looks like the politician Boss Tweed, ready to put a penny in his pocket. The tin mechanical banks at left, dating from 1905 to 1936, were all made in Germany, except for the Home Bank, an American favorite that provided a one-cent deposit receipt when a penny was inserted.

During the period of their greatest popularity—from the 1870s to the early 1930s—mechanical banks were manufactured mainly by American companies. While some of these banks were produced in tin and wood, the most inventive designs were made of cast iron, which was not only inexpensive but also provided a strong housing for the levers, gears, and springs that controlled the action.

Although fewer than four hundred different cast-iron mechanical bank designs were patented, many more variations exist because compet-

ing companies often copied one another, changing a design just enough to prevent a lawsuit. In each, something magical happened that was worth the sacrifice of a penny: a clown's tongue might stick out, a rabbit's ears spring up, or perhaps an artilleryman would take a shot at a target. Often, children's interests or storybooks inspired the bank designs, but some also had moral, historical, or political themes.

By the turn of the century, cast-iron banks were joined on the market by light tinplate banks that were simpler mechanically. While American companies produced some of the new banks, most were imported from Germany.

Carnival subjects and shooting themes were favorites for cast-iron mechanical banks like those shown at left, dating from the 1880s to the 1920s.

The rare circa 1880 clockwork Freedman's Bank above was the only bank made by Jerome B. Secor, a Bridgeport, Connecticut, manufacturer of other types of clockwork toys. When a coin is placed on the desk, the cashier deposits the money, thumbs his nose defiantly, and nods his head.

FOUR

Favorite Pastimes

*familiar diversions intended
to please and instruct*

During the 19th century, a range of toys and games that could keep children suitably occupied became extremely popular in America. Some were ideal for outdoor recreation; it was not unusual, for example, to find a few young comrades shooting marbles in the back yard on any given afternoon. Board games, puzzles, and card games, on the other hand, brought children and parents together indoors by the parlor fire for an evening of healthy family activity.

By the beginning of the Victorian era, the idea that playing with toys and games was an advantageous way to educate children was also firmly in place. Partly to justify their use, toys and games made before the mid-1800s were invariably designed to impart some sort of moral lesson. They were also used as a pleasant means to learn everything from the ABCs, taught with building blocks, to fairly complex scientific principles, demonstrated by optical toys. By the second half of the 1800s, however, the emphasis had shifted from facts to fun, as many games took on purely comical themes.

*Blocks, books, games, and even doll furniture were designed to teach
children the alphabet while they played.*

Building Blocks

Continued

Made in Germany about 1900, the lithographed blocks above have animal pictures on two sides and letters of the alphabet on the other four.

Easy for young hands to hold, blocks have long been among a toddler's first toys. While the exact origins of these familiar playthings are unclear, it is known that alphabet blocks made of wood or bone were used in England in the late 1600s. The toys also caught on in this country, and wooden alphabet blocks were probably made here by carpenters early on; ivory blocks were advertised by the 1800s.

The first blocks made in any quantity in America, however, were those produced by S. L. Hill of Brooklyn, New York, who in 1858 patented his paper-covered Spelling Blocks, featuring letters, numerals, and pictures. The printing on

Dating from the 1890s to the 1920s, the paper-covered picture blocks opposite were all designed to present a child with simple puzzles to solve. With some sets, six different pictures could be made by unscrambling the blocks; illustrations of the completed pictures were often provided.

With the circa 1900 wood building block sets above it was possible to make an early American town and a pavilion like those on the Atlantic City boardwalk.

most blocks of this period was generally limited to engravings, but by the 1870s, brilliantly hued lithographs were being widely used. Blocks came alive with appealing images inspired by fairy tales and nursery rhymes, as well as with the artwork of popular illustrators such as Kate Greenaway.

By 1880, one hundred and seventy-three toy and game manufacturers were listed by the U.S. Census Bureau, and most were offering such colorful blocks, made of wood or cardboard. The most creative makers of all were Jesse and Charles M. Crandall, distant cousins who each had their own toy business. Among Jesse's inventions were nesting blocks, while the many original designs patented by Charles included

interlocking blocks and his whimsical Expression Blocks. These were actually a puzzle; the alphabet on one side was the key to the picture—of Crandall himself—on the other.

Another well-known innovator in block design was the F. Ad. Richter Company of New York, which in 1880 patented their Anchor Building Bricks, made of cast cement. Extreme-

ly popular through the 1920s, these construction sets included pillars, arches, and triangles—ideal for parapets and towers. Other construction sets of the period came with "logs," for frontier cabins, and even tin walls, windows, and balconies that could be assembled into skyscrapers—or anything else that a young architect or engineer could dream up.

Bridges and skyscrapers rose from the construction blocks above. The 1924 Bilt-E-Z skyscraper set came with enameled tin parts; the other sets are of cast cement.

111

CHARLES M. CRANDALL, TOYMAKER

If nothing else, Charles Crandall was sure of his ability to amuse: "C. M. Crandall has done it again! has made another splendid thing that will perfectly charm all the LITTLE FOLKS..." boasted an 1875 ad by the toymaker. Crandall, in fact, lived up to that promise repeatedly, producing one of the broadest selections of toys, games, and puzzles offered in Victorian America.

Charles was still a child himself when, in 1845, at the age of twelve, he went to work in his family's Covington, Pennsylvania, furniture factory. He began designing wooden toys on the side, and when his father died four years later, young Crandall took over the company, eventually shifting the emphasis of its business to toymaking.

Sometime in the 1860s, the firm moved to Montrose, Pennsylvania, and it was in this period that Charles introduced many of his most innovative toys. After the Civil War, croquet became a fad, and Crandall was a major producer of croquet sets, which he packed in boxes assembled with tongue-and-groove joints. One day the toymaker brought home some boxmaking scraps, and found that his children could amuse themselves for hours fitting the interlocking pieces together. An idea was born, and Crandall's blocks were patented in 1867.

Flat, interlocking rectangles, Crandall's blocks were the simplest of many toys he made based on the tongue-and-groove principle. One of the most whimsical was The Acrobats, also issued under the 1867 patent. A boxed set came with four torsos, four grinning heads, eight arms, and eight legs, which could be

Among Crandall's most popular toys was The Acrobats, above, which sold for fifty cents a box in the 1870s.

fitted together in all manner of daring acrobatic poses.

In 1876, the toymaker patented a method for using rivet joints so that the shoulders, hips, elbows, and knees of his figures could actually be moved. Crandall was soon offering a line of toys in which the rivets were combined with the tongue-and-groove fittings. These included Crandall's Menagerie, in which fifty-six interchangeable animal and human body parts could be used to make "tens of thousands of the most laughter-provoking figures."

Other toys manufactured by the Charles M. Crandall Company included a rubber-band powered cannon that was able to propel a rubber ball a distance of thirty feet. The cannon came with a company of soldiers and with building blocks for erecting fortifications—all of which could be satisfactorily destroyed in the heat of battle. Crandall also made an assortment of clever pull toys, including the Lively Horseman, which was designed to "perform" on the box in which it was packed.

Some of Crandall's success in the toy business can be attributed to the company's wholesale agent, the Orange Judd Company of New York City. This firm published a popular magazine entitled *The American Agriculturist,* and Crandall's ads often appeared on its pages. Because few 19th-century American toymakers advertised nationally, this gave Crandall a competitive edge.

In 1865, Charles moved to Waverly, New York, and opened the Waverly Toy Company, leaving his son Fred in charge of the Montrose firm. Charles died in 1905, but only after, according to a *New York Tribune* article, furnishing "more pleasure through toys and puzzles than any other person in the country."

Children's Puzzles

The first picture puzzle is believed to have been made in the 1760s by an English printmaker named John Spilsbury, who mounted hand-colored maps of Europe on thin sheets of mahogany and then cut out the various countries with a coping saw. Spilsbury called his creations "dissected maps," and their sole purpose was to teach geography to children. The emphasis of most early puzzles, made mainly in England, France, and Germany, remained educational until the first half of the 1800s. At that time, images focusing on school and Bible sub-

Made in both Europe and America, the puzzles at left date from around 1880 to the early 1900s and depict subjects designed to capture a young imagination: train crashes, shipwrecks, circus scenes, and storybook characters. The best puzzles were backed with mahogany, but makers usually preferred cheaper softwoods. By the end of the 1800s, cardboard had all but replaced wood.

jects gradually gave way to those from fairy tales, nursery rhymes, and adventure stories.

Although puzzles were imported, few were made in America before the Cut Up Pictures first seen in the 1867 catalog of McLoughlin Brothers of New York City. Most puzzles of the time were just that: cut-up pictures with simple flat-edged shapes. In their 1875-1876 catalog, McLoughlin Brothers, however, boasted puzzles "dissected in a novel manner," with the more complex interlocking pieces that would eventually become standard in puzzle making.

115

Parlor Games

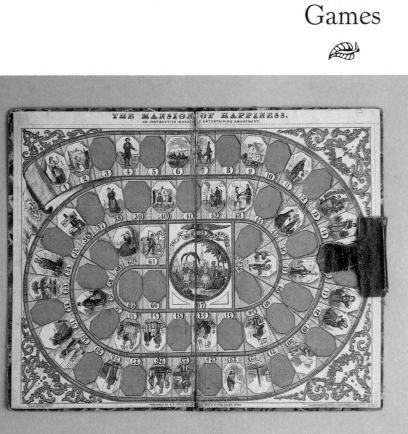

Parlor games were essentially the product of the 19th century, a period when more and more people enjoyed leisure time, and the entertainment of the young centered around the family. According to their manufacturers, games amused children, educated them, and promoted togetherness. "They tend to make happy firesides," asserted McLoughlin Brothers, a major producer, "and keep children at home, instead of compelling them to seek amusement away from the family circle."

One of the first American manufacturers of board games was W. & S. B. Ives of Salem, Massachusetts, a stationer who issued The Mansion of Happiness in 1843. Games were generally of-

Continued

Based on an English board game, The Mansion of Happiness suggested that leading a moral life ensured a place in heaven. It was created by Anne W. Abbot, a minister's daughter, and first issued in 1843 by the W. & S. B. Ives Company of Salem, Massachusetts; the board above dates to 1864.

Showing themes very much of their time, the board games at left date from the 1880s to 1920.

McLoughlin Brothers billed their 1909 creation, The Pussy Cat Ten Pins, above, as a "Skill and Action Game." Based on bowling, this game was played on a tabletop and came with ten cardboard cats on detachable bases and three balls used to knock them over.

fered as a sideline by stationers and booksellers until after the Civil War, when firms such as Milton Bradley of Springfield, Massachusetts, Selchow & Righter of New York City, and Parker Brothers (which acquired Ives in 1887) were formed and started manufacturing games fulltime. Competition was fierce, and the makers frequently issued old games under new names.

The early games usually imparted a religious message, educating players about the Bible, perhaps, or demonstrating an allegorical way to reach heaven, as in The Mansion of Happiness. As America's economy expanded in the second half of the 19th century, however, a new and

very different morality became dominant: financial and material success. In games like The Errand Boy or Failure and Success, lowly company employees competed to rise through the ranks of their firm to become president.

Science, literature, geography, and sports were also themes of games, as was magic. The Chiromagica, which sold for two dollars, featured a magnetic hand that answered "quite correctly in a mysterious manner a great many questions." Games of skill, on the other hand, relied on manual dexterity, and generally involved rolling or throwing balls at colorful targets, or "fishing" for elusive objects with magnets.

The table games opposite were both issued by McLoughlin Brothers. Fish Pond, a favorite party game in the 1890s, involved fishing with a magnet "bait." In the 1895 Brownie Artillery game, cannonballs were used to knock down the Brownie figures, originated by the popular illustrator Palmer Cox.

Card Games

The educational card games above, dating from the mid-1800s to about 1910, drilled players in such subjects as nature, history, and geography.

The first record of a card game being played in America dates to 1633, and although the Puritan mind associated the pastime with gambling and the devil, cards were nevertheless fairly common by the 18th century. It was a popular concept at the time that the young should learn through play, and most children's card games found in this country during the 1700s were based on a question-and-answer format, designed to teach facts about such dry subjects as mathematics, science, and geography. The questions were generally so difficult, and the facts so obscure, however, that the games could hardly be considered fun.

Most card games were imported to America from England until the 1820s, when several domestic manufacturers began producing them. At about the same time, the market for the tedious educational card games started to decline, and after around 1850 packs that focused purely on fun began to take their place. Amusing games such as Rook, Old Maid and Old Bachelor, and Komical Konversation Kards, which was a variation on a number of popular games requiring players to converse on a topic listed on the card, became common. These remained favorites among both children and adults throughout the early 20th century and, in some cases, beyond.

The card games above, primarily from the late 1800s and early 1900s, were "merry and laughable," and meant purely to amuse.

Marbles

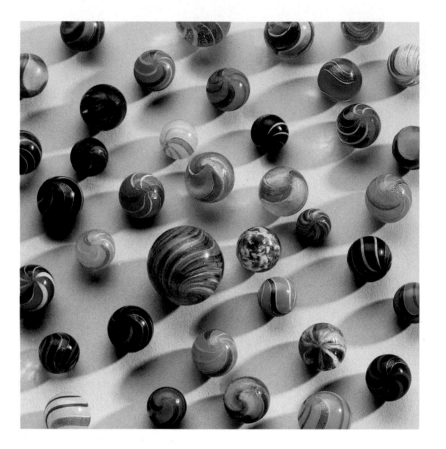

Shooting marbles is among the oldest games known to man, dating at least as far back as ancient classical times. Played with stone or clay marbles, the game appeared in Britain in the first century, after the Roman conquest, and eventually spread throughout the rest of Europe.

The great age of marbles in America was the late 1800s and early 1900s, when few boys were without a bag of "aggies" (marbles made of agate) and some prized "taws," or shooters, used to knock an opponent's marbles out of a circle.

On a nice day, a ring marked in the dirt would suffice, but if it was raining, the children might go indoors for a game of Persian, played on the circle patterns found in Oriental carpets.

In the Victorian era, marbles made of stone, pottery, clay, and china were all widely used. Among the most coveted, however, were the lovely swirled glass marbles that came chiefly from Germany. The queen of all marbles, the delicate hand-blown sulphide, with a tiny clay figure or object trapped inside, was also made primarily in that country.

The "Lutz-type goldstones" above, featuring swirls and gold bands, are named after Nicholas Lutz, a glass designer who worked at the Boston & Sandwich Glass Company in the late 1800s. Most Lutz-type marbles, however, actually came from Germany, and the "gold" was really finely ground copper.

Measuring as large as 2½ inches in diameter, the glass marbles shown here were made primarily in Germany. At top are "swirls"; at center, "onionskins," also called "clouds" or "end-of-day marbles"; and at bottom, sulphides, containing tiny molded images. While animals in sulphides were quite common, human figures and everyday objects, such as watches, were rare.

Marble Games

During the late 1800s, tabletop marble games became very popular. Miniature pinball games were a sensation, as were Chinese Checkers and games made with vertical backboards, such as Tip I Tip. In these, a marble might roll down a tunnel or drop through a series of cups until it rang a bell or fell into a hole marked with a point value.

Made of wood or cardboard, such games were invariably covered with colorful lithographed pictures, often printed with circus scenes or cartoon characters. They were widely played by adults as well as children, and at the turn of the century, one known as Pigs in Clover even became quite notorious. This game, introduced by Charles M. Crandall in 1889, called for patience and manual dexterity, requiring the player to maneuver four marble "pigs" simultaneously through a maze from a "field" into a "pen" by tipping the round playing board.

Meeting the challenge could apparently be quite addictive. "Driving pigs" became a craze among members of Congress, causing a scandal that was aggravated when President Benjamin Harrison was pictured in a political cartoon playing the game. Newspaper reports brought international fame to Pigs in Clover and it eventually reached England, where it was heralded as "A new American device for the propagation of insanity in Great Britain."

The popular marble games made between the late 1800s and the 1930s at left include Poosh-M-Up, a pinball game, and the famous Pigs in Clover, in the round box.

The volume above, published in Germany, came with an envelope of flower cutouts that could be arranged in precut slots.

Books specifically designed to delight young readers did not appear in any number until the mid-19th century, which marked the beginning of a new taste for volumes richly decorated with fanciful illustrations. Publishers who had heretofore been limited to dry primers and schoolbooks with uninspired engravings now faced a world of possibilities opened up by advancements in color lithography—and by the new idea that it was acceptable, and even desirable, for books to be fun.

The most imaginative book designers sometimes dispensed with text altogether, and did not stop with images that lay flat on a page; instead, they found a way to make their pictures move, metamorphose, or come to life in three dimensions. Pull a ribbon and a bird might fly across the sky; pull a paper lever and venetian blind-like slats would flip to make one picture dissolve into another. Some books even had tabs that caused a three-dimensional scene to pop up when the page was opened, or paper accordians that enabled various figures to spring from a background illustration. The "action" could also come from the reader, who might be provided with cutouts meant to be inserted into slots. Facial features were added to various heads appearing throughout a story, for example, or flowers "arranged" in wreaths and vases.

Most of the early action books were published in Germany and in England, where inexpensive folding books were extremely popular in the late

Continued

Action Books

The "overlay," or "trans-formation," books at left were produced in England in the mid-1800s by Dean & Son, one of the first publishers of action books for children. As the pages of these books were turned, a three-dimensional head inside the back cover popped through a hole to fit a new body and scene.

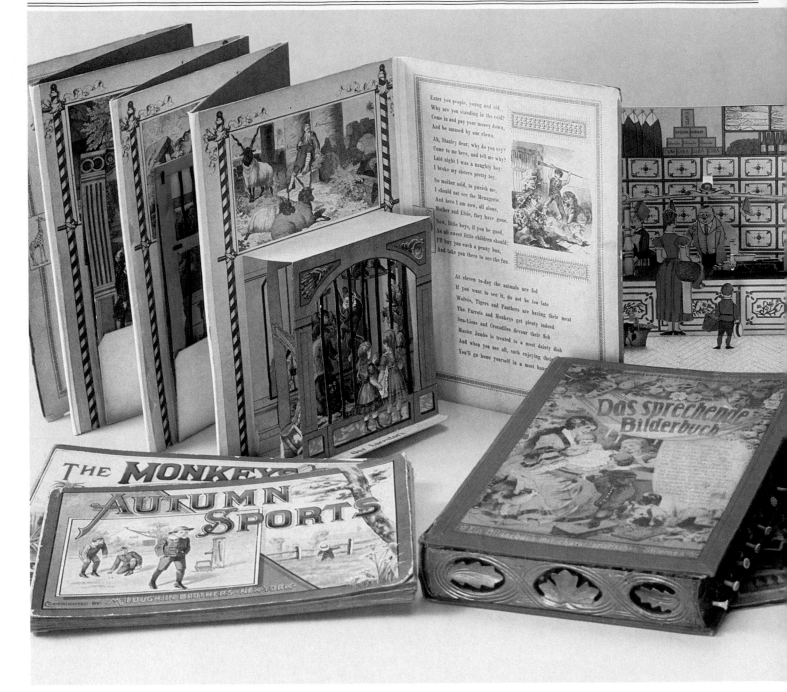

1700s. Such amusements, however, were primarily for adults until the 1840s, when the London firm of Thomas Dean founded a company specializing in children's publishing. Dean was known particularly for his "overlay," or "transformation," books, which featured a face on the inside back cover that gained a different costumed body as each page was turned. He also excelled in making scenic books; when these remarkable volumes were opened, intricately layered panoramas popped up into perspective.

While Thomas Dean and his son George were responsible for producing many ingenious volumes, a German puppeteer named Lothar Meggendorfer is considered by many to be the real "father" of action books. Born in Munich in 1847, Meggendorfer started designing books in the 1880s, and produced more than sixty cre-

ations during his thirty-two-year career. Printed in numerous editions and translated into several languages, the volumes incorporated all the various types of action devices, which were cleverly concealed by the covers and bindings. His most popular work, *Internationaler Circus,* a pop-up book that appeared in 1887, opened into six full scenes, including an audience of four hundred and fifty individual figures, but was only about an inch thick when it was closed.

Both English and German makers produced numerous action books for distribution in this country, which proved to be a major market for these volumes. But there were also publishers here; the leading 19th- and early-20th-century producer of action books in America was probably McLoughlin Brothers, whose six-volume *Little Showman's Series* made its debut in 1884.

The action books above include volumes published in both Germany and America between around 1875 and 1900.

The action books at right were designed by Lothar Meggendorfer of Munich, who was renowned for his ingenious paper mechanics. *Internationaler Circus, first* published in 1887, was a panorama book that opened to reveal six fold-out scenes.

Lustiges Automaten Theater ("Comical Automated Theater"), designed in 1890, featured a grinning musician. When a lever was pulled, he bowed the strings of his violin as he danced on the page.

The World of Mother Goose

Among the earliest books published for the entertainment of children were those containing nursery rhymes. While a few verses had appeared in English volumes by the early 1700s, the first known collection of any size is generally thought to be *Tommy Thumb's Pretty Songbook,* printed in the 1740s. Illustrated with simple woodcuts, the volume contained thirty-eight ditties detailing the activities of such familiar nursery characters as Little Robin Red Breast and Mistress Mary Quite Contrary. Including many of the same verses, a book called *Mother Goose's Melody* was brought out in London around 1765, and became extremely popular in both England and America. Before long, all nursery rhymes were known as Mother Goose rhymes.

Scholars have never found an author responsible for Mother Goose verses, and it is most likely that they are simply folk rhymes, many of which were passed on orally for generations before they were written down. As a folk figure, however, "Mother Goose" was an appropriate head of the nursery, since the barnyard species is well-known for watching over her large broods with fierce protectiveness.

Yet, despite Mother Goose's nurturing persona, her rhymes are hardly typical nursery fare. Cradles fall, houses burn, children are whipped, and animals maimed with surprising frequency. Few of the verses, in fact, were written specifically for children. Instead they were generally the inventions of whoever was minding the baby, and it was not unusual for bits of plays, popular drinking songs, political satire, and familiar verses to find their way into the compositions. "Diddle diddle dumpling/My son John/Went to bed with his trousers on," for example, originated as the street cry of hot-dumpling sellers in London. And, according to legend, "Little Jack Horner" tells the story of how one Thomas Horner secured a "plum" of an estate for himself during the reign of Henry VIII.

Most attempts to find history lessons in Mother Goose, however, have proved unsuccessful, as have efforts to coax morals from the verses. Except for the occasional alphabet book brought out under her name, Mother Goose volumes are not meant to be didactic. Instead, it is the very absurdity of the verses—the rub-a-dub-dubs and dishes running off with spoons—that captures a child's imagination. Their economy and wit, in turn, delight the parents who read them aloud.

Unprotected by copyright, Mother Goose rhymes have appeared again and again, in countless variations. The sampling at right includes volumes published in England and America between 1870 and 1950.

Optical Toys

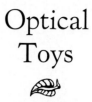

As advancements in the field of science captured the public's imagination throughout the 1800s, devices demonstrating natural and physical principles became the rage. None proved more fascinating than those involving optics: magic lanterns, kaleidoscopes, and countless gadgets with convoluted "scientific" names that relied on reflections, light, and moving images to create a special effect.

Optical toys were produced on both sides of the Atlantic. While they originated as adult amusements, they were eventually marketed for the enjoyment of children. Some, such as the kaleidoscope and the anamorphic picture device, "tricked the eye" by altering an image with mirrors. Most, however, were based on the "persistence of vision" principle, which holds that the eye continues to see an image for a brief moment after it has vanished from view.

Among the earliest of these amusements was the Thaumatrope, first offered in England in 1825. Really quite simple, the device was nothing more than a set of paper disks with different parts of the same image printed on either side.

Continued

The circa 1790 anamorphic picture device above used a curved mirror to correct an intentionally distorted drawing. The optical toys at left include two circa 1875 drum-shaped Zoetropes, and a candlelit kaleidoscope patented by a Rhode Island maker in 1872.

The Praxinoscope Theater, above, patented in 1877 by Emile Reynaud of Paris, combined the illusion of motion with a background scene. A typical "film" strip might show a dog jumping through a hoop or an acrobatic horseback rider.

When a disk was spun on strings, the eye superimposed the pictures so they appeared as one. That idea was taken a step farther by the Phenakistoscope, introduced in the early 1830s. In this toy, the disks were printed on one side with a series of related pictures, and slotted at even intervals. As the disk was spun before a mirror, the viewer looked through the slots and the reflected images merged into a series of movements; a snake might slither out of a hole, for example, or a tadpole might grow into a frog.

The pleasure of the Thaumatrope and the Phenakistoscope increased with the Zoetrope, popular beginning in the 1860s. When a strip of paper printed with a series of images was placed inside a slotted drum and the drum rotated, any number of people could watch with delight as the "moving picture" flitted past the slots. A more complex variation on this toy was the Praxinoscope, invented in 1877, which used mirrors and lamplight to clarify the moving images, and came with detailed background scenes.

The Thaumatrope, which consisted of disks printed on two sides, was introduced by the 1820s; the version at top left was made in France around 1900. The Phenakistoscope at center was produced by Ackermann & Company in London in 1833. The designs on the hand-colored disks included graphic geometric shapes and wonderfully weird ghouls, which delighted the eye when spun into "action." The "phasmagoric images" in the circa 1830 German viewer at bottom transformed their appearance as they were exposed to different amounts of light.

On the Move

*toys that captured the spirit
of travel and progress*

As the effects of the Industrial Revolution became fully felt, the public's attention was focused on the technological advances that were rapidly changing the world. Nowhere did those developments have more impact than in the field of transportation. By the 1850s, American railroads linked eastern settlements to western frontiers, and paddle-wheelers were plying the country's major waterways; by the 1890s, the automobile had begun to replace the horse-drawn carriage, and ocean liners were crossing the Atlantic. In 1903, the Wright brothers took off at Kitty Hawk.

To the delight of children, toymakers were quick to produce miniature replicas of nearly everything that was traveling by land, sea, and air. Any improvements made in the full-size vehicles were almost immediately copied by toy manufacturers so that they could keep offering up-to-date models. While American firms produced many innovative transportation toys, the cars, trucks, planes, boats, and trains made by European companies in the early part of the 20th century were particularly coveted for their quality and detail.

Tinplate was a popular material for toy boats because it could be used to make inexpensive vessels with colorful detailing.

Toy Boats

Made in the 1840s by Francis, Field & Francis of Philadelphia, the rare side-wheel steamer above was one of the earliest tin toys to be commercially produced in America. The boat is named for General Zachary Taylor, a hero of the Mexican War who became President of the United States in 1849.

By the 1840s, steam-powered vessels were not only plying America's rivers but also regularly crossing the Atlantic. While boats had moved under sail for centuries, steamboats were still new enough to fascinate the public, and toymakers were quick to pick up on the interest. Soon children had their own miniature paddle-wheelers—with romantic names like *River Queen* and *Giant*. Most of these early boats were pull toys or clockwork toys meant for use on land rather than in the water. By the 1890s, however, some American manufacturers had also begun to make toy boats with more powerful clockwork engines and watertight hulls, which were intended to float.

Although toy steamers would continue to be

Continued

The 19th-century side-wheelers at right include (clockwise from the top) a lithographed wooden boat, a windup toy with a "smoke" key, a tin clockwork boat, and a steam-driven vessel.

popular into the 20th century, by the early 1900s manufacturers were also producing replicas of nearly every type of craft that sailed the seas. Especially notable were the warships and ocean liners made by the firms Gebrüder Märklin, Gebrüder Bing, and Georges Carette of Nuremburg, Germany. These coveted toy boats were made in many sizes, with the largest measuring over three feet long. Some featured officers, deck hands, and passengers, and most had working propellers, anchors that could be dropped, and either clockwork, steam, or electric motors (the

last could run up to six hours). It was not uncommon to find a child standing forlornly on the shore of a lake or pond watching as his powerful new liner sailed off without him.

Not surprisingly, these European-made boats were expensive, and only the wealthiest families could afford them. To extend sales, manufacturers often adapted the same model for export simply by changing the flags and the name—one boat, for example, might appear as the *Puritan* in the United States, the *Prince of Wales* in England, and the *Rotterdam* in Holland.

Christened the Ocean Wave, *the thirty-one-inch lithograph-covered wooden pull-toy sailing ship above was made by the W. S. Reed Toy Company of Massachusetts in 1882. Its mizzen, main, and foresails are cardboard.*

The tin clockwork boats opposite, manufactured by the German company Carette in the early 1900s, were designed to be used in the water. The twenty-inch ocean liner at top features removable crow's nests; the eighteen-inch launch at bottom has an anchor that can be dropped.

Horse-drawn trolleys were among the most common forms of public transportation in the 19th century. Those above include a yellow and red tin model, made by Stevens & Brown of Cromwell, Connecticut, in the early 1870s, and two smaller vehicles produced by James Fallows of Philadelphia around 1890.

By the mid-1800s, great numbers of horse-drawn vehicles filled the streets of America's cities. Along with surreys, traps, phaetons, gigs, and other types of fancy carriages, there were omnibuses, trolleys, and hansom cabs for public transportation. These vied for the right of way with fire engines, delivery wagons, and commercial carts of every description.

Producing faithful imitations of horse-drawn vehicles proved to be extremely lucrative for American toy manufacturers from the 1860s until the early years of the 20th century, when the automobile became the favored form of transport. By copying in miniature what appeared on the streets, toymakers could continually offer their customers new products.

Most of these playthings were designed to be rolled along by hand. The earliest examples were made of tin with cast-iron wheels by companies such as George W. Brown of Forestville, Connecticut, and James Fallows of Philadelphia, who specialized in all types of tinplate toys. By the late 19th century, the Ives Manufacturing Company of Bridgeport, Connecticut, and the Kenton Hardware Company of Kenton, Ohio, had become two of the most important producers of the toys in more durable cast iron.

While the vehicles themselves varied greatly—ranging from simple boxlike carts to elaborate carriages with simulated leather interiors—the horses were commonly made in just a few styles that could be used with most of the different vehicles a single company produced. Generally, these toys were given to small boys, who found it easy to imagine themselves as bus drivers, deliverymen, or peddlers hawking their wares along the streets.

Horse-Drawn Vehicles

The 19th-century delivery vehicles at left include a tin cart, top, made by James Fallows in the 1880s; a circa 1880 tin Pedler Wagon, center, by an unknown maker; and a cast-iron ice wagon, bottom, produced around 1900 by the Ives Manufacturing Company. This last features a removable driver and delivery boy, and blocks of "ice" made of glass.

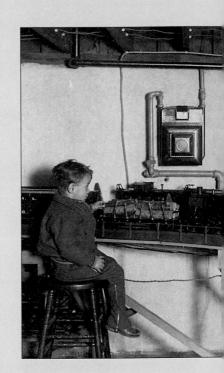

CHILDHOOD MEMORIES

Ever since the Victorian period, children have been fascinated by the expanding world of transportation, and by the many toys that world has inspired. Puddles easily become oceans, and sidewalks highways, as boys and girls skipper their sailing ships to safe port or race a fire truck to put out the flames of a burning building. As these old photographs attest, there is no limit to the possibilities for play when young imaginations are involved.

Fire-Fighting Equipment

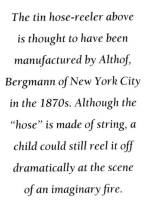

The tin hose-reeler above is thought to have been manufactured by Althof, Bergmann of New York City in the 1870s. Although the "hose" is made of string, a child could still reel it off dramatically at the scene of an imaginary fire.

For a 19th-century child probably no occurrence was more terrifying—and thrilling—than a fire. In an age of gas lamps and coal stoves, fires were all too common, but along with the horror also came the excitement of horses thundering down streets and firemen heroically saving lives.

By the Victorian age firefighting had come a long way from the bucket brigades of colonial America. In the second half of the century large towns were apt to have several firefighting companies, generally staffed by volunteers and equipped with gleaming carriages and wagons.

Continued

The 1885 ladder wagon above right, by Ives Manufacturing of Bridgeport, Connecticut, and the circa 1900 hose-reeler at right, by Dent Hardware of Fullerton, Pennsylvania, feature galloping steeds.

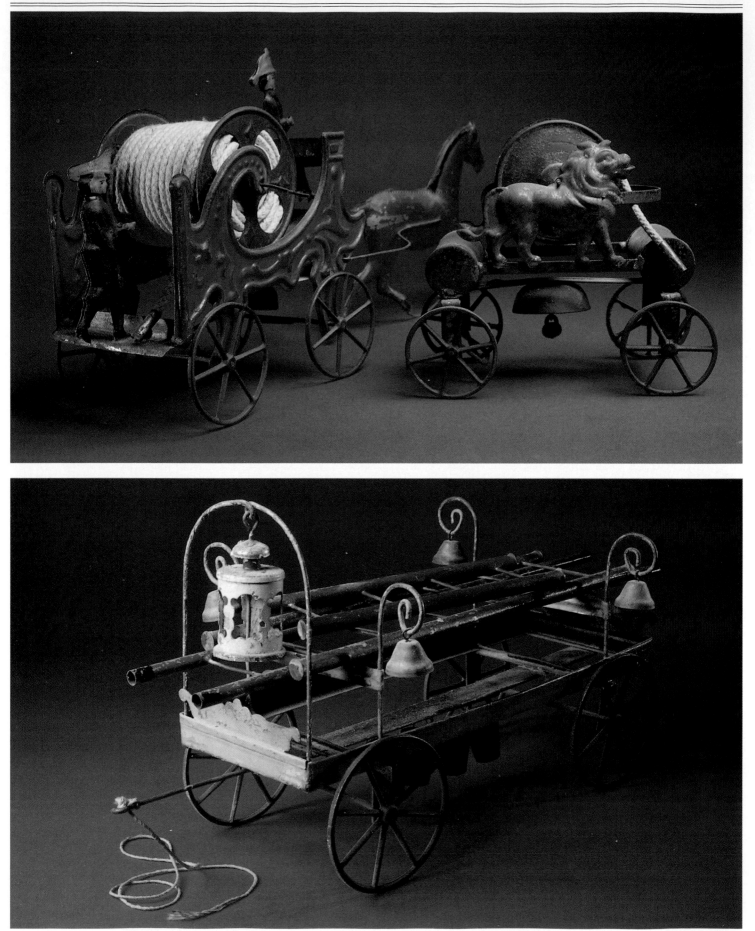

Among the vehicles were hook-and-ladder wagons with long, flat beds to carry extension ladders, and hose-reel wagons that made it possible to unwind enormous lengths of hose quickly and efficiently. The hoses, in turn, were connected to pumper wagons that drew water from hydrants or other water sources. Early pumper wagons were operated manually, but by the 1880s many companies also had pumpers that were run by heavy steam engines.

Toymakers were quick to capitalize on children's fascination with firefighting, producing replicas of full-size vehicles that were correct down to the smallest details. Horses galloped and bells rang, ladders could be extended and hoses unreeled. The most expensive toy pumper wagon (which sold for $6.50 in the 1880s) was even equipped with a miniature live-steam engine—heated by an alcohol burner—that actually pumped water. And for the child who had to have a truly complete set of equipment, there were also auxiliary vehicles, including fire chiefs' carriages and the showy hose-reelers that were pulled by firemen in parades, as well as miniature firehouses equipped with doors that swung open at the sound of a clanging alarm.

One of the earliest toy steam pumpers, the brass and cast-iron Weedens Upright Engine No. 2, above, was patented in 1885 by the Weeden Manufacturing Company of New Bedford, Massachusetts. The toy could actually shoot water, which was pumped through rubber hoses.

Firefighting toys like those opposite were made more realistic by the addition of bells. The tin hose-reelers at top include a circa 1890 horse-drawn vehicle by James Fallows of Philadelphia and a circa 1880 parade vehicle by Merriam Manufacturing Company of Durham, Connecticut. The tin ladder wagon at bottom, made around 1875 by Althof, Bergmann, is a replica of a wagon pulled by men.

Toy Trains

The first passenger railroad was built in America in 1828. By 1840 there would be over four hundred different rail companies servicing major cities from New England to Georgia. Caught up in the progressive spirit of railroading, toymakers began producing miniature trains in the mid-1800s. The earliest types, known as floor or carpet runners, were designed to roll along without tracks. Made through the end of the century in both tin and cast iron, they derived much of their charm from their painted and stenciled decoration.

Not all floor trains lacked power, however. In 1856, George W. Brown of Forestville, Connecticut, produced the first American clockwork floor train. A decade later a number of other American companies were turning out clockwork models, some featuring automatic air whistles, and smokestacks that belched clouds of real smoke (produced by tiny pellets). Toymakers in Europe, meanwhile, had been experimenting with steam-powered models, which might come with a small set of tracks.

An important breakthrough in the toy train

Continued

Trackless carpet runners like those shown here were designed to be pushed or pulled along the floor. Known as the Lyon, *the stenciled tin train at top was made by Stevens & Brown of Connecticut in the 1870s. The tin* Flash, *at bottom, was patented by James Fallows of Philadelphia in 1883.*

153

industry came in 1884, when an American inventor, Murray Bacon, patented the first electric train. By the early years of the 20th century, companies such as Bing and Märklin in Germany, Frank Hornby in England, and Lionel and American Flyer in the United States were producing elaborate electric train sets that imitated many of the contemporary train lines. On these accurate replicas, cars often had brass and copper fittings, doors that opened and closed, windows that were glazed with mica, and even tiny toilets with seats that could be lifted.

The English firm of Frank Hornby produced the twenty-two-piece clockwork tin train set above in 1929.

Although it came with only four pieces of track, more could be purchased separately.

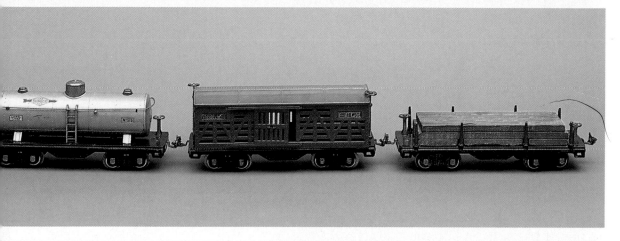

From the early 1900s until the 1960s, Lionel and American Flyer were the major competitors for the American electric train market. The 1931 Lionel freight train above came with a steam engine and eleven realistic cars, seven of which are shown. The 1927 American Flyer President's Special, at left, had working doors and brass fittings on its cars; included here are a locomotive, a Pullman, a mail car, and an observation car.

Railroad
Accessories

Toy train "sets" essentially consisted of a train and a circular track, until the late 1880s when Gebrüder Bing started making sets with more elaborate layouts. By the early 1900s toymakers in both Europe and America were producing a wide range of realis-

tic train accessories in tin, steel, or cast iron—including station houses, warning signals, and tiny people—which could be purchased individually. These railside attractions added considerably to the cost of setting up a miniature railroad, yet fathers gladly spent the money,

The railroad accessories at left were made by American and European toymakers from about 1900 to 1935. Included are a waiting room and a two-lamp signal tower, both by Lionel of New York City, a ticket office made by Ives Manufacturing of Connecticut, and an elaborate station with an imitation clock, made by Märklin of Germany. The tiny electric lights in the towers, signals, lamps, and buildings worked.

since they enjoyed playing "engineer" as much as their sons did.

One of the first American manufacturers to realize that children would lose interest if trains did not come with added diversions was Joshua Lionel Cowen, who founded Lionel Manufactur-ing in 1900. Without these little extras, the toy-maker suggested, "the little nippers will wander off and squeeze out some toothpaste or set fire to the curtains." Not surprisingly, Lionel catalogs offered especially complete lines of accessories, all intended to make toy railroading more fun.

THE GEORGE BROWN SKETCHBOOK

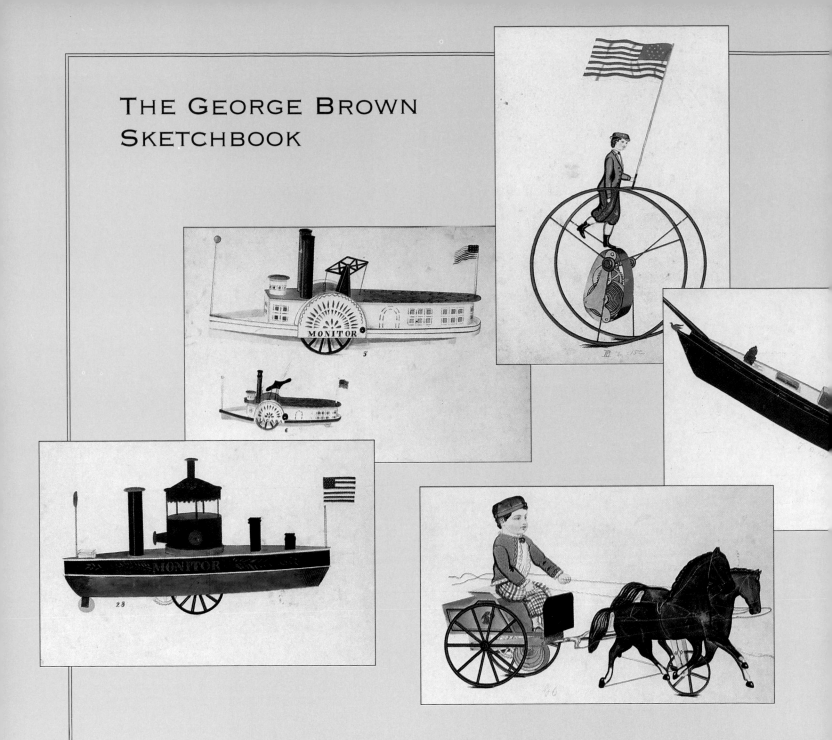

Of all the popular tin playthings that were turned out by American toy manufacturers in the second half of the 1800s, perhaps none were more indicative of their time than those of George Brown. Brown came to Forestville, Connecticut, in 1845 as a clockmaker's apprentice, and there, in 1856, formed George W. Brown & Company, the first firm in America to mass-produce clockwork toys. An incurable inventor, Brown was constantly updating his mechanical devices. His numerous designs for transportation toys further reveal that he was caught up in the fascination with speed, motion, and technology then sweeping the newly industrialized country.

The watercolor illustrations above are from a sixty-five-page sketchbook of Brown's mechanical toy designs that was discovered years after his death. Containing pictures of tinplate knickknacks as well as patterns for self-propelled locomotives, gigs, streetcars, paddle-wheelers, fire engines, and hoop toys, the book was evidently a kind of "working" catalog. In it the toymaker recorded

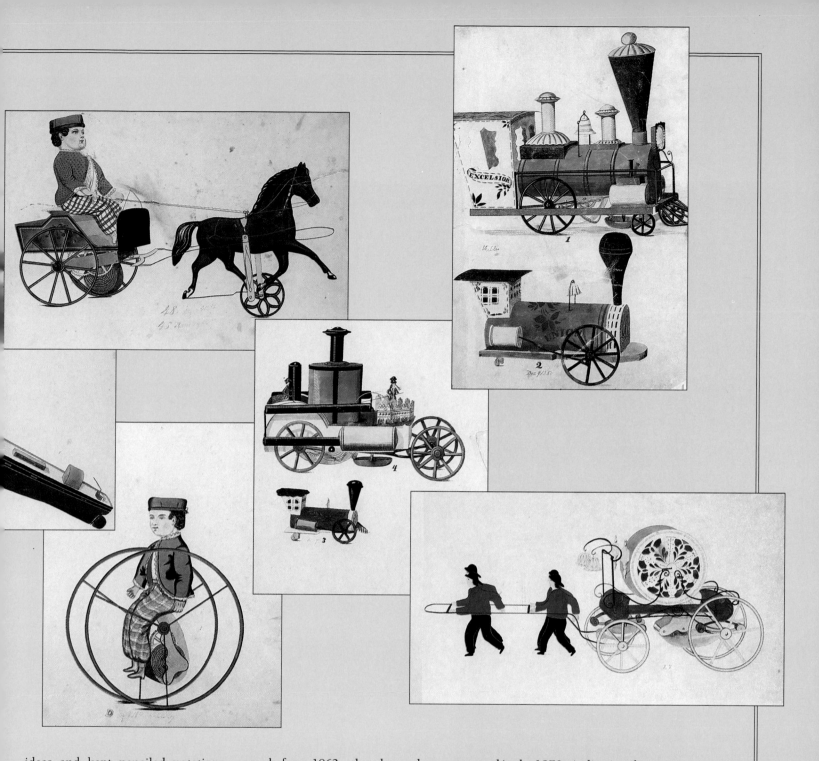

ideas and kept penciled notations of wholesale prices. It is uncertain whether the illustrations were done by Brown himself or by a professional artist. Almost all the toys were rendered in the actual sizes and colors of the finished products, many of which appeared in the firm's official trade catalogs.

The sketchbook was probably begun before 1862, the date when Brown apparently left toymaking temporarily to make oil burners for lamps. He sold his burner business in 1868, and the following year joined forces with the J. & E. Stevens toy manufacturing firm, forming Stevens & Brown, located in Cromwell, Connecticut. A number of the toys in the sketchbook were patented in the 1870s, indicating that the volume was in use while Stevens & Brown was in business. That company was dissolved in 1880, and Brown died nine years later. Ironically, his obituary dwelled on his career as a burner manufacturer, and only briefly mentioned his importance as one of America's early toymakers.

Cars and
Trucks

Thought to have been made in the 1890s by a French firm, the tin horseless carriage above left is one of the earliest toy cars known. The 1903 Bing De Dion clockwork runabout above right has an adjustable steering wheel and rubber tires.

In the early 1890s, when the first motor cars, or horseless carriages as they were then called, appeared on the roads, toymakers—like the general public—were slow to accept them. It would not be until after 1900 that toy cars were represented in any quantity in manufacturers' catalogs, but once they were, they quickly became best sellers.

From the start, the toys were made as passable copies of full-size cars. As the look of automobiles rapidly changed from designs that truly resembled carriages without horses to sleek, closed-body styles, toymakers were kept busy updating their own lines. As a result, it was not uncommon for a particular toy to be discontinued after a year—as the full-size models were.

Many of the toy cars that American children enjoyed in the early 1900s were European imports. Just as the automobile had caught on in this country, so it had abroad, and European toy firms were quick to fashion many of their cars after American models, such as Ford's famous

Model T. Particularly popular in this country were painted-tin cars from the German manufacturers Bing and Carette, whose toys were especially well made. Many had finished interiors and features such as rubber tires, brass- or nickel-plated trim, and glass windshields. While clockwork or lightweight spring-driven windup motors were the main means of propulsion for these vehicles, cars with steam or electric engines were also made.

During World War I many German toy com-

panies were forced to close, and Carette, for one, never resumed operation. In the postwar years American toy manufacturing grew considerably stronger. Companies such as Hubley Manufacturing of Lancaster, Pennsylvania, which had produced only a few cast-iron vehicles before the war, now began developing an expansive selection. And new toy companies, such as Kingsbury of Keene, New Hampshire, sprang up. Among the best sellers made by Kingsbury was a series of "record cars," which were replicas of

Continued

The two German chauffeur-driven cars above include, at left, an open town car made by H. Fischer & Company around 1912, and, at right, a sedan produced by Bing around 1928, which can be turned by means of a squeeze mechanism.

the automobiles that competed each year for the world's land speed record.

The end of the war also saw an increase in the number of specialized cars and trucks on the road, and toymakers raced to keep pace. There were, for example, whole fleets of cast-iron toy taxicabs designed to look just like the Checker, Red Top, and Yellow Cabs that were now servicing many cities. And every toy catalog had at least one wrecker, dump truck, and cement mixer, as well as trucks and vans that bore the

names of nationally known companies such as Bell Telephone and Standard Oil.

But even with all the new vehicular possibilities, toy passenger cars remained children's favorites, and manufacturers continued to record every design change. The boxy Pierce-Arrow and Pontiac roadsters of the 1920s and the curvaceous Airflow Chryslers and DeSotos of the 1930s were just some of the hundreds of models that rolled off the toymakers' production lines and into stores.

The cast-iron taxis at left were made between 1923 and 1930 by Arcade Manufacturing of Freeport,

Illinois, and Dent Hardware of Fullerton, Pennsylvania. Parked in front of the 1925 filling station,

above, made of wood, paper, and pressed steel by Gibbs Manufacturing of Canton, Ohio, is a 1929

cast-iron roadster by Kilgore Manufacturing of Westerville, Ohio.

The lithographed tin vehicles at left are only a sampling of the vast number of penny toys that were produced and exported by such German toy companies as Georg Kellermann, Johann Meier, and Johann Distler from about 1900 to 1917.

Flying Machines

When the Wright brothers made their historic first flight at Kitty Hawk, North Carolina, in 1903, flying was still too much of a novelty for toy-makers to pay much attention. But by 1908, when Wilbur Wright was demonstrating his improved biplanes near Paris, and Frenchman Louis Blériot crossed the English Channel in a monoplane, the world took notice. That same year tinplate biplanes and monoplanes started appearing in German toy catalogs, and from then on the Germans would remain the leading manufacturers of aeronautical toys.

Many early toy planes were designed to be pulled along the ground or swooped through the air by hand. Manufacturers, however, also experimented with clockwork mechanisms that allowed a plane to taxi down the runway on rubber wheels or fly along a tautly stretched wire threaded through a pulley. At first, the range of toy planes was limited, but after World War I, and with the rapid development of commercial aviation in the 1920s, manufacturers were soon turning out all types of aircraft, from fighters to mail planes. And when, in the 1930s, Märklin in Germany and Meccano in England introduced constructor sets, children could enjoy building flying machines themselves.

The early toy biplane above could "fly" across a wire on a pulley; the circa 1935 clockwork Pitcairn mail plane at right taxied along the floor. The 1930s biplane opposite was made from a kit.

AEROPLANE CONSTRUCTOR

Selected Reading

Barenholtz, Bernard, and Inez McClintock. *American Antique Toys, 1830-1900*. New York: Harry N. Abrams, 1980.

Bartholomew, Charles. *Mechanical Toys*. Secaucus, N.J.: Chartwell Books, 1979.

Coleman, Dorothy S., Elizabeth A., and Evelyn J. *The Collector's Encyclopedia of Dolls*. New York: Crown Publishers, 1989.

Davidson, Al. *Penny Lane, A History of Antique Mechanical Toy Banks*. Mokelumne Hill, Calif.: Long's Americana, 1987.

Fraser, Antonia. *A History of Toys*. New York: Spring Books, 1972.

Gardiner, Gordon, and Alistair Morris. *The Illustrated Encyclopedia of Metal Toys: An All-Color Guide to the Art of Collecting International Playthings*. New York: Harmony Books, 1984.

Gottschalk, Lillian. *American Toy Cars & Trucks, 1894-1942*. New York: Abbeville Press, 1986.

Hewitt, Karen, and Louise Roomet. *Educational Toys in America, 1800 to the Present*. Burlington, Vt.: The Robert Hull Fleming Museum, University of Vermont, 1979.

Hillier, Mary. *Automata & Mechanical Toys*. London: Jupiter, 1976.

King, Constance. *Metal Toys & Automata*. Secaucus, N J.: Chartwell Books, 1989.

King, Constance Eileen. *The Collector's History of Dolls*. New York: St. Martin's Press, 1978.

King, Constance Eileen. *The Encyclopedia of Toys*. New York, Crown Publishers, 1978.

McClinton, Katharine Morrison. *Antiques of American Childhood*. New York, Bramhall House, 1970.

Milet, Jacques, and Robert Forbes. *Toy Boats, 1870-1955: A Pictorial History*. New York: Charles Scribner's Sons, 1979.

Norman, Bill. *The Bank Book: The Encyclopedia of Mechanical Bank Collecting*. San Diego, Calif.: Accent Studios, 1985.

Opie, Iona and Robert, and Brian Alderson. *The Treasures of Childhood: Books, Toys, and Games from the Opie Collection*. New York: Arcade Publishing, 1989.

Pinsky, Maxine A. *Greenberg's Guide to Marx Toys, Vol. 1: 1923-1950*. Sykesville, Md.: Greenberg Publishing Company, 1988.

Pressland, David. *The Art of the Tin Toy*. London: New Cavendish Books, 1976.

Richardson, Katherine W., ed. *Instructive and Amusing: Essays on Toys, Games, and Education in New England*, Essex Institute Historical Collections, vol. 123, no. 2, special issue. Salem, Mass.: Essex Institute, April, 1987.

Spilhaus, Athelstan and Kathleen. *Mechanical Toys: How Old Toys Work*. New York: Crown Publishers, 1989.

White, Gwen. *Toys, Dolls, Automata Marks & Labels*. London: B. T. Batsford Ltd., 1985.

Whitton, Blair. *American Clockwork Toys, 1862-1900*. Exton, Pa.: Schiffer Publishing, 1981.

Whitton, Blair. *Paper Toys of the World*. Cumberland, Md.: Hobby House Press, 1986.

Museum, Collection, and Photography Credits

Cover, Frontispiece, and **Page 8**: The Lawrence Scripps Wilkinson Collection of Toys, Detroit, MI/photos by George Ross. **Pages 10, 11**: (all) private collection/photos by Steven Mays. **Page 12**: Museum of the City of New York, NYC/photo by Steven Mays. **Page 13**: private collection/photo by Steven Mays. **Page 14**: Museum of the City of New York, NYC/photo by Steven Mays. **Page 15**: The Lawrence Scripps Wilkinson Collection of Toys, Detroit, MI/photo by George Ross. **Page 16**: (both) Museum of the City of New York, NYC/photos by Steven Mays. **Page 17**: The Lawrence Scripps Wilkinson Collection of Toys, Detroit, MI/photo by George Ross. **Pages 18-21**: (all) Museum of the City of New York, NYC/photos by Steven Mays. **Pages 22-23**: The Lawrence Scripps Wilkinson Collection of Toys, Detroit, MI, and Detroit Historical Department, Detroit, MI/photo by George Ross. **Pages 24-26**: Museum of the City of New York, NYC/photos by Steven Mays. **Page 27**: The Lawrence Scripps Wilkinson Collection of Toys, Detroit, MI, and Detroit Historical Department, Detroit, MI/photo by George Ross. **Pages 28, 29**: The Lawrence Scripps Wilkinson Collection of Toys, Detroit, MI/photos by George Ross. **Pages 30-31**: dolls—collection of Jonathan Green, NYC; books—private collection/photo by Steven Mays. **Page 32**: The Lawrence Scripps Wilkinson Collection of Toys, Detroit, MI/photo by George Ross. **Pages 33-35**: The Lawrence Scripps Wilkinson Collection of Toys, Detroit, MI, and Detroit Historical Department, Detroit, MI/photos by George Ross. **Pages 36-39**: (all) collection of Margaret and Blair Whitton/photos by Steven Mays. **Page 40**: private collection/photo by Steven Mays. **Page 41**: (both) collection of Margaret and Blair Whitton/photos by Steven Mays. **Pages 42, 43**: (all) Museum of the City of New York, NYC/photos by Steven Mays. **Page 44**: The Lawrence Scripps Wilkinson Collection of Toys, Detroit, MI/photo by George Ross. **Pages 46-49**: (all) Museum of the City of New York, NYC/photos by Steven Mays. **Pages**

50-51: The Lawrence Scripps Wilkinson Collection of Toys/photo by George Ross. **Pages 52-53**: Schoenhut collection (except Rolly-Dollys, catalog pages)—Keith and Donna Kaonis, The Inside Collector, Elmont, NY; Rolly-Dollys—collection of Neil Weissman, NYC; catalog pages—collection of Norman Bowers, Schoenhut Collectors Club, Evanston, IL/photo by Keith Kaonis. **Pages 54-58**: (all) collection of Margaret and Blair Whitton/photos by Steven Mays. **Page 59**: (top) private collection/photo by Steven Mays; (bottom) collection of Margaret and Blair Whitton/photo by Steven Mays. **Page 60**: (top) Museum of the City of New York, NYC/photo by Steven Mays; (bottom) private collection/photo by Steven Mays. **Pages 61-63**: (all) private collection/photos by Steven Mays. **Pages 64-67**: private collection/photos by Stephen Donelian. **Pages 68-69**: The Lawrence Scripps Wilkinson Collection of Toys, Detroit, MI/photo by George Ross. **Pages 70-73**: (all) Detroit Historical Department, Detroit, MI/photos by George Ross. **Pages 74, 76-77**: The Lawrence Scripps Wilkinson Collection of Toys, Detroit, MI/photos by George Ross. **Page 78**: (left) The Lawrence Scripps Wilkinson Collection of Toys, Detroit, MI/photo by George Ross; (right) Museum of the City of New York, NYC/photo by Steven Mays. **Page 79**: (both) private collection/photos by Steven Mays. **Pages 80, 81**: The Lawrence Scripps Wilkinson Collection of Toys, Detroit, MI/photos by George Ross. **Page 82**: photo by Bill Holland. **Page 83**: The Lawrence Scripps Wilkinson Collection of Toys, Detroit, MI/photo by George Ross. **Pages 84-85**: private collection/photo by Steven Mays. **Page 86**: National Gallery of Art, Washington, DC, gift of Edgar William and Bernice Chrysler Garbisch. **Page 87**: (top) Hirschl & Adler Folk, NYC; (bottom left) National Gallery of Art, Washington, DC, gift of Edgar William and Bernice Chrysler Garbisch; (bottom right) Abby Aldrich Rockefeller Folk Art Center, Williamsburg, VA. **Page 88**: private collection/photo by Steven Mays. **Page 89**: The Lawrence

Scripps Wilkinson Collection of Toys, Detroit, MI/photo by George Ross. **Page 90**: private collection/photo by Steven Mays. **Page 91**: (top) The Lawrence Scripps Wilkinson Collection of Toys, Detroit, MI/photo by George Ross; (bottom) private collection/photo by Steven Mays. **Page 92**: (top left) The Lawrence Scripps Wilkinson Collection of Toys, Detroit, MI/photo by George Ross; (top right and bottom left) Hillman-Gemini Gallery, NYC/photos by Steven Mays; (bottom right) photo by Bill Holland. **Page 93**: The Lawrence Scripps Wilkinson Collection of Toys, Detroit, MI/photo by George Ross. **Page 94**: photo by Bill Holland. **Page 95**: (top) private collection/photo by Steven Mays; (bottom) Museum of the City of New York, NYC/photo by Steven Mays. **Pages 96-99**: (all) The Lawrence Scripps Wilkinson Collection of Toys, Detroit, MI/photos by George Ross. **Pages 100-101**: collection of Mythology Unlimited, Inc., NYC/photo by Steven Mays. **Pages 102-104**: Hillman-Gemini Gallery, NYC/photos by Steven Mays. **Page 105**: photo by Bill Holland. **Page 106**: The Lawrence Scripps Wilkinson Collection of Toys, Detroit, MI, and Detroit Historical Department, Detroit, MI/photo by George Ross. **Pages 108-110**: (all) The Lawrence Scripps Wilkinson Collection of Toys, Detroit, MI/photos by George Ross. **Page 111**: The Lawrence Scripps Wilkinson Collection of Toys, Detroit, MI, and Detroit Historical Department, Detroit, MI/photo by George Ross. **Page 112**: The Lawrence Scripps Wilkinson Collection of Toys, Detroit, MI/photo by George Ross. **Page 113**: from the collections of The Essex Institute, Salem, MA, a reprint by the Antique Toy Collectors of America. **Pages 114-115**: The Lawrence Scripps Wilkinson Collection of Toys, Detroit, MI/photo by George Ross. **Page 116**: The Lawrence Scripps Wilkinson Collection of Toys, Detroit, MI, and Detroit Historical Department, Detroit, MI/photo by George Ross. **Pages 117-119**: (all) The Lawrence Scripps Wilkinson Collection of Toys, Detroit, MI/photos by George Ross. **Pages**

120, 121: The Lawrence Scripps Wilkinson Collection of Toys, Detroit, MI, and Detroit Historical Department, Detroit, MI/photos by George Ross. **Pages 122-123**: collection of Arnold D. Cohen, Washington, DC/photos by Stephen Donelian. **Pages 124-125**: collection of Bertram M. Cohen, Boston, MA/photo by Stephen Donelian. **Pages 126-129**: (all) collection of Margaret and Blair Whitton/photos by Steven Mays. **Pages 130-131**: private collection/photo by Steven Mays. **Pages 132-133**: Kendra Krienke, Original Art for Children, NYC; Susan Weiser Liebegott, Enchanted Books, Brooklyn, NY; Second Childhood, NYC/photo by Steven Mays. **Pages 134-137**: (all) private collection/photos by Steven Mays. **Page 138**: The Lawrence Scripps Wilkinson Collection of Toys, Detroit, MI/photo by George Ross. **Page 140**: photo by Bill Holland. **Page 141**: The Lawrence Scripps Wilkinson Collection of Toys, Detroit, MI/photo by George Ross. **Page 142**: (top) The Lawrence Scripps Wilkinson Collection of Toys, Detroit, MI/photo by George Ross; (bottom) Museum of the City of New York, NYC/photo by Steven Mays. **Page 143**: The Lawrence Scripps Wilkinson Collection of Toys, Detroit, MI/photo by George Ross. **Page 144**: photo by Bill Holland. **Page 145**: (top and middle) private collection/photos by Steven Mays; (bottom) Hillman-Gemini Gallery/photo by Steven Mays. **Pages 146-147**: (top row, left to right) from the collections of the Library of Congress, Washington, DC; from the collections of the Library of Congress; The Bettmann Archive, NYC; from the collections of the Library of Congress; (middle row, left to right) collection of Bill Holland; The Bettmann Archive, NYC; from the collections of the Library of Congress; Culver Pictures, NYC; (bottom row, left to right) from the collections of the Library of Congress; Culver Pictures; photo by Roy. Pinney; from the collections of the Library of Congress. **Page 148**: photo by Bill Holland. **Page 149**: (both) The Lawrence Scripps Wilkinson Collection of Toys, Detroit, MI/photos by George Ross. **Page 150**: (both) photos by Bill Holland. **Page 151**: Detroit Historical Department, Detroit, MI/photo by George Ross. **Pages 152-153**: (both) private collection/photos by Steven Mays. **Page 154**: The Lawrence Scripps Wilkinson Collection of Toys, Detroit, MI/photos by George Ross. **Page 155**: (all) The Lawrence Scripps Wilkinson Collection of Toys, Detroit, MI/top train photo by Steven Mays, bottom train photo by George Ross. **Pages 156-157**: The Lawrence Scripps Wilkinson Collection of Toys, Detroit, MI/photo by George Ross. **Pages 158-159**: Alexander Gallery, NYC/photos by Stephen Donelian. **Pages 160, 161**: Hillman-Gemini Gallery, NYC/photos by Steven Mays. **Pages 162-165**: (all) from *American Motor Toys* by Lillian Gottschalk/photos by Bill Holland. **Page 166**: (both) photos by Bill Holland. **Page 167**: Hillman-Gemini Gallery, NYC/photo by Steven Mays.

Index

Acknowledgments

Our thanks to Alexander Acevedo, Terry Ackerman, William Bailey and Lauren Eichengreen of Mythology Unlimited, Inc., Nan and Bill Bopp, Norman Bowers, Arnold Cohen, Bertram Cohen, Jane Hirschkowitz of the Museum of the City of New York, Bill Holland, Patience Nauta of the Detroit Historical Department, Barbara Niman of The Lawrence Scripps Wilkinson Collection of Toys, Elizabeth Prime, Leon and Steven Weiss of the Hillman-Gemini Gallery, Margaret and Blair Whitton, Lawrence Scripps Wilkinson, and Cynthia Young of the Detroit Historical Department for their help on this book.

First printing
Published simultaneously in Canada
School and library distribution by Silver Burdett Company,
Morristown, New Jersey

TIME-LIFE is a trademark of Time Incorporated U.S.A.

Production by Giga Communications, Inc.
Printed in U.S.A.

Library of Congress Cataloging-in-Publication Data

Toys and games
p.   cm. — (American country)
Includes index.
ISBN 0-8094-7054-3 — ISBN 0-8094-7055-1 (lib. bdg.)
1. Toys—United States—Collectors and collecting.
2. Games—United States—Collectors and collecting.
I. Time-Life Books.   II. Series.
NK9509.65.U6T69   1991   688.7'075—dc20   90-42314
CIP

American Country was created by Rebus, Inc., and published by Time-Life Books.

REBUS, INC.

Publisher: RODNEY FRIEDMAN • Editor: MARYA DALRYMPLE
Executive Editor: RACHEL D. CARLEY • Managing Editor: BRENDA SAVARD • Consulting Editor: CHARLES L. MEE, JR.
Copy Editor: ALEXA RIPLEY BARRE • Writers: JUDITH CRESSY, ROSEMARY G. RENNICKE
Freelance Writer: JOE ROSSON • Design Editors: NANCY MERNIT, CATHRYN SCHWING
Test Kitchen Director: GRACE YOUNG WIERTZ
Contributing Editors: LEE CUTRONE, ANNE MOFFAT, KATE TOMKIEVICZ
Indexer: MARILYN FLAIG

Art Director: JUDITH HENRY • Associate Art Director: SARA REYNOLDS
Designers: AMY BERNIKER, TIMOTHY JEFFS
Photographer: STEVEN MAYS • Photo Editor: SUE ISRAEL
Photo Assistant: ROB WHITCOMB • Freelance Photographers: STEPHEN DONELIAN, GEORGE ROSS
Freelance Photo Stylist: DEE SHAPIRO • Set Carpenter: MARCOS SORENSEN

Special Consultants for this book: BILL BOPP, JANE HIRSCHKOWITZ, LEON AND STEVEN WEISS
Series Consultants: BOB CAHN, HELAINE W. FENDELMAN, LINDA C. FRANKLIN, GLORIA GALE,
KATHLEEN EAGEN JOHNSON, JUNE SPRIGG, CLAIRE WHITCOMB

Time-Life Books Inc. is a wholly owned subsidiary of THE TIME INC. BOOK COMPANY.

TIME-LIFE BOOKS INC.

Managing Editor: THOMAS H. FLAHERTY
Director of Editorial Resources: ELISE D. RITTER-CLOUGH
Director of Photography and Research: JOHN CONRAD WEISER
Editorial Board: DALE M. BROWN, ROBERTA CONLAN, LAURA FOREMAN, LEE HASSIG,
JIM HICKS, BLAINE MARSHALL, RITA THIEVON MULLIN, HENRY WOODHEAD

Publisher: JOSEPH J. WARD

Associate Publisher: TREVOR LUNN • Editorial Director: DONIA STEELE
Marketing Director: REGINA HALL • Director of Design: LOUIS KLEIN
Production Manager: MARLENE ZACK • Supervisor of Quality Control: JAMES KING

For information about any Time-Life book please call 1-800-621-7026, or write:
Reader Information, Time-Life Customer Service
P.O. Box C-32068, Richmond, Virginia 23261-2068

Time-Life Books Inc. offers a wide range of fine recordings, including a Rock 'n' Roll Era series.
For subscription information, call 1-800-621-7026, or write TIME-LIFE MUSIC,
P.O. Box C-32068, Richmond, Virginia 23261-2068.